W9-BMU-750

THE WAY SHE LOOKS TONIGHT

BY THE SAME AUTHOR

The Embroidered Tent: Five Gentlewomen in Early Canada (1982)

Redney: A Life of Sara Jeannette Duncan (1983)

Below the Peacock Fan: First Ladies of the Raj (1987)

Blenheim: Biography of a Palace (1989)

In a Gilded Cage: From Heiress to Duchess (1993)

The Way She Looks Tonight

FIVE WOMEN OF STYLE

Marian Fowler

St. Martin's Press New York

 For information, address St. Martin's Press, 175 Fifth Avenue, New York, N.Y. 10010.

Library of Congress Cataloging-in-Publication Data

Fowler, Marian
The way she looks tonight : five women of style / Marian Fowler.
p. cm.
Includes bibliographical references.
ISBN 0-312-14757-0
1. Fashion–Biography. 2. Women–Biography. I. Title.
GT1720.F69 1996
391'.008922–dc20
[B] 96-3117 CIP

First published in Canada by Random House

First U.S. Edition: November 1996

10 9 8 7 6 5 4 3 2 1

This book is dedicated

with love

to Byron Bellows,

who keeps me dancing

Contents

Introduction

All five women had their favorite metaphors of self. Empress Eugénie defined her womanly sphere by the width of her crinoline. Elinor Glyn undulated happily on tiger skins. Marlene Dietrich danced for both sexes in top hat and tails. The Duchess of Windsor bedecked herself in an ex-King's ransom of jewels, and Jacqueline Kennedy crowned herself with pillboxes. Each woman, with great discipline and dedication, mastered a special language which is universal, intriguing, cryptic and highly effective: the language of clothes. These five women wrote their life stories in fabric and feathers and furs.

In my previous biographical works, I researched a woman's life in the conventional way, by reading or recording a great many words: hers, to begin with, in diaries and letters and other writings; those of her family and friends; and those of previous biographers and journalists. Words and more words – such an avalanche of them that digging out the real woman from underneath was a slow and laborious process: a fingernail of her personality here, two hairs of it there.

Was it possible, I wondered idly one day, to write a woman's life using a very different source, namely the constant, immediate shorthand of clothing? Eagerly, using the contents of their closets as the primary source, I began researching the lives of these five women who grasped the imagery of clothes: Eugénie Bonaparte, Empress of France (1826–1920); Elinor Glyn (1864–1943); Marlene Dietrich (1901–1992); Wallis Warfield Simpson, Duchess of Windsor (1895–1986), and Jacqueline Kennedy Onassis (1929–1994).

I chose these five not only because they seemed to me to be exemplary women of style, but also because all of them were famous enough to imprint their image, via newspapers, magazines, film or television, on masses of women who rushed to copy them. Eugénie, in fact, was the first Western woman whose style achieved wide currency, due to fashion's coming of age in her time through the advent of clothing factories and retail outlets. Three of my subjects – Eugénie, Wallis and Jackie – found themselves in the public spotlight when they married; Elinor and Marlene's professions launched them into the media glare. Since these two were both early Hollywood image-makers, Elinor through silent films and Marlene in talkies, I have placed their chapters back to back, ignoring the strict chronology of birth dates.

I read and observed, focusing on verbal descriptions of their wardrobes, supplemented by plenty of visual images in paintings, photographs and films, gradually discovering what these women kept on hangers, in drawers and hatboxes – and under wraps. I tried to be thorough and I questioned everything. Why did Marlene Dietrich keep every fur she ever owned, no matter how dry and cracked? Why did Jacqueline Onassis insist that her maid iron her pantyhose so that they would lie in flat, neat piles in her drawer?

In my search for answers I read what psychoanalysts, social anthropologists, philosophers of aesthetics, art critics and social historians had to say about clothing. I hadn't progressed very far in my reading before I realized that there was a problem: the academic experts knew how to theorize and generalize brilliantly but, being for the most part male, they knew woefully little about the details of female finery. Their specialty, after all, was psychology or sociology or economics, not fashion. The fashion experts, on the other hand – couturiers, women's magazine editors and others in the trade – had mastered the details but couldn't see the larger picture. However, I pushed on, grateful to such writers as James Laver, who understood both actual garment and historical overview, and to Alison Lurie and Roland Barthes, who viewed clothes primarily as signs and symbols. I began to see that one should never underestimate the power of a wardrobe, that apparel, however old or dowdy or nondescript, always – to borrow fashion jargon – "makes a statement."

It was Victorian historian Thomas Carlyle, in his work of transcendental philosophy *Sartor Resartus* (1839), who first saw apparel as highly symbolic. His book is based on the "grand proposition" that humankind's earthly interests "are all hooked and buttoned together, and held up by clothes." Carlyle viewed the world as a series of garments; the body is merely a suit of clothing for the soul, and the universe itself is one giant "living garment of God," showing the invisible beyond the visible. If, as Carlyle maintained, "Society is founded upon cloth," then, surely, one small portion of it, namely a woman's life, could also be founded on cloth. I determined to examine these five lives-in-costume, paying attention to what each woman was communicating and why; to connections between her apparel and the socio-historical background of her time; to her influence on other women's dress; and, finally, to lessons to be learned from her example concerning the pleasures, and pitfalls, of style.

As I carried out my research, I was encouraged and excited to find my chosen five gradually revealing their psyches to me through a lifetime's garments and accessories. All of them were brilliant, dazzling practitioners of that special lingo in which, as Alison Lurie writes in *The Language of Clothes*, "for thousands of years human beings have communicated with one another first." Since Victorian times, women have signified much more than men because their fashions change more frequently and more radically. They have, one might say, a much larger vocabulary.

Long before a woman is near enough to us to speak, she is already announcing her sex, age, class status, and giving clues as to her nationality, personality, taste, mood and sexual desire. By the time she begins to talk about herself, there is almost no need for words. We have already "read" her, if we have the necessary skill and knowledge. Even when she keeps her mouth shut and remains resolutely mute, or even if she is a chosen biographical subject, now deceased, her clothes go right on rapping and whispering, with a real gift of the gab.

Like that of all women, the clothing of these five suggested, persuaded, advertised, insinuated, told the truth or lied, for every choice a woman makes in deciding what to wear sends its message, whether she intends it to or not. As Volumnia says in Shakespeare's *Coriolanus*, "Should we be silent, and not speak, our raiment / And state of bodies would betray what life / We have led."

Women think their clothes cover them. They are wrong. Instead, clothes uncover, and strip them bare. Outer garb is always directly connected to the mind of the wearer. A woman's apparel "is a continual manifestation of intimate thoughts, a language, a symbol," wrote Balzac in *Daughter of Eve* (1830). It is a mistake to group costume with other applied arts such as architecture, furniture, silver or china. Clothes are different from all these because they are inseparable from the self. They give a visual aspect to consciousness itself, and not just to its surroundings.

The attire of Eugénie, Marlene or Wallis didn't always aim its language at others; sometimes it wasn't trying to communicate except to the self in an ongoing interior monologue which could occasionally censure and scold, more often comfort and cosset. "A sense of being perfectly well dressed," a lady once told Ralph Waldo Emerson, "gives a feeling of inward tranquillity which religion is powerless to bestow."

Internal or external, the language of dress is both conscious and unconscious. Every woman makes thousands of decisions a year about her wardrobe: what to buy, what to put on each morning, what to discard, and at least half the time she lets character and training decide for her, without conscious thought. For the five women in this book, their mind was more consistently tuned to clothing than is the case with most women; their choices were more often conscious than unconscious, and so easier to determine. Of course, such repressed feelings as guilt, narcissism, compromise or renunciation sometimes played their part, too.

Dreams in both our sleeping and wakeful states are often tied to dress, and cling to the psyche in an amazingly persistent way. All of us have had dreams of appearing in public half naked. "I dreamt I went to the opera in my Maidenform bra," said the girl in the fifties ad, expressing a universal fear. And, sometimes, we dream of wearing something wondrous and unattainable. As V.S. Pritchett wisely notes, "we live by our inner life and our illusions." Like all women, these five often expressed their wish fulfillment in dress by appearing richer or younger or sexier or more powerful than they actually were. Their clothes were at the same time real artifact and ideal archetype, both vehicle and vision.

While all women send messages in the language of clothes, the five I have chosen sent ones that were remarkably clear, consistent, original and unified. They stand out from the mass of women in thc same way that professional writers do from other people, all of whom write, but perhaps only letters and checks. Just as writers are artists with words, these five ladies were artists in cloth, skilled in expressing themselves in a way that was instantly recognizable, distinctive and memorable. They also knew exactly how fabric and color could be used to accentuate their physical charms and disguise their defects. The generating force of mind behind the wardrobe choices of such women we call *style*. "Style is the dress of thoughts," declared Lord Chesterfield in 1749, the clever packaging of the mind, the invisible cord which holds apparel and accessories together and attaches them securely, superbly, to the self.

It is unfortunate that "style" is an overworked word with so many meanings and such banality that it has grown gray and threadbare. Given its stretch and breadth and long history, I felt it necessary to define it anew.

The etymology is from *stylus*, the pointed rod used by Greeks and Romans for writing on wax. A person's style was originally his or her way of shaping letters, and then expanded to include their choice of words. In the beginning, it was always used in the context of an *individual*'s style, which is how I intend to use it, although the word has long since acquired a social context as well, so that we speak of "the French style of cooking" or "the lifestyles of the rich and famous."

After looking at definitions of style offered by E. H. Gombrich, Meyer Schapiro, Paul Nystrom, George Kubler, A.L. Kroeber and Leonard B. Meyer, I decided to tailor one to fit the specific needs of this book. I shall use the word style to mean a mode of expression which is laudable in its order, conspicuousness, consistency and cohesion of separate elements. Style implies admirable choice within a series of social and cultural constraints.

The woman of style, with will, energy, talent, discipline, confidence and a strong ego, with a little help from her subconscious and a lot from her bank account, creates a unified and arresting image, not on paper, canvas or celluloid, although it may well end up there, but on her body, using all kinds of materials. She reaches out to sheep on a hillside, furtive animals in the forest, silk worms at their spinning, fields of blue-flowering flax, exotic long-tailed birds, oysters on the ocean floor, rocks below the earth's crust, and from all these disparate bits and pieces she creates an artistic whole, a masterpiece.

She never confuses style with fashion, which is always her minion, never her master. She knows that whereas style is particular, fashion is general, being what the majority decides is appropriate garb. She understands how strong a pull towards conformity fashion exerts. Eighteenth-century playwright Colley Cibber summed it up: "One might as well be out of the world as out of fashion." The woman of style is ready, sometimes, to defy custom. Often her daring innovation will become the fashion, adopted by the masses. She habitually walks a tight-rope stretched midway between conformity to current fashion and timeless eccentricity, managing always to keep her own sure-footed poise. Any woman can buy fashion; style, on the other hand, is a gift from a fairy godmother bestowed on a female while she's still wearing her first, and probably her last, boring, anonymous garment: a diaper.

It was Georges Louis Leclerc de Buffon, addressing the French academy in 1753, who declared: "*Le style c'est l'homme même*" or – with a gender switch – "the style is the woman herself." Style is nothing, doesn't even exist, without the body: vibrant, pulsing, constantly in motion. The style needs the life. A dress on a hanger always looks empty and forlorn; it has no essence until a woman puts it on, smoothing the fabric over her hips, doing up the tiny buttons at her wrist. She does her magician's act every time she gets dressed, using arms and legs as magic wands, making limp cloth spring instantly to life and beauty.

The French philosopher Descartes concluded in 1637 that the basic premise of existence was *Cogito ergo sum.* The woman of style's existence, however, is predicated on *Vesto ergo sum*: I dress, therefore I am. She lives to dress and dresses to live. The Latin verb *habitare* means to live, and the Latin noun *habitus* means both character and style of dress. From *habitus* comes the English word habit, which means both a settled practice and the dress of a particular class, so that we speak of a nun's habit or of a riding habit. For the five women in this book, style is their habit, using the word with all its Latin and English meanings: style is character and life – routine and uniform.

The woman of style loves clothes with a sheer, unadulterated, faithful love. There are many females who think clothes a bore, a necessary evil, an annoyance, a chore. They panic in the stores, never knowing what to choose. Others shop for apparel with more attention to price tag than aesthetics. But a deep, real, abiding passion for clothes is rare, and these five women had it.

The chapters that follow will show how, in their attire, they all revealed what it meant to them to be female and how they envisioned their female role. Their clothes showed their creativity and artistic originality; they advertised the self and made a delightful package and powerful tool for achieving goals and ambitions, whether they were political, social or career-oriented. Elinor and Marlene, for example, used their finery and its image-making as a main vehicle for advancing their careers. Elinor once made an unforgettable entrance at a London literary luncheon with her marmalade cat Candide draped around her neck as fur-piece.

It is important to distinguish between the public image these women projected and the private self. In some cases, the gap widened considerably as the years passed. For all five, the public image which they cleverly contrived was spectacular. Each had a personal magnetism and magic so powerful that she could always make heads turn, spotlights swivel and cameras click. Each, in her own way, became a cult figure, celebrity and icon, focus for the wish fulfillment of women in the western world. The medium of the message changed, beginning, in Eugénie's case, with painted portraits by Winterhalter and steel engravings, and ending, in Jackie's case, with tabloid journalism and television, but some form of media was always focused on them.

Examining *what* each woman was communicating through apparel is fascinating, but equally so is *why* she chose as she did. Each had her own main motive but taken together they cover the gamut of general female reasons for clothing choices. Utility is always the very least of it. No woman wears clothes primarily to cover her nakedness or to keep out the cold. If practicality were a factor, Empress Eugénie and her fashion imitators would not have worn crinolines three feet across at a time when railway carriages were at their narrowest.

Class status, as it was for one of our five, may be the main consideration. Thorstein Veblen takes this view in *The Theory of the Leisure Class* (1899) where he talks about dress demonstrating conspicuous consumption, conspicuous leisure and conspicuous waste to indicate superior wealth and social status. To Veblen's three class-related motives Quentin Bell, in *On Human Finery*, adds a fourth: conspicuous outrage, practised by those who pride themselves on being above and beyond plebeian fashion, and so entitled to defy its norms. Marlene, for example, wore trousers in Hollywood when no other woman dared.

More important, however, than either the desire to raise status or eyebrows is the need for decoration. Epictetus in his *Discourses* wisely wrote: "Know first who you are, and then adorn yourself accordingly." Legend has it that when Adam and Eve plucked fig leaves to cover their shame, only Adam did so; Eve wove hers into a wreath for her head. Images of tribal figures posing in bronzed nakedness wearing only beads and nose-rings prove the primacy of decoration. Like them, the stylish five understood that dress signifies magic and mystery, and the Duchess of Windsor, in particular, could feel a jewel's awesome power.

For one of the five, as for many females, sex appeal was an important motive. As Robert Burton notes in *The Anatomy of Melancholy*, "The greatest provocation of lust comes from our apparel." J. C. Flügel in *The Psychology of Dress* stresses the ongoing conflict between modesty and sexual allure, both rooted in the sex urge, denied in one, acknowledged in the other. James Laver calls this "the Seduction Principle" and charts the shifting erogenous zones wherein one part of the female body – breasts or buttocks or legs – is emphasized either by exposing it, drawing cloth tightly over it, or even padding it. Personally, I feel that Laver, Flügel and other male writers place too much emphasis on sex appeal as a motive for dress. Perhaps this is because they themselves are susceptible to female charms.

I believe that women dress more to please themselves than to please men or other women, in accordance with their own concept of beauty. Anne Hollander, in *Seeing Through Clothes*, emphasizes aesthetics as motive and sees the art of dress as having its own autonomous history, a self-perpetuating flow of images derived from earlier images. During the nineteenth and twentieth centuries when these five ladies lived, visual images of clothes were steadily, as the years passed, increasing, in newspapers, advertising, movies and television. Consequently, the stylish woman's eye, and that of her imitators, was being trained to ever more sophisticated and finely discriminating levels of seeing. As a result, the majority of women attached more and more importance to their appearance and to the presentation of self through clothing, with the celebrity style-setter as main instigator and leader. Pictures of her were everywhere, and her influence was enormous, not just on the height of a heel, but on the configuration of the female soul, and the gestalt of the female psyche.

In order to appreciate the vernacular of style in all its implications of meaning and motive, we need to place it in its setting. I shall pay some attention to interior décor, but only where it exemplifies and amplifies personal style. Moving farther afield, I shall connect attire, where it seems relevant to do so, to its geographical or historical context. These five women were a cosmopolitan lot: a Spaniard who lived mainly in France; a Canadian who lived for the most part in England; a German who lived chiefly in America; and two Americans who traveled around the world. Their lives span the years 1826 to 1994, and their clothes are a key to the whole era. Anatole France once declared that if he were allowed to look into all the books published a century after his death, he would choose a fashion journal as the best source of information about the world as it was, far more revealing than books of philosophy, literature or science. James Laver agrees in *Style in Costume* that "woman is the mould into which the spirit of the age pours itself." We can, for example, read the history of female emancipation through hats. Where woman has no power at all, her face is hidden behind veils; where she has very little power, she wears a face-obscuring bonnet; where she has a little more, she reveals her face wearing a tiny, tentative confection, at a precarious angle over one eye, as Eugénie did, or, if she's grasped more power, she boldly claps a man's top hat on her head, as did Marlene. Today, when women claim equality with men, they most often, like Jacqueline once she'd left the formality of the White House, wear no hat at all.

The matter of headgear leads us directly to women's history. Since woman's dress always reflects changing attitudes to her role and place in society, I shall look at such items as Eugénie's military braid, Elinor's trailing chiffons and Marlene's trouser suits in this particular feminist context, to examine how the individual's concept of what it meant to be female conformed to, or deviated from, the consensus.

This brings us to the question of influence. Why did the female half of the Western world in the 1870s follow Eugénie's lead and step into crinolines, and in the late 1930s glide across a dance floor in gowns of Wallis blue? Was it simply a matter of Mrs. Average wanting to identify with an icon, or did Mrs. Average have some prior aesthetic or psychological need for a crinoline or a Wallis blue gown? Can a celebrity's style only catch on where it finds an answering desire in the female heart?

We know that people tend to model themselves on pictures of other people, who also look like pictures because they are doing it too. We also know that the *image* of the clothed figure can have more power over eye and ego than does the actual clothed person. One suspects, however, that whereas Mrs. Average is influenced by a picture of someone else, the woman of style is more often inspired by a picture of herself which both clarifies and reinforces her distinctive self-image.

The best-dressed five influenced women in their own day, but they also have a message for today's woman. These life-histories of applied self-imagery can be read as a how-to book, teaching readers not only how to avoid the slippery slopes of style which *can* lead down, down into solipsism, but also how to master a new language, a new form of pleasure and a revitalized concept of what it means to be female.

In line and colour and texture, Eugénie, Elinor, Marlene, Wallis and Jackie limned their lives and left their mark. Now it's time to find out how they did it, and what they kept in their closets.

THE WAY SHE LOOKS TONIGHT

CHAPTER 1

Eugénie Bonaparte

Eugénie's "habit," the costume in which, as a young woman, she felt most herself, was exactly that – a riding habit. She was wearing it on November 13, 1852, the day when France's new president and future emperor, Louis Napoléon Bonaparte, fell in love with her. At a great stag hunt in the forest of Fontainebleau, one of France's royal residences, Eugénie was in her element, mounted on a fine thoroughbred from Louis Napoléon's own stables. For the first time since her wild girlhood in Spain, as she cracked her dainty pearl-handled whip against sweating horseflesh, she reveled in all the daring and dash of the chase. She loved the trim, masculine fit of her tailored coat, hated the usual feminine impediment below it of yards and yards of heavy skirt, dragging almost to the ground as she thundered ahead. Ladies were expected to ride side-saddle, but Eugénie, eager to flaunt convention, was riding astride.

She raced through tall oaks which blurred into wide green ribbons unwinding on either side, while hounds bayed in rising pitch and forest guards at intervals, in green coats and knickerbockers above high yellow gaiters, stood as firmly planted as trees. Eugénie spurred her horse, determined to be in the vanguard, the auburn ringlets clustered at the nape of her neck bouncing high beneath veiled top hat, its upright ostrich feathers bent almost flat by rushing wind.

She was first in at the kill, the usually pale skin of face and throat flushing pink with excitement. Almost at once, Louis Napoléon reined in beside her. Born April 20, 1808, forty-four-year-old Louis was the son of Hortense de Beauharnais, daughter of Empress Josephine by her first husband before she married Napoléon I. Louis' father, Louis Bonaparte, King of Holland, Napoléon I's youngest brother, always claimed that some other man, and there were plenty of possibles, had fathered Hortense's son, a sickly child who grew into an odd-looking man. Louis Napoléon looked his best, and knew it, on a horse, where one didn't notice his short legs or awkward way of walking, with body and too-large head leaning to the left, toes turned out, arms making great play to help propel him forward. Louis had a large hooked nose and small, foxy, pale blue eyes. Today they had a new light, and the waxed ends of his large moustache pointed jauntily skywards. His burly form was splendid in a gold-braided green coat with crimson velvet lapels, green three-cornered hat, white gloves and neckcloth and white kid knickerbockers. This was the uniform for all members of Louis Napoléon's hunt, but only he had white plumes exploding on his tricorne. Whenever he made some worthy courtier a member of his hunt, Louis Napoléon would send him for his jacket the requisite solid silver buttons embossed with gold stags. The similar green uniforms of forest guards, whippers-in and kennelmen bore cheap metal buttons, without stags. Eugénie always noticed such things.

She had first met Louis Napoléon at an April reception three years before, and thereafter at occasional dinners and balls, where he would cast a lecherous eye over the ladies bunched together in sweet pea-colored tulle, never even noticing Eugénie. Now, she could feel his hot, heavy-lidded gaze on the black serge stretched taut across her breasts, as if he hoped to see right through to camisole and corset. Eugénie had heard the gossip, knew that at Fontainebleau dinners the President often filled a straw basket with feminine trinkets, while ladies crowded round to draw for the so-called "prize" – Louis Napoléon himself. At evening balls, he was even less subtle; he would sidle up to a woman, leer at her low décolletage, twist his moustachios and mumble "later" into her ear. Eugénie gave her reins a sharp jerk – she could handle this man as easily as she could his big, powerful horse.

It seems fitting, given her temperament, that Eugénie was born during an earthquake, in Granada, Spain, on May 5, 1826, to the Count and Countess of Teba. Her father looked like a Byronic hero; Lord Byron, that tempestuous Romantic who lived with passion and defied convention, was Eugénie's favorite poet. Beneath locks of auburn hair and pale brow, Count Teba wore a black patch over the eye lost while serving Napoléon I in the Peninsular War, where he also acquired a Byronic limp from a badly wounded leg. Eugénie adored her father, who told her stories of her great hero, Napoléon I, but she had plenty of friction with her domineering mother, Dona Manuela, daughter of Scotsman William Kirkpatrick, who had left his native land for Malaga in 1788. There he'd become a prosperous wine exporter, numbering George Washington among his customers, and cannily applying for American citizenship so that he could become Malaga's American consul.

Eugénie's father ran his household on strict, frugal, military lines. She and her sister Paca had to wear the same few dresses summer and winter, along with cheap cotton stockings, silk ones being considered an unnecessary luxury. (Later in life, Eugénie would more than compensate for these deprivations.) Her father believed in fresh air, exercise, obedience, self-denial. He had a rather strange habit of putting little Eugénie astride a cannon that stood on Granada's walls, and then firing the cannon so that the hard iron vibrated alarmingly between her legs – and deeply, permanently, in her psyche.

Eugénie was a wild little thing, always in motion: swimming, doing gymnastics, galloping bareback about the countryside (her father wouldn't let the girls travel by carriage), dancing the fandango with some wandering gypsy band. She craved novelty and change in everything; she even tried smoking and fencing, and when her mother's friend, French novelist Prosper Mérimée, came to visit, she got him to teach her how to load and fire a pistol. She was daredevil and tomboy, "all fire and flame," high-spirited, over-excitable, so intense one couldn't bear her company for long. Her abrupt changes of mood would become more marked as the years passed. She could flash from good humor to hysteria as quickly as shot-silk changed color.

When her uncle died in Madrid in July 1834, Eugénie's father inherited his elder brother's title of Count de Montijo, along with plenty of money, a spacious house in Madrid, and a small castle called Carabanchel in the country. Dona Manuela went off at once to Paris, for the first of many extended stays, taking Paca and Eugénie with her. It was their first heady exposure, in their plain frocks and cotton stockings, to all the dream fripperies of Paris. The girls were schooled at the Sacred Heart Convent and, briefly, at a boarding school in England where the English students called Eugénie "Carrots," causing her to comb her auburn hair with leaden combs in a vain effort to darken it.

By the age of twelve, Eugénie had already found her one true love: clothes. From Paris she wrote to her father: "Please send me black lace, and also money to buy a muff. I am now very big [five feet tall, seventy-four pounds] and want to be in fashion."

Her father died the following year, and as Eugénie stood beside his Madrid grave on a raw March day, she felt her childhood, with all its wild adventure and romantic impulse, being buried with him.

By the time she was seventeen, Eugénie had grown into breathtaking beauty: small-boned, perfectly proportioned, her Titian-red hair glinting gold in certain lights, her oval face white as camellias. Her eyebrows drooped a little at the outer corners above eyes which a servant described as "of a bright, deep blue, full of soul, energy and sweetness." Only her mouth was less than ideal; its upper lip showed a hint of lining, as if a giant thumb had pushed its bow upward. Portraits and photos could never quite catch Eugénie's beauty, which was essentially one of coloring and mobility. Every emotion showed in face and body and she moved with unconscious, fluid grace, seemingly incapable of an awkward movement or of staying still.

Only in these early years was Eugénie all-of-a-piece, a Romantic inside and out, in mind and expression, preferring simple, flowing, uncomplicated clothes. She fell passionately in love with the handsome young Duke of Alba but, to her chagrin, he preferred her tranquil, dark-haired sister Paca. "You will say that I am romantic," wrote Eugénie to the duke just after he became engaged to Paca in the spring of 1843. "I love and hate in excess and I don't know which is better, my love or my hate; passions mingle in me, some terrible, all of them strong."

Paca married the duke a year later and Eugénie grew more restless and reckless, riding bareback through the streets of Madrid and turning up at bullfights, as one contemporary recalls, "on a wild Andalusian horse," with "her dainty hand armed with a riding-whip instead of a fan," and in her belt, "a sharp-pointed dagger." Once, at a resort in the Pyrenées, she shocked the guests with a favorite trick: sliding down the bannisters, skirts flying, legs far too much in evidence.

In 1847, Eugénie suffered through another unrequited love affair, this one with the Marquis of Alcanisez, a most eligible bachelor: handsome, amusing and rich. They exchanged love notes twice a day, and every morning he sang beneath the windows of the Palacio de Liria, the Duke of Alba's Madrid mansion where Eugénie was then staying. In her mind floated the frothing lace and pink ribbon love-knots of an extensive trousseau – until the day she found out that the marquis was merely using her to gain access to Paca, his real love. Eugénie felt betrayed, humiliated, as if her large store of vanity and pride had been snipped to shreds. She took poison, trying to kill herself – but taking care not to succeed. After that, she buried her passions deep inside her, vowing never to fall in love again. And she never did. However, sublimated feelings have a way of resurfacing...

Eugénie grew even more volatile: in private, she stormed and screamed and threw things; in public, she glided gracefully about, charming everyone, cocking her exquisitely poised little head. When neither technique worked to get her what she wanted – her will was strong and stubborn – she cried floods of tears. That usually did the trick.

Early in 1848, Eugénie was back in Paris, in rented quarters at 12 Avenue Vendôme, dragged to social events by a mother desperate to get her mettlesome daughter married and permanently bridled. Dona Manuela ordered Eugénie "a charming dress from Palmyre," one of the best Parisian dressmakers, and paraded her at the opera. "I am very much upset today. I have to go with Mama to see Princess Mathilde [Louis Napoléon's cousin] and do not know anyone there," Eugénie confided to Paca, whose calm and counsel she sorely missed. "I fear I shall begin to cry, which I feel more like doing than anything else." Only one thing could give Eugénie courage and comfort. "I shall put on my blue dress."

That same year witnessed Louis Napoléon's rise to prominence. What he lacked in leg-length and romantic gallantry, he made up for with single-minded, steely ambition. He was a Madison-Avenue type advertising genius before his time, for he created out of thin air a public demand for a product nobody really wanted; he persuaded the French people to switch from Bourbon monarchy to Republic to Bonaparte Empire with the same alacrity with which women changed hats. Firstly, on February 24, 1848, the French drove their king, Louis Philippe, into exile, sacked the Tuileries Palace, and heaved his throne out a window. There was plenty of rioting and looting, but Eugénie's only comment writing to Paca from 12 Avenue Vendôme was: "The revolution left nothing more for Palmyre," for the women of Paris discarded their silks and expensive lace and donned cheap cotton dresses costing ten francs each. They also shortened their skirts a few inches in anticipation of life without carriages. Louis Napoléon kept on writing pamphlets of self-promotion and amusing himself in his off hours with Harriet Howard, daughter of a Brighton bootmaker, who had surrendered her virginity to a racehorse jockey at age thirteen, gone on the stage at fifteen, and worked her way up from man to man until she reached Louis Napoléon. She gave him money, bestowed on her by former grateful gentlemen, to help stage his *coup d'état* on December 2, 1851, whereby he became president of the new Republic. Eleven months later, at his Fontainebleau hunt, came the *coup de foudre* in which he fell in love with Eugénie.

On the morning after the hunt, Louis Napoléon offered her the horse on which she had triumphed, a large bouquet of flowers

– and a place in his bed. Eugénie settled for the horse and the flowers. That night at dinner, gentlemen took bets on "when the walls [would] be breached and the fortress surrender." "You cannot imagine what they are saying about me for having accepted that damned horse!" scrawled Eugénie to the Duke of Alba's younger brother.

The next month, on December 2, 1852, Louis Napoléon declared himself emperor and launched the Second Empire. Drapers and dressmakers rubbed their hands in glee thinking of all the bolts of silk and velvet to be sold and made up for Court functions after the lean years of plain clothes and patching. Women let their old dresses down to sweep the ground again, rushed off to their dressmakers to order new ones, and crowded the aisles of Paris' first department store, Au Bon Marché, opened that year, scooping up fans and parasols and bonnets.

The ladies of France, including Eugénie, looked forward eagerly to a new age of luxury and style. Certainly the previous decade had seen the dullest, most insipid fashions of the entire century, with no style-setter in the courts of Europe to lead the way. The only well-dressed woman in Paris was said to be Marie Duplessis, the golden-hearted courtesan who served as model for Dumas' heroine in *Lady of the Camellias* and Verdi's Violetta in *La Traviata*, which had premiered in Paris in March 1843. In the 1840s, a lady's closet contained a mantle, several silk gowns made with a view to hard and prolonged wear, and a bonnet or two. If she was married, she probably had an Indian cashmere shawl as well, an expensive item acquired on her wedding day.

Two weeks after ushering in the new *luxe* by declaring himself emperor, Napoléon III invited Eugénie and her mother to join the first Imperial house party at Compiègne, the royal château some fifty miles north of Paris, built in an oak forest famous for its wild boars. Eugénie, Dona Manuela and ninety-nine other guests left Paris' Gare du Nord station on December 17, aboard a special Imperial train with six parlor cars for guests, six first-class ones for servants and a long, long line of baggage vans. Eugénie felt all the excitement of a new adventure beginning as the train pulled into Compiègne station one hour later, where carriages awaited whose coachmen and postillions wore powdered wigs above green, gold-braided livery. It took a long time to load the hundreds of trunks into wagons, for each woman had brought four different voluminous-skirted outfits, with matching accessories, for each day of their stay.

Like everything else in the Second Empire, from skirts to industry to territorial demands, the house party expanded. Planned to last four days, it lasted eleven, while ladies switched sashes and lace collars frantically among their sixteen outfits. The 101 guests hunted and flirted and dined each evening off gold plates and Sèvres porcelain. There were 183 servants to tend them, and Louis Napoléon never left Eugénie's side. "In Compiègne he first spoke to me of love, but I did not take it seriously, almost as a joke," Eugénie would later recall. One evening, as they strolled together in the gardens, Eugénie admired a clover leaf sprinkled with dew. At once Louis Napoléon sent for his first chamberlain, Count Marius Bacciochi, who then procured his women, to Paris post-haste to bring back a cloverleaf whose petals were four emeralds spread wide in a dew of diamonds. Eugénie grabbed it eagerly with her small hands, but when, during a game of hide-and-seek, the emperor found her behind a curtain and grabbed *her*, she pushed him away, crying, "Not until I'm empress!" She was playing a clever game; the prize would be high style and a crown on her head.

Following the Compiègne house party, Eugénie, with her mother as chaperone, appeared at every fête at the royal residences of Saint-Cloud, Fontainebleau and Compiègne, while Louis

Napoléon ogled and salivated. However, Eugénie held him at arm's length – no mean gymnastic feat in itself – with one small silk-clad arm. She must have realized Louis wanted only to bed her, for rumor had it he was looking frantically but fruitlessly among Europe's royal houses for a wife.

For a Court ball at the restored Tuileries Palace, given on January 12, 1853, just after the Emperor had moved in, Eugénie called in dressmaker Madame Barenne to fashion her a magnificent ballgown. Madame Barenne obliged with one of ivory brocade, made with the usual tight basque bodice, off-the-shoulder décolleté and very full skirt. The gown was lavishly trimmed with sparkling silver tassels which swayed provocatively as Eugénie moved. Louis Napoléon seemed "woefully out of sorts" at the ball, as well he might, for he had just been rejected as spouse by Princess Adelaide of Hohenlohe-Langenburg, Queen Victoria's niece, the latest of many humiliating rejections from Spanish, Portuguese, Russian and Bavarian royal houses, whose blue-blood rulers considered France's new emperor a vulgar parvenu. Consequently, on that January 12, Louis Napoléon lowered his sights to Eugénie's pink-flushed bosom and decided to propose. She had given him a strong hint that she would accept him, for on her auburn curls she wore a wreath of orange blossoms. The other female guests had clucked disapprovingly; no woman wore orange blossoms except on her wedding day! Thus properly primed, the emperor asked Eugénie to become his empress and she gave a resounding "Yes!" She certainly wasn't in love; it was mainly her romantic regard for heroes which impelled her: "The Napoleonic creed was in my blood, and I felt it was easy for me to give my life for the heir of such a name," she would later write. Like her other hero, Lord Byron, Eugénie was a fatalist; she believed her destiny was to join Louis Napoléon on the throne of France, and to play out her role in splendid, memorable, spectacular attire.

The next day she wrote excitedly to Paca: "I want to be the first to tell you of my marriage with the emperor. He has been so noble, so generous. He has shown me so much love, that I am quite overcome." But not so overcome that she couldn't still focus on her wardrobe. "Be kind enough," continues Eugénie, "to buy me two scarlet fans, the finest you can find; if none please you, send as far as Cadiz in search of them. Please try to find another sandalwood [fan] with silver filigree, and another one gilded, the most elegant you can lay your hands on. I am sending you for your birthday a charming mantle from Madame Doucet. I am very busy. Goodbye."

When Louis Napoléon informed his cousin Princess Mathilde, an intellectual focused on art and politics, that he intended to marry Eugénie, the princess called her a shallow creature who could think of nothing but clothes. When Eugénie heard this criticism, she sniffed that Princess Mathilde, who liked to paint, "always dressed in her own watercolors."

Once the engagement was announced, Eugénie moved into the Elysée Palace with her mother, her official residence until the wedding, set for January 29, and turned her attention to her trousseau. The emperor visited his fiancée every day, and Miss Howard every night at Saint-Cloud, where she was packing up her sleazy flounces preparing to vacate. Louis Napoléon arranged for Eugénie to have an annual income of 250,000 francs ($250,000 in today's currency) and gave her unlimited credit to buy her trousseau. Somehow, in only two weeks, Madame Vignon made thirty-two day dresses and Madame Palmyre twenty-two evening gowns, while Eugénie flew about seeing to the new settings of crown jewels, choosing antique lace and standing still only for fittings on her gowns. They were put on exhibition shortly before the wedding, and the women of Paris, still starved for finery, flocked to see them. (Eugénie's influence would soon cross the

Atlantic – the following May *Godey's Lady's Book* published a detailed list of every trousseau item.)

The trousseau included a scarlet velvet dress embroidered in gold thread with the Napoleonic symbols of bees and eagles; a pink watered silk, trimmed with lace, fringe and curling white feathers; a green silk dress also trimmed with feathers; a mauve silk with Brussels lace; and three identical afternoon dresses in white, pink and blue. There was nothing novel or particularly noteworthy about any of these creations, for Eugénie had not yet found her distinctive style.

She tried to endear herself to the French by refusing to accept the City of Paris' gift of a 600,000-franc diamond necklace. Instead, declared Eugénie with a sigh, she would use the money to build an orphanage in the shape of a necklace in the suburb of Saint-Antoine.

On the eve of her marriage, Eugénie wrote, with great prescience, to Paca: "When I shall play my part as empress I don't know that I shall play it from nature." There were two marriage ceremonies to go through: a civil one on January 29, and a religious one the following day. The civil rites took place at the Tuileries Palace. Eugénie wore a pink silk gown with antique lace trim, a wreath of jasmine and a diamond crescent in her hair. She also sported a necklace of many large pearls, ignoring the old Spanish superstition which said that the pearls a bride wears at her wedding would be the tears she will shed afterwards. "I cannot describe to you how much I suffered during the three quarters of an hour, sitting on a throne, facing the guests," she told her sister. "I was paler than the jasmine in my hair." One newspaper reporter present wrote that the new empress appeared "agitated" and trembled as she signed the register, and another journalist noted that the air of the great salon was full of a delicious new scent: Monsieur Guerlain's newest perfume, Bouquet Eugénie.

After the ceremony, the bride returned to the Elysée with her mother, and the bridegroom went off to spend his wedding night with Miss Howard.

Sunday, January 30, was a fine, clear, frosty day. Eugénie climbed into her wedding gown of white silk satin with a four-yard train, its tight bodice sewn with diamonds. The gown was trimmed with Alençon lace patterned in violets, the empire's official flower. Lastly, Eugénie put on the matching long lace veil. Playing no favorites, she wore the sapphire and diamond coronet belonging to her hero Napoléon's first wife, Josephine, and the sapphire belt belonging to his second, Marie-Louise. The sapphires in the diadem matched Eugénie's blue eyes and complemented her beautiful hair, curled and coiled by the fashionable coiffeur Félix. Once she was dressed, Eugénie sat down, carefully, and dashed off a note to Paca, wishing she were there to support her. "I fear the responsibilities that will weigh upon me, and yet I am *accomplishing my destiny.*" Then the empress was driven to the Tuileries. To all the laurel bushes in its gardens, flower-makers had fastened artificial white-satin roses. Those fake flowers would prove to be fine portents of Second Empire style. At the Tuileries, Eugénie was joined by her bridegroom, who wore a scarlet military uniform inexplicably one size too small. His oversized, waxed moustache and the surfeit of medals and orders blazoned across his chest gave him a comic-opera air. Shortly after noon, the bridal pair climbed into the same golden state coach with golden eagle which Napoléon I had used for his 1802 coronation, and his 1810 marriage to Marie-Louise. The carriage was drawn by six black horses in scarlet harness, preceded by a squadron of the *Garde Impériale* and followed by a division of heavy cavalry. Down the rue de Rivoli they all clattered, the street festooned with assorted banners and green velvet hangings glittering with gold Napoleonic bees, and the letters "N" and "E" entwined. Sun glinted on the gleaming breastplates and helmets of the troops, and brass bands at every intersection crashed out First Empire marches. There were huge, gold eagles everywhere, on triumphal arches and public buildings, but, like the Tuileries' white satin roses, the eagles weren't quite what they seemed, being mere plaster covered in gold paint.

Eugénie sat erect, "pale as death," as cries of "*Vive l'Impératrice!*" buffeted her like waves. She was feeling far too many conflicting emotions, there inside her misty cloud of lace, as the procession made its slow progress towards Notre Dame Cathedral.

Inside the church, where 15,000 candles flickered, she and Louis Napoléon took their places on an ermine-covered stage, under a red velvet canopy well sprinkled with golden bees, and surmounted by yet one more color-of-gold eagle. The ceremony proceeded. "Do you promise and swear to remain faithful to her in all things which a faithful husband owes to his wife according to the commandment of God?" the Archbishop of Paris asked Louis Napoléon sternly. The emperor looked him square in the eye and replied, "I do."

Romance, every trace, disappeared forever for Eugénie as soon as she took off her enveloping cloud of lace mist. She put on her going-away outfit, crimson velvet chosen for its royal implications, with lavish edgings of fur, chosen for comfort, and walked hopefully, trembling but smiling, towards her future.

Of the imperial wedding night nothing is known, but much can be inferred. For Eugénie it was probably short, nasty and brutish, and she may well have conjured up the childhood memory of an iron cannon between her legs. The over-sexed emperor, physically infatuated with his pretty young wife, proved insatiable. Later, he claimed that for the first six months of marriage, perhaps remembering the words of the Archbishop, he had sworn off all other women, including Miss Howard, and concentrated all his lust upon his lawful wedded wife. Eugénie bided her time; then one day when she and Louis Napoléon were walking in the garden and he bent over to examine some plants, she pushed him, hard, so that he landed awkwardly on all fours, a position which made him look, just for a moment, not at all like an emperor and very much like an animal.

All too soon Eugénie found herself pregnant and knew that soon she would be unable to fit into her pretty trousseau dresses. On April 27, three months after her wedding, she suffered seventeen hours of excruciating pains which ended in a miscarriage. While confined to bed for a month, she took a good hard look at her new life, and at the satyr she shared it with. For a woman, particularly a woman of style, nature was a seductive, cruel enemy, leading to physical humiliation, an ugly body, terrible pain. She was finished with sexual love; let the rest of the court cavort around her as they pleased. Reclining in her gilded bed, which was elevated on a platform and suitably canopied, Eugénie, her face like marble, there in her romantic excess of lace and ribbons, became from that day forward an asexual woman. Years later, she would express the sentiments which became hers on that spring day. "After all, men are worth very little," a woman friend said to her, describing some man's sexual intrigues. Eugénie replied: "Since we are alone, I will tell you: they are worth nothing." On another occasion she asked a friend plaintively, as well she might, "Why do men never think of anything but *that*?" She also confided to her ladies-in-waiting that she thought the whole business of sex was "disgusting."

But the satyr was intent on producing an heir, and Eugénie soon found herself pregnant again, and again endured a painful miscarriage.

In addition to the burden of conjugal duties, she felt the weight of court formality pressing down upon her. At all the royal residences, even at the seaside villa he would later build at

Biarritz, the emperor insisted on a rigid, stifling formality. At every doorway stood ushers in chestnut-colored coats with powdered wigs and plumed hats, ready to shout "*L'Impératrice!*" if Eugénie passed by, or "*L'Empereur!*" if a listing Napoléon III tacked his way through, leaning on his favorite rhinoceros-penis walking stick. When on the main floor of the Tuileries Palace, whose interior was so dark that even in summer lamps were lit all day in its stuffy, unventilated corridors, Eugénie had to wear a hat, and she moved always in a knot of people, none of them friends, but merely court attendants: the *Grande Maîtresse*, Princesse d'Essling, a cold, severe woman; the *Dame d'Honneur*, Duchesse de Bassano, slightly more approachable; two chamberlains and two equerries in blue uniforms with silver braid; her "reader" who never read because Eugénie preferred to read for herself; six ladies-in-waiting (later increased to twelve). The latter wore their hair so tightly drawn back from their faces that, as one observer noted, "they can hardly close their eyes, and they wear scarlet jackets and mantles, which go very badly with their complexions." The ladies-in-waiting preened and gossiped and twittered endlessly to Eugénie about their lovers, a scarlet pool always there, spreading around her. Every day the same routine. In the mornings, Eugénie wrote letters and saw to her wardrobe, ordering from a stream of tradesmen who came to the palace; at noon she had to sit patiently through the daily report of each attendant while they droned on and on. After lunch she made her stately progress in the carriage, with postilions and outriders in green and gold livery, round and round the lake in the Bois de Boulogne, while her mounted equerry rode round and round the imperial carriage. There were never less than fourteen guests for dinner. Footmen came and went with two soups; two *relevés*; four entrées; two roasts..., while Eugénie felt the whalebone of her corset growing ever more constricting.

During the winter season at the Tuileries, there were receptions every Monday for six hundred guests; banquets every Thursday; between January and Lent, four balls for five thousand guests, plus a fancy-dress ball during Carnival; and four concerts in Lent.

"Every fate has its sad side. I, who was always so excited at the mere mention of freedom," wrote Eugénie to Paca, "am never free from court etiquette, of which I am the victim." "I am the slave of my kingdom," she complained, "isolated in a crown, without a woman friend and, it goes without saying, without a man friend either; never alone for a moment; an insufferable existence."

She paced up and down her suite of ten rooms on the Tuileries' second floor, which had a small private staircase linking them to the emperor's suite below, up which he stumbled and puffed whenever he felt the urge. The empress had lately begun to wear outfits all in one color: dress, hat, parasol, shoes. And that was also how she chose to decorate her rooms. The first salon was all in shades of green: walls, carpet, upholstered furniture and Sèvres china ornaments. The second salon was blue, in tones ranging from pale blue to ultramarine, with a thick, Prussian-blue carpet and cerulean silk gauze curtains. The third salon was pink, with a ceiling painted by Chaplin of the Triumph of Flora, peony-pink curtains and pale pink walls with arabesques in brighter pink. There were little tables and glass-fronted cabinets everywhere in all Eugénie's rooms, all of them crammed to excess with jeweled boxes, china figures, silver-framed photos and costly *objets d'art* in ivory, jade and lapis lazuli. Eugénie moved restlessly from room to room, ruefully eyeing the tropical birds in bright plumage painted above one door. "Tell me what has happened to the fans," she scrawled to Paca from her study. "I would like to know if I must give up hope of receiving them." The study had flamboyant purple satin curtains and upholstery, and a screen of gilded bamboo, up which exotic, rambling plants had been trained to cling. "But I have made a rule," continued Eugénie to Paca, "not to want what I cannot get."

By July of 1853, Louis Napoléon had returned to Miss Howard's bed, but was on the hunt for a new mistress. In his upright moments, he was busy supervising Georges Eugène Haussmann's transformation of Paris – by means of great landscaped boulevards, five thousand acres of parks and impressive cream-stone buildings – into the Paris we know today. On every broad new façade and bridge, fake-gold eagles spread their plaster wings.

In 1854, Napoléon III allowed France to be drawn into the Crimean War and Eugénie ordered gowns in two new colors that had just become popular: Crimean green and Sebastopol blue. Next year, Winterhalter did a lovely painting of the Empress with her ladies-in-waiting, in which they look like large, voluptuous flowers dropped lightly onto grass. Eugénie wears a dress of filmy white gauze over white silk, with blue ribbons to match her eyes. She'd ordered it from Maison Gagelin, and, unbeknownst to her, it was made by the man who, in another five years, would dramatically change her life.

Eugénie and Louis Napoléon made a state visit to England in April 1855, where Eugénie began her life-long friendship with Queen Victoria. Eugénie thought the latter's dresses terribly dowdy, but admired her riding clothes. They were made, the queen told her, by Henry Creed. At once, Eugénie ordered him to make her several riding habits, which, when delivered, fitted so perfectly that she persuaded him, in the fall of 1855, to open a tailoring establishment in Paris, in the rue de la Paix. (The Parisian House of Creed would be carried on by sons and grandsons until World War II, when it returned to England.) Eugénie's new riding clothes soon grew too tight, for that fall she was pregnant again, and feeling ill and exhausted. Her final outing before her confinement was to accompany the emperor to see the imperial layette, on display at Madame Félicie's in the rue Varenne. Newspapers reported that the layette cost the equivalent of $100,000: all hand-sewn with tiny, invisible stitches in finest white lawn, silk or muslin, with plenty of embroidery and lace. The baptismal robe alone cost $1000.

Eugénie went into labor in the early hours of Friday, March 14, 1856, and was in agony throughout Friday and Saturday; at times she had to be kept standing, supported by attendants, to recover her breath after the terrible spasms. The doctors finally had to use forceps to deliver the Prince Imperial, Louis Jean Joseph (soon to be nicknamed Lou-Lou). Not until May could Eugénie walk unsupported. The doctors told her that she could never have another child, and Eugénie made it clear to Louis Napoléon that never again at bedtime was he to come lunging up the private staircase to her boudoir.

It was in that year, 1856, that a few of the most fashionable women stopped wearing multiple petticoats to puff out their dresses. Up to that time they'd worn at least five petticoats: two cambric, two flannel and one of really stiff material woven from horsehair. Now they happily discarded all that weight, and put on crinolines. Invented by Frenchman R.C. Milliet, whose patent was dated April 24, 1856, and made possible by the improved quality of steel, the crinoline was a lightweight arrangement of eight hoops of thin, flexible steel in increasing diameter from waist to hem, with vertical tapes to anchor them. It made the dress fabric worn over it balloon to amazing new breadth. Eugénie, in the beginning, opted to keep the thick, insulating armor of her many petticoats. Since Lou-Lou's birth, her skin had "yellowed," as her doctor remembers, and she was plagued by kidney problems and annoying pain. When she sat, she placed a large leather cushion at her lower back, and when she traveled she took with her a smaller one stuffed with horsehair.

Along with the vexing question of whether or not to switch to crinolines, as more and more women were doing, there was the beautiful nineteen-year-old Countess of Castiglione to make Eugénie reach for her back cushion. The countess had arrived in Paris that year, and Louis Napoléon had immediately taken her to bed and made her his official mistress, giving her an emerald worth $100,000, a pearl necklace worth $442,000 and a house in the rue de la Pompe.

The countess didn't fancy herself in colors, so she always wore black – except when she sat naked, hour after hour, regarding her curves in her large boudoir mirror. She covered the walls of her drawing room in black silk and put black satin sheets on her bed and black taffeta covers on all her furniture. She soon let her friends know that when she died she wished to be buried in the lace-trimmed nightie she'd worn on that blissful night when her emperor had first sat astride. She turned up at a June evening fête at Villeneuve l'Etang in a dress of see-through black muslin with her dark hair tumbling to her shoulders from beneath a large hat pendulous with maribou. The mesmerized emperor rowed her about the illuminated lake and then led her into the dark shrubbery. Eugénie nursed her wounded pride and vanity, and translated her agitation, as always, into movement; she began to dance, but not being fully recovered from her confinement, she fell heavily in plain sight of the whole company.

When Count Walewski gave a costume ball on February 17, 1857, at the newly opened Quai d'Orsay, Countess Castiglione swanned about in a black gauze dress – so sheer that it was plain to all, including the pop-eyed emperor, that she wore no undergarments, relying on cut-out hearts to cover strategic places. When the countess curtseyed to her empress, Eugénie looked at her coldly and said: "Your heart seems a little low tonight." This was a rare lapse, for in public Eugénie usually managed to keep her emotions under wraps. "I live in a world," she told Paca, "where I must play two parts – my public life, my private life," and she took care to keep them separate. Her public self was stoical, stately and dressed to the nines. Her private self was impetuous, volatile and simply dressed, Bohemian style, in a jacket of red flannel or knitted black wool, worn with a plain black skirt.

The public charade continued. "How did you know that I cough?" Eugénie asked Paca on January 2, 1858, at the start of yet another winter round of parties. "I have not mentioned it to you or Mama in order not to alarm you. The doctors want to condemn me to silence, but at these receptions I have to talk to everybody. What would commerce say if I shut myself away without giving balls? And if you give them you must go to them. Pale or pink – what does it matter? The winter season must be gay, that is what matters."

Occasionally, she could throw off the empress' heavy responsibilities. In September 1858, she made a visit to the Basque country, and as her doctor reported, "after dinner, when the Basques began to dance to the sound of the guitar the dances of their country, the empress could hold out no longer and, flinging aside her hat and mantle, she began to dance a most graceful fandango."

France went to war with Austria in the following year over the unity of Italy, while Louis Napoléon switched his amorous allegiance to Countess Walewska before mounting his horse and galloping off to war. Eugénie acted as regent while he was away, garbed in leather belts and severely tailored jackets whose braid at hem and wrist gave them a distinctly military air and a hint of male authority. The rest of the female population ordered dresses in the new shade called magenta, following the emperor's triumph at the Battle of Magenta.

Then, at a memorable Tuileries ball during the winter of 1860, Eugénie's whole life changed. The ball began like all the others, at 10:30 in the evening. The Tuileries' façade was outlined in burning gas jets, as if hung with yellow-diamond necklaces, as coaches arrived and discharged their passengers. Inside, lining the staircases, as guests ascended, were the *Cent-Gardes* splendid in sky-blue uniforms, white breeches and silver helmets with long, flowing manes of white horsehair. As they mounted the stairs, ladies in clouds of pale silk would pause to study their hairdos in a guard's gleaming breastplate, resettling coronets of diamonds, or garlands of fresh flowers if that was all they could afford.

Ballrooms were lighted with wax candles; Johann Strauss himself, from a balcony, conducted his waltzes while five thousand guests whirled and twirled. At promptly 11 p.m. the emperor and empress arrived, entered the Salle des Maréchaux, paraded slowly to one end where a raised platform stood, with crimson velvet canopy and the ubiquitous gold eagle. Then the empress, as always, faced the room, made one deep curtsey to the princes seated on her right; one to the diplomatic corps on her left; and one to the general throng. Then, as always, she danced the opening quadrille, not, thank God, with Napoléon III and his two left feet, but with the highest-ranking male guest. After that she and the emperor circulated through the various ballrooms. It was while she was nodding and smiling and doing her empress thing that Eugénie spotted twenty-two-year-old Pauline de Metternich, wife of the Austrian ambassador, Prince Richard de Metternich. Pauline wasn't at all pretty; she had a dark-skinned little face with a too-large mouth and a figure far too skinny. When Louis' cousin Princess Mathilde called her "a little histrionic monkey with her thirty-six flounces and her forty trunks," Pauline retorted, "At least I'm a fashionable monkey!" Pauline made up for her lack of beauty by tremendous chic. She had been in Paris for a year, rattling about town in a carriage painted bright yellow with a coachman in yellow and black livery. She danced the cancan at parties, sang naughty songs and sometimes smoked cigars.

In the Tuileries ballroom, Eugénie stood transfixed. She couldn't take her eyes off Pauline's dress, like none she'd ever seen. It was white silver-threaded tulle, with bunches of pink-centred daisies half-hidden in wisps of wild grasses, all of it dewed with diamonds and misted over with more white tulle. It spoke directly to Eugénie's heart. It expressed, in tulle and tracery, all her stifled romantic yearnings, all the sweet, sweeping feelings tangled up inside her. She learned, with growing excitement, that the gown was designed by Charles Frederick Worth, who, Pauline told her, had opened a salon at 7 rue de la Paix two years before. "Tell him to come and see me tomorrow morning at ten o'clock!" cried Eugénie.

She couldn't concentrate on the voices buzzing round her in the Gallery de Diane as she toyed with the food spread there for a stand-up buffet supper. At long last, 12:30 came; time for the empress and emperor to leave, although the dancing would go on until three or four a.m. She placed her hand on the Emperor's arm and they departed, Eugénie with her graceful step lighter and quicker than usual, Louis Napoléon with his usual shuffle, as if he had one foot in a ditch, and behind them came the usual crocodile of court attendants, in blue, scarlet or green jackets with white breeches and hose, clanking their swords and insignia.

Usually, when she returned to her second-floor rooms, Eugénie would be so tired that already on the way upstairs she would be removing the weight of crown and jewels from her aching head and wrists so that, at the door of her dressing room she could toss them pell-mell into her maid's skirt, held out to receive them. But tonight Eugénie bounced up the stairs, full of a new energy and eager for the morrow.

Worth arrived promptly at the palace next morning, but showed his self-confidence by coming in his normal everyday clothes rather than in the evening dress all tradesmen visiting the palace were expected to wear. He also sported a velvet beret, which, ever since Rembrandt had painted his famous self-portrait, denoted the artistic temperament. Born in Bourne, Lincolnshire, on October 13, 1825, thirty-four-year-old Worth (one year younger than Eugénie) was a handsome man, full of smiles, with a round, shiny pink-and-white face, fair hair parted in the middle, and moustaches that glittered like gold. At age twelve, Charles Worth had apprenticed himself to Swan and Edgar's in London to learn the dress goods trade, selling not only silks and muslins by the yard, but bonnets and shawls as well. He had taught himself dress design by studying portraits in the National Gallery. At twenty, speaking not one word of French and with only five pounds in his pocket, Worth had come to Paris and been hired as salesman by Gagelin and Opigez, a shop which sold fabrics but not, of course, dresses, which could only be obtained through dressmakers. There Worth met and married pretty staff member Marie Vernet, on June 21, 1851. He persuaded the firm to let him dress his wife in original designs made up from Gagelin cloth. His employers took some convincing, for this was all very radical. Up to that point, no man had ever made women's apparel, except for riding clothes, and no live model had ever modeled it. Women's clothes were made by women and the design depended on each customer's own initiative, with no shop displays to guide her. Women dressmakers in France had formed a guild for making women's clothes as early as 1675, and at the time Worth appeared on the scene the three most important women were Palmyre, Vignon and Victorine (whose creations Balzac and Stendhal praised). None of them were truly original or particularly talented.

At Paris' World Fair in 1855, Worth, still at Gagelin's, won first prize for his design for a court train. He then arranged to sell some of his designs to foreign buyers with permission to copy them, and the French couture trade as we know it was launched. (Before that, fashionable women outside France saw French clothes only on dressed dolls, dispatched to foreign capitals.) Sewing machines were then just coming into use, and copies of Worth's Paris dresses were soon on sale in European and American cities.

Worth left Gagelin and Opigez in 1858 to open a business of his own in the rue de la Paix, which was becoming quite the fashionable street. Other women besides Pauline de Metternich had already found their way to Worth's Salon de Lumière, where walls were mirrored from floor to ceiling, and Monsieur Worth, Mademoiselle Mary or Mademoiselle Esther were ready to pin and advise.

Now Worth smiled at Eugénie and she smiled back, happy, as always, to be focusing on style. She was about to begin what one fashion critic calls "her greatest achievement: her collaboration with her couturier." It was a union made in heaven. They were both arch romantics, both lovers of drama, sentiment and everything new. The empress told him her requirements, opened her heart, through the metaphor of frill and flower, and gave him an order. She had found at the same time her ideal man and manner of expression. And this man would service her body and her vanity in the way she preferred – by keeping a respectful distance.

With Eugénie's patronage, Worth prospered, and also ushered in fashion's modern era, becoming the first real couturier; the first to see that clothes could be both creative and commercial, both art and big business; the first to proudly "sign" his dresses, by means of a label sewn inside, just as an artist such as Rembrandt signed his paintings. On the strength of his imperial appointment, Worth steadily gained new customers among the courts and courtesans of Europe. He always came to Eugénie at the palace, but all other women had to come to his salon. Their men folk were shocked by the very idea of a man in woman's preserve, a fox in the hen-house. "Would you believe," wrote Charles Dickens in February 1863, "that there are bearded milliners, man-milliners [there was no English equivalent for *couturier*] who with their solid fingers, take the exact dimensions of the highest titled women in Paris – robe them and unrobe them."

It wasn't long before Worth persuaded Eugénie to throw away her many petticoats and step into a crinoline instead. By 1860 the crinoline was approaching its maximum diameter, about ten yards of fabric at the hem, giving Worth plenty of ground on which to strew his romantic appliquéd or embroidered blossoms, crescent-moons, doves, love-knots and other charming conceits.

The crinoline very quickly became not only Eugénie's favored metaphor but also that of the Second Empire itself. The crinoline, first appearing as it did in 1856, made its debut when masculine and feminine polarities of gender definition and role in a patriarchal society were as far apart as they would ever get. The crinoline was the essential prop which made the female silhouette look as distinct as possible from the masculine one. The Womanly Woman in tight-waisted, crinolined gown and bonnet and the Manly Man in frock coat, stove-pipe trousers and top hat looked so different they might well have been two distinct species.

Now, with her heavy impeding petticoats gone, Eugénie suddenly felt light as air, and wonderfully free. Her legs could bend, stretch, cross, scissor back and forth, move continually, do whatever she wanted them to do, there inside her correct steel cage. And no one, given her surface decorum and formal deportment, would ever suspect all that activity going on underneath. The crinoline became not only her freedom flag but her weapon as well, for it kept all male fools at a distance. After Eugénie had been swaying about in her unapproachable sphere for several weeks, the disgruntled emperor commissioned a farce in which the leading lady appeared in a crinoline grotesquely wide. The joke, however, misfired. Eugénie sent her maid for its measurements, and had one made at once in the exact same size.

Like Eugénie's temperament, the crinolined skirt was changeable and unpredictable, tilting up behind when she stood close to a table, swaying from side to side when she walked, tilting up in front when she sat down. And like Eugénie herself, the crinoline gave forth an ambiguous message. In the first place, it said: from the waist down, I'm frigid, I'm an igloo, don't dare approach; but it also said: I'm a passionate woman, a fertility symbol, just look at the width across my hips. Secondly, the empress' crinoline declared: I'm seizing more space and more power; but also: I'm as different as possible from a man, who holds it all.

Like Eugénie's public image and so much else in the Second Empire, the crinoline was a sham. It made a skirt look as roundly solid as an architectural dome but in actual fact was nothing but wire, with no real substance or stable position at all. It yielded to the slightest pressure, and it was never quite the same two minutes running.

With Eugénie and Worth leading the way, the crinoline became so wide during the years 1860–62 that it was impossible for two women to go through a doorway together or sit on the same sofa. Women could no longer wear any kind of coat as outer garment, but only capes or shawls. The shawl gave Eugénie's restless little hands as much activity as the crinoline did her legs, for shawls had to be constantly clutched, rearranged, adjusted. She bought a large store of cashmere ones from Les Compagnie des Indes in the rue de Richelieu.

Eugénie looked so charming in her Worth creations that soon he was being asked to dress all the other empresses and queens of Europe, including wasp-waisted Elizabeth of Austria, lovely Alexandra of Russia and dumpy little Queen Victoria, who needed all the help she could get. He also acquired more and more newly rich American customers whose husbands were making fortunes in railroads or oil or manufacturing. The American ladies bought their gowns directly, if they were in Paris, or ordered them sight unseen to be shipped to New York. We can draw a straight line of influence from Eugénie as dressed and crinolined by Worth to the Southern belle Scarlett O'Hara in the 1939 film *Gone With the Wind*, based on Margaret Mitchell's novel. In the 1994 eight-hour CBS television mini-series *Scarlett*, based on Alexandra Ripley's sequel, its heroine aped both Eugénie's skirt-width and variety, for she changed her costume 120 times – once every four minutes.

Eugénie's new-found joy in dress, and in the new man in her life, was interrupted by a cruel blow. Her beloved sister Paca, her one confidante and true friend, became gravely ill. She came to Paris for treatment, but by July 1860 she was so ill that she could no longer walk and lay all day on a couch, eyes half closed, gasping for breath. By August, it was clear that Paca was dying from advanced cancer of the spine. Eugénie called on her every evening, and on Paca's good days they drove together in the Bois, where one spectator remembers the Duchess of Alba as "elegant, beautiful, immobile, pale, dying." Eugénie was depressed and distraught, for, as one friend recalls, she "idolized her sister – in my humble opinion this was the strongest emotion of her life." Eugénie had to leave her sister to accompany the emperor on a trip to Algiers; while there, on Sunday, September 16, Paca died, but the emperor put off telling Eugénie until they reached Marseilles on September 21, not wanting to interrupt the tour. Eugénie never forgave him; she lost not only the sister she adored, but all remaining faith in her husband.

Eugénie, who never did things by halves, gave way utterly to grief. She wept, sobbed, moaned. "No one must live in the room where my sister died!" she cried, and tried to have the house torn down. "It seemed to me as if my soul had been torn from me," she later wrote. Now the only really soothing, restraining influence on Eugénie's violent feelings was gone. Her temper tantrums grew louder and more frequent; she would fly into a fury if her maid forgot to put her back cushion in her carriage. In between, she was mute and listless. In December, she packed her black mourning gowns and went off to Scotland, where the damp gray mists matched her mood, stopping briefly in London to see Queen Victoria, who thought her "thin and pale and unusually melancholy" and noted that her friend only mentioned the emperor once.

After some months, Eugénie switched from black dresses to pearl gray ones, and eventually back to bright colors, but it was a very long time before she again put on her favorite color, an intense sky blue which matched her eyes.

Her crinolines, meanwhile, were still expanding, for as the Second Empire grew more prosperous and more material, so grew the crinoline, demanding, quite literally, more material. Ladies' dresses became a special kind of financial statement, showing increasing prosperity in the width of skirt and the luxury of trimmings. Instead of costing 300 francs, which is what Pauline de Metternich had paid for her first Worth gown, they now cost several thousand. Second Empire France, like Victorian England and America in its Gilded Age, was experiencing its first era of rapid industrial growth. Napoléon's real backers, supporting Second Empire goals the way the crinoline underwrote its women, were bankers, industrialists and capitalists. They formed, with Empress Eugénie leading the way, not only the first generation of conspicuous consumers, but also the first generation to consider clothes as self-expression, to consciously, with a lot of help from Worth and others, tailor them to the psyche, with special emphasis on class status as motive for dress.

The Tuileries Palace balls served the same function then as runway fashion shows do now. They showed the new styles and started the new trends, with Eugénie as most important model and *première-vendeuse.* With five thousand guests crowded together, whirling around "La Reine Crinoline," as they called the Empress, all the latest novelties could be displayed in a short space of time to a great many people. The ladies invited to the Tuileries included a large number of newly rich Americans, as well as Russians, English, Italians, Spaniards, Germans and Mexicans. Fashion began at the palace and fanned out to the rest of Paris, the rest of France and the rest of the world. As a fashion authority noted in 1854, every new form of dress for the past two hundred years had always originated at the highest social level and then worked its way down. Eugénie was the last of that long unbroken line of royal and titled fashion leaders, but she was, so to speak, balanced on the cusp, because she was also the first fashion leader in the modern, democratic age, where all it takes to lead is enough money and enough conspicuous consuming. Eugénie herself was not of royal blood, but a parvenu at a short-lived, precarious court. She had a large state bankroll and a great talent for spending it. It was Parisian wit Nestor Roqueplan who summed up the Second Empire attitude to fashion. "Money," said Nestor, "is always chic." The Best-Dressed lists have been underlining that view ever since.

Women were feeling an exhilarating new sense of self-importance, which explains why they reveled in their widening crinolines, and why they discarded delicate, pastel hues in favor of colors made possible by the recent invention of aniline dyes, colors that would knock your eye out at a hundred paces: garish shades of orange, parrot green, turquoise and purple. For the first time, women had become a market. Whereas formerly they were mere buyers of food and other domestic necessities, now they became a prime target for consumer exploitation. They still had no civil rights, but all through the western world, women, inside their newly enlarged, brightly colored spheres, took their first steps towards eminence and emancipation. Style was the new byword. In addition to Au Bon Marché, other department stores opened in Paris: Le Louvre (1855), Le Printemps (1865) and La Samaritaine (1865). In 1850, Paris had 158 establishments selling women's wear; in 1898 it had 1,932. By 1860, Au Bon Marché was doing 5 million francs worth of business a year, compared to 500,000 in its opening year, 1852. A new crime was classified in police precincts and textbooks: kleptomania. Newspapers and magazines, also for the first time, devoted an enormous amount of space to fashion. The number of words written on the pros and cons of the crinoline alone exceeds human understanding.

Following Paca's death, Eugénie began to channel all her emotional energy into her clothes. Romance had lost its tongue but found its tailor. She became obsessed with style to the same extent that Louis Napoléon was obsessed with women. Her motives for dress were personal, but only partly. She knew herself to be the only woman in that morally lax, frantically coupling court circle who never took a lover. Consequently she needed all her arsenal of femininity, a great passionate outpouring of lace, fans, parasols, furs and jewels. In her public life, she had found an avenue of expression for her blocked emotions and sexuality. Her gloves were embroidered in birds, butterflies and flowers. Her parasols had ivory or silver handles and were creamy with lace. Her velvet garters were ornamented with worked pansies and silver tears, or made of gold and silver filigree by Froment-Meurice in the rue Saint-Honoré. When it came to accentuating the feminine, Empress Eugénie could teach modern-day women a thing or two. Shc loved shoes and how they looked on her tiny feet, and ordered hundreds of pairs in the current style of flat-heeled slipper, from Massez, in violet, bronze or scarlet leather. She never wore a pair twice, sending the used slippers to the children's orphanage which she'd founded for three hundred orphans selected from the poor of Paris, who were trained to embroider and make artificial flowers.

Eugénie's second motive for dress was political. She was a dutiful enough Empress to know that she had to lead the commercialism and industrialism of her day by example: to stand at the apex, setting the style, encouraging women to spend, spend, spend, but never once taking them where they didn't want to go. She spent the equivalent of $100,000 a year on clothes at a time when the Louvre director got $7000 per annum for his purchases.

Excess was stamped deep in her nature. "You never get an idea," Louis Napoléon once told her, "an idea gets you!" She appeared at a Tuileries ball wearing a white satin gown trimmed with 103 tulle flounces. One Worth gown of cherry red velvet had a skirt entirely covered in handmade Alençon lace and cost the equivalent of $25,000. When a lady turned up one day at court wearing something new: a locket on a ribbon round her neck, Eugénie appeared next day with seventeen lockets dangling from a velvet choker. When she became attached to a trimming, she wanted it on all her new dresses. When she liked a certain color, she ordered dress after dress in that same intense shade. She plunged into fashion, talking of dress incessantly, as if it were the most important thing in the world. "*Si vous aller au diable*," Eugénie liked to say, as she pirouetted before a mirror, adjusting flounce upon flounce upon flounce, quoting a Spanish proverb, "*au moins allez-y en voiture!*" [If you want to go to the devil, at least go in a carriage!]

Worth was on call at all times, and Eugénie had him rushing to the Palace almost daily while she ordered a new gown for every official occasion, never appearing in the same dress twice. And she wanted her newest robe *at once*. Worth records in his memoir that he "once made a gown for the Empress Eugénie in three and a half hours!" Political pamphleteers began to write of "the frivolity of the Empress" and of "her immoderate love of fine clothes." It was in the provinces of France that she was judged most severely, and people began to mutter that she should take warning from Marie Antoinette's fate.

In spite of these dissident voices, Eugénie's influence spread. Everything she wore was noted, and described in France's daily papers and in such fashion journals as *Le Follet, La Psyché* and *Le Petit Courrier des Dames*. The American fashion bible, *Godey's Lady's Book*, published in Philadelphia, in its "Chitchat on Fashions" column detailed Eugénie's latest craze, writing often of "Empress blue" and "Empress cloth." Women coiled and braided their hair into elaborate chignons like Eugénie's, for she'd moved beyond flying ringlets to a hairstyle with more weight and substance. The new style for doing the hair, *Godey's Lady's Book* reported in November 1862, was off the face in two rolled coils "*à la Impératrice*," separated by small side combs "now all the rage," in tortoise shell for daytime and gem-studded gold or ivory for evening. Many women dyed their hair trying to emulate Eugénie's auburn tints; the chemicals they used were primitive, so some of them went bald in the process. But if that happened, they could easily buy "Eugénie curls" by the cluster. Portraits of Eugénie were displayed in shop windows in the principal cities of Europe, as well as in North and South America. Inferior copies of her dresses could be bought in London for under two pounds, and fabric shops told their customers that the fringes and ribbons they were selling had found favor with the French Empress.

In her crinoline, Eugénie covered a lot of ground, and her new feeling of empowerment went to her well-coiffed head. She became a perfect autocrat. She gave orders that for formal balls at the Tuileries all women were to wear white, in the tradition of her hero Napoléon I's court. No woman was to appear in the same gown twice; they were to dress in latest fashion and deck themselves in plenty of diamonds. The wife of a New York banker, and the daughter of a Baltimore manufacturer "have been notified by the master of ceremonies of the Empress Eugénie," noted *Godey's Lady's Book* in April 1869, "that the permission formerly granted to them to appear at the Monday evening receptions of the Empress has been withdrawn. Cause – unbecoming dresses at the last soirée in the Tuileries."

All those white evening gowns taxed Worth's ingenuity but he was equal to the task, deftly interlacing white tulle with silk flowers, and experimenting with different textures. In 1863, for instance, he put Eugénie into white tulle with red velvet bows and gold fringes; in 1866, white trimmed lavishly with ivy; in 1867, white spangled in silver; and white tulle with black velvet sash.

Eugénie's clothes obsession grew. She had her ballgowns made in duplicate so that half-way through the evening she could change, then reappear looking fresh and dazzling. Every article purchased for her wardrobe received a number on its arrival at the Tuileries and an entry was made in a register, of which there was one for dresses, one for hats, one for shoes, and so on. There was simply no other way to keep track of the sheer volume of apparel. Two rooms of her Tuileries suite were used as workrooms by needlewomen who were constantly sewing there, hunched over long tables. Here the empress, in addition to Worth's magnificent and expensive creations, could have plain morning dresses made up to her own design. Four dress forms with Eugénie's measurements stood at the ready, where gowns could be fitted and pinned.

Eugénie bought clothes at the beginning of each of the four seasons when various tradespeople streamed in and out of her rooms. She ordered day dresses from Laferrière; mantles from Madame Félicie; hats from Madame Virot and Madame Lebel.

In her compulsive and excessive spending on clothes, Eugénie was precursor and prototype for another First Lady who, like her, presided over a court (this one in Washington, "Versailles on the Potomac" as Lewis Lapham calls it in *The Wish for Kings*); had an over-sexed, bed-hopping husband; set the fashion for all women of the western world; found an ingenious way to dispose of discarded clothing; and, in all probability, used too-much consumption as compensation for too-little love.

Eugénie kept active by changing her costume seven times a day. She owned one linen wrapper but no dressing-gown; she had no need of one since she got fully dressed first thing in the morning and stayed fully dressed until she retired for the night. Only with all her clothes on did Eugénie feel truly herself.

She had a most ingenious method of getting dressed. Directly above her dressing room, which had great revolving mirrors and a dressing table skirted in white lace with blue ribbons, was a large room of oak closets with sliding doors where all her apparel was stored. While Eugénie slipped off her linen wrapper, her maid spoke into a speaking tube, giving instructions to another servant above. Then she pressed a button which activated a trap-door in the ceiling. Next, a wicker-work figure of Eugénie's measurements slowly descended, dressed in gown, crinoline, underwear and accessories. With her maid's help, Eugénie could put everything on in fifteen minutes. This arrangement kept her clothes from wrinkling and bunching as they would have if carried down the nearest narrow staircase. After adding necklace, earrings and bracelets, Eugénie summoned her hairdresser, "for the Empress, contrary to the usual fashion," reported *Godey's Lady's Book* in

1869, "leaves her coiffure to the last." Assisting Eugénie in this seven-times-a-day ritual was Madame Pépa Pollet, in charge of wardrobe and known as "the treasurer." She had tended Eugénie as a girl in Spain, and had married a Frenchman after coming to Paris. Pépa was small, dark, bony; no one but Eugénie liked her. She fought with all the other servants, screaming at them in her heavy Spanish accent, and pocketed bribes from tradesmen.

With a steady stream of new apparel flowing *into* the palace, where space had to be left for people and furniture, Eugénie devised a method to keep used clothing flowing *out* again. Once a year she held a sale in a long gallery in the Tuileries basement. Opened oak wardrobes against its two long walls contained dresses; shawls and mantles were folded over stretchers down the middle; shelves at one end held underwear and a counter at the other displayed hats on wooden stands. Most of the customers were female court servants, who walked about, noted the number attached to an article, and then announced their chosen numbers to a clerk. Gowns worn on some historic occasion were tagged with highest prices; apparel not sold by day's end went off to Paris' second-hand clothing dealers, who resold it to their clients for immense sums. The money Eugénie raised from this annual event went, ostensibly, to charity.

One day, when Worth was making one of his frequent visits to Eugénie's humming workroom, he brought her a ballgown he'd designed, as he explained, for his beautiful Empress. It was made of beige Lyons silk brocade woven in a flower motif copied from a rare Chinese shawl. He explained to her that the Lyons silk mills were in decline, their hand-looms threatened by the new steam-driven power looms of English and German manufacture. The Lyons workers were starving, continued Worth, as his empress re-entered the room attired in the beige brocade. Eugénie liked tulle and gossamer silks for evening, fabrics that floated on air and skin as lightly as butterfly wings. The Lyons brocade was what *Godey's* would later describe as "the heaviest, never-wear-out style of silk." "I won't wear it," exclaimed Eugénie firmly, "it makes me look like a curtain!" Wasn't it enough in the cause of Empire that she often went about in velvet covered with regimented rows of little bees? Just then, Louis Napoléon listed into the room and stood looking at his wife, his head even nearer than usual to his left shoulder. Worth explained the plight of the Lyons workers, and the emperor thereupon decreed that the empress must not only wear the gown but order others. Eugénie capitulated, and thereafter wore what she called her "*robes politiques.*" In time, although she disliked the weight of the fabric, her romantic soul responded to the sprays of roses, showers of stars and other conceits repeating on the gleaming surface. Sometimes she indulged her own fancies, and dictated the design to be woven into warp and woof. Soon women everywhere were wearing Lyons silks; the looms could hardly keep up with the demand, and in the years 1860–70 the number of Lyons silk looms doubled.

By 1862, although Eugénie still missed Paca dreadfully, she was back in all her usual bright colors except "Eugénie blue." Sometimes, however, her sense of style faltered. "The Empress almost for the first time since she occupied her present elevated position," reported *Godey's Lady's Book* in December, "was very unbecomingly dressed, as the color of her gown did not at all suit her complexion." Her green silk dress was "long, wide, flowing and flounceless" and over it she wore, as a last hint of mourning, a black lace shawl which fell at the back "in large, heavy folds; neither brooch nor bracelet was visible."

For the Carnival fancy-dress ball of 1863, Eugénie dressed as wife to a Renaissance Doge of Venice, her bodice "literally *cuirasée* in diamonds." She "glittered like a sun goddess" in a robe of scarlet satin, but failed to upstage Countess Castiglione who slithered in black satin, skirt slit to waist to reveal shapely legs in black-silk tights. To keep the legs in full view, the countess had conscripted a young boy in black-face to walk behind her as an Egyptian page, holding her train as high as his arms could reach.

Eugénie tried to stay focused on whether her sash should be pink or crimson, or where to place a silk rosette; she tried to float on the dreamy surface of life, heeding the words of the popular song from the 1863 hit musical revue *Paris S'Amuse*: "Without finery and pleasure, we must agree, life is just a stupidity." But it got increasingly harder to see only the empire's gilding and not the rough plaster cracking alarmingly beneath.

Louis Napoléon began to suffer intense pain from stones in his bladder. His hair matted on his forehead and his moustache drooped. In spite of declining health, he acquired yet another mistress, blonde Marguerite Bellanger. Eugénie called her "*cette crapule*" and found a new form of exercise. She took up skating on the lake in the Bois de Boulogne. Very quickly the empress became an expert skater, her silver blades fixed to cuban-heeled pointed boots, skimming over the ice in short jacket warmly trimmed in sable or chinchilla, a short crinolined skirt with velvet knickers below, and a small velvet toque on her head. She liked the freedom of the short skirt so much that she had all the hems to her walking dresses shortened six inches; since this revealed her ankles, she stopped wearing the usual flat-heeled slippers and got into laced-up, high-heeled boots made feminine by jet beading or silk tassels.

Worth made her a short dress of Scottish tartan, which she wore with a closely fitted jacket and small toque. The rest of the females of the western world shortened their skirts, too, and put on boots whose heels added to their height and sense of importance. A few indecisive women compromised with the new fashion by keeping their day dresses long but adding strings (*tirettes*) from waist to hem which could be pulled up as required and wound around a button at the waist.

On August 30, 1864, Louis Napoléon suffered another acute bladder attack, summoning his doctor at six a.m. and keeping to his rooms for several days. In September he was brought back from Passy in a state of complete collapse. Eugénie went straight to Marguerite Bellanger and told her that she was "killing the Emperor and must give him up."

Eugénie herself that September was suffering from "nervous spasms," loss of appetite and "a state of extreme weakness." She went off to a German spa at Schwalbach in an attempt to throw off her public role completely, but at Baden, when she was relaxing in her linen wrapper, feeling too tired to dress, the King of Prussia paid a surprise visit. She had to climb quickly back into her traveling clothes, and suffocate in her sealskin cloak for half an hour while he droned his inanities. By 1865, as Prosper Mérimée noted, "Eugénie is no more; there is only an Empress. I mourn and I admire."

Louis Napoléon's military campaigns, like his health, were failing, including a disastrous attempt to put the Austrian emperor's brother Maximilian on Mexico's throne. The whole Second Empire, along with the crinoline, was showing definite signs of collapse. Eugénie stepped up the surface show. According to Maxime de Camp, the empress became "preoccupied with the impression she made, parading her shoulders and bosom, her hair dyed, her face painted, her lips rouged." Eugénie piled on make-up with a rabbit's foot, blackened her eyebrows and eyelashes, and drew a black line underneath each eye. She hired a Nubian servant to stand behind her chair at dinner and dressed him in an elaborate Venetian get-up. Her hairdresser, garbed in silk knee breeches and sword, carefully did her hair with pads to add thickness, and false braids dyed the same unnatural red as her real hair.

The whole Second Empire society grew more decorative on the surface, more decadent beneath, as the gap between appearance and reality widened. The Goncourt brothers, famous diarists of the period, noted that every face in Paris had the unwholesome look of the morning after a masked ball. Paris had become the brothel of Europe and venereal disease was everywhere, treated, but never cured, by Dr. Ricord at 52 rue de Tournon. Jules de Goncourt himself would die of syphilis, along with Alexandre Dumas, Manet and Baudelaire. The *Cent-Gardes*, still elegant on Tuileries staircases in their sky-blue and silver uniforms, almost all suffered from venereal diseases, acquired as they serviced the ladies of the court – and the gentlemen. During one three-month period the larger *Garde Impériale* lost over 20,000 duty days in hospital being treated for syphilis.

Beyond the copulating court, where only Eugénie was still chaste, the high-class whores of Paris, whose patrons included Russian grand dukes, Turkish pashas and American millionaires, spent most of their generous allowances on clothes, and rivaled the empress as style-setters. They, too, were dressed by Worth, with the difference that they wore red camellias to indicate when they were menstruating and temporarily off duty. One *demi-mondaine*, Anne Deslions, routinely sent her gentleman a duplicate invoice for the gown she would wear that evening, as a hint of what she expected to be paid. Cora Pearl's price was $5000 to $10,000 per night; for the higher fee she posed in a bath of champagne and danced naked on a carpet of orchids. Sex, like everything in the Second Empire, came with style.

The madness whirled on. Eugénie grew tired of plain white silk stockings, and invented striped ones. On the day she wore blue and white stripes, "all the courtiers proclaimed the union of the two colors ravishing to behold," according to *Godey's Lady's Book* for July 1865. There was a mania for butterflies, "all sizes, in gayest colors," embroidered or appliquéd on dresses, bonnets, collars, cuffs, even handkerchiefs. In the same year, cholera struck Paris' slums, which had plenty of rats but no butterflies. When the empress visited patients in three hospitals, the ragged, deprived women in the streets ripped pieces from her beautiful silk dress, leaving gaping holes everywhere, and making Eugénie feel as if her very self was being devoured.

By 1866, tensions between emperor and empress had increased to the point that they were barely speaking. She berated him, in rising decibels, for his sexual intrigues, and he would roar: "Eugénie, you go too far!" Rumors of divorce crept up and down the dark corridors of the Tuileries. One night at Compiègne, the guests played a favorite game, *Cheval Fondu*, in which one gentleman knelt on the floor with his head burrowing into a lady's lap while the rest of the company – all but the empress – climbed on top in a hilarious heap. That evening, when the guests had picked themselves up off the floor, they noticed that the gentleman who had initially buried his head in the lady's erogenous zone still had it there. The gentleman, of course, was the emperor.

Eugénie had never succeeded in winning the love and approval of the French. They had called Marie Antoinette "that Austrian woman" and they called Eugénie "that Spaniard." "If they knew," she once cried out in anguish, "what I would give to be really loved!" One day her ten-year-old son Lou-Lou was loudly hissed at when he appeared on a platform, and Eugénie had hysterics; all that evening, as she moved like an automaton among her guests, she muttered "my little boy, my little boy." The French public objected to Eugénie's participation in cabinet meetings, which she attended regularly in place of the emperor, so ill he could neither sleep nor walk and whose mental powers were waning. At one meeting of the Council of Ministers, the empress appeared in masculine, armored guise, wearing a dress of "extremely thick grosgrain, so thick that it could have easily passed for leather." "I assure you," Eugénie wrote to Metternich, the Austrian ambassador, "we are moving towards our fall."

As her self-confidence shrank, so did the circumference of Eugénie's skirts. By 1867, the fullness which remained had retreated to the rear and skirts at the hem were only two and a half yards instead of ten. Eugénie became obsessed with Marie Antoinette, and when she put on that poor queen's magnificent earrings, with huge diamonds shaped like pears, it was Marie Antoinette's frightened face that stared back at Eugénie from the mirror. At the annual Carnival-week masked ball, the empress dressed in imitation of Lebrun's portrait of the guillotined queen. "Madame," leered one courtier as Eugénie swished by, "your costume is such that one might lose one's head over it!"

Meanwhile, in her dressing room, the wicker-work figure of the empress still went up and down, up and down, resplendent as ever in lilac-plumed hats and sealskin cloaks. The favorite color of 1867 was Bismarck brown, named for the German Count Otto von Bismarck, who was very busy wooing the French and consolidating Prussian power. In spite of the fact that Pauline de Metternich protested that Bismarck brown reminded her of "petrified shit," the color, like the man himself, became all the rage.

Worth and Eugénie together designed a radical new kind of dress in 1868: straight and narrow in front with a bias-cut, gored skirt which suited her thickening waist better than a full, gathered one, and which signified the end of the crinoline's reign, and the takeover of the bustle. Bonnets gave way to very small hats perched well forward above a great coiled mass of braids and chignon at the nape of the neck, so that the head in silhouette matched the skirt. These much more insignificant hats had more surface embellishment than substance: one was trimmed with four stuffed hummingbirds and another with a whole feathered songbird, perched at a precarious angle.

In the autumn of 1869, Eugénie went off to Egypt to represent France at the opening of the Suez canal, designed by her cousin Ferdinand de Lesseps. The emperor was too ill to accompany her; she put up a brave front by taking 250 different outfits, including 100 Worth ballgowns, all with much shorter trains but more gold and silver threads than usual, used either as embroidery or woven into the fabric. As she chattered of these new creations, Princess Mathilde commented dryly that the empress seemed as mad about clothes as on her wedding day. "I would wish to put out of my memory everything in my life which has tarnished the bright colors of my illusions," wrote Eugénie to Louis Napoléon as she floated down the Nile.

In the summer of 1870, war broke out between Prussia and France. Louis Napoléon appointed Eugénie as Regent and, although he could barely stand the pain of being lifted on and off his horse, put on make-up to hide his pallor and went off to fight the Prussians, taking fourteen-year-old son Lou-Lou with him. The Eugénie-shod girls at the empress' orphanage stopped doing their gold and silver embroidery, and began sewing earth-bags for the fortifications. Worth tossed his bolts of silk and tulle to the back of a cupboard and turned his workrooms into a hospital for the wounded. Rich American ladies and other foreigners who had crowded the Tuileries parties packed up their newest Worth gored dresses and striped stockings and went back to wherever they'd come from.

Reports from the front were not encouraging. Eugénie handed over the crown jewels to the ministry on her own initiative and, shrewdly, got a receipt, "for I knew," she said later, "that if it came to a revolution, I should be accused of having stolen them."

Her private jewels she entrusted to Princess Metternich. The war ended on September 1, in the sleepy town of Sedan, where Louis Napoléon surrendered his army of 80,000 troops to the victorious Prussians. Eugénie came rushing down her staircase at the Tuileries and confronted the emperor's secretary, Conti. "Do you know what they're saying? That the emperor has surrendered. Never I tell you!" exclaimed the empress. "Surely it can't be true? A Napoléon never capitulates – never!" When Conti told her it was indeed true, she screamed: "Why didn't he get himself killed?" "A rush of incoherent and mad words followed," according to an onlooker, Augustin Filon. For "five long, terrible minutes" the empress raved and ranted. "We remained speechless and stunned, like men who have come through an earthquake," wrote Filon.

On September 4, the French denounced Napoléon III, voted his empire at an end and proclaimed a new republic. The women of France put off their finery and got back into plain clothes, as they had in 1848. It was an ironic note for Eugénie that the Third Republic was declared at Lyons, whose chief trade of silk manufacture she herself had revived. She could hardly eat and could only sleep with the help of chloral. What was to become of her? An angry mob surrounded the Tuileries, shouting "Down with the empire!" and – most frightening – "Down with the Spaniard!" All over Paris, gilded plaster eagles were torn from their standards.

She knew she must flee. She quickly donned a black cashmere dress with narrow white collar; thin, waterproof cloak; dark gloves; black hat. She ate a bit of bread from her untouched lunch tray and left by a back door, taking Mme. Le Breton, her "reader," with her. She fled to her American dentist, Dr. Evans, and asked him to get her out of Paris. She then borrowed a round Derby hat with a thick black veil from Mrs. Evans and left for the coast, with Mme. Le Breton and Dr. Evans, in a plain, brown, unmarked carriage. She had no change of clothes; no money; no jewels. She was stripped of all her accoutrements of self, and shook with the terror of it, thinking of Marie Antoinette.

As the carriage rumbled ahead, Eugénie couldn't stop chattering and sometimes gave a hectic, nervous laugh. What a strange adventure life was! She fleeing, the emperor taken prisoner by the Prussians! "Everything seems a short, evil dream," she sighed, her black-gloved hands twisting and tapping on her plain black skirt.

Towards the end of September, the ex-empress found a house in England which she considered suitable called Camden Palace, at Chislehurst. Not all that suitable – unbeknownst to Eugénie, the house had been owned in the 1840s by the Rowles family, whose daughter Emily had been one of Louis Napoléon's many consorts when he resided in England. The ex-emperor, ill and demoralized, and young Lou-Lou soon joined Eugénie at Chislehurst.

One suspects that Eugénie was relieved to be rid of the whole crazy French circus. Perhaps she reflected that it was not immorality that had destroyed the Second Empire nor unsound finances nor even the warring, ambitious Prussians. It was the total denial of reality fed by an overweening desire for luxury, for the lace-trimmings of life. And she had been the guilty ringleader. According to an English friend, Eugénie became "the least Second Empire lady imaginable. She is the only woman I know whose whole aspect, from her clothes to her attitudes, does not bear the imprint of the times of her greatest glory."

In England, where she lived for the rest of her life, Eugénie found again a quiet self and renewed sanity. She wore simple clothes in dark colors or black; took to religion and good works; cemented her friendship with Queen Victoria. The queen came to see her on a dreary, raw day in late November 1870 and found Eugénie "thin and pale, simply dressed, no jewelry, her beautiful hair held in a net." In December, the queen wrote to her daughter Vicky, Empress of Prussia, that Eugénie "bears her sad fate with the greatest dignity. Not one word of complaint or bitterness is ever heard from her, and she accuses no one."

Eugénie sold her private jewels in June 1872; friend Pauline de Metternich had deposited them, through a minor Austrian diplomat, at the Bank of England. They brought Eugénie $300,000 to keep her in comfort for the rest of her long life.

The deposed emperor never regained his health and died at Chislehurst on January 9, 1873, of kidney failure, with Eugénie and Lou-Lou at his bedside. Lou-Lou was then enrolled at Woolwich Academy to learn to be a soldier. He was killed six years later, on June 1, 1879, in South Africa, where he'd gone to help the British fight the Zulu war. When a servant came to tell Eugénie of her only child's death, she burst into a great fit of sobbing and fainted several times that day. A few days later she wrote to her mother, "I hide myself away as far as possible. My grief is savage, quiet, irascible. I am in no way resigned and I don't want to be consoled, I want to be left in peace."

The Prince Imperial had written a will before his death, stipulating that the splendid uniform he died in, however muddied and tattered, and the underwear beneath it, be sent to his mother. When the clothing arrived, Eugénie placed it in Lou-Lou's former study at Camden Place, where she kept his smoking cap, pipes and even a ration biscuit from his knapsack in a cabinet rarely, if ever, opened. Found later among her papers was the sentence: "I am left alone, the sole remnant of a shipwreck, which proves how fragile and vain are the grandeurs of this world."

She built a large house at Farnborough Hill, Hampshire, in 1881, and a museum nearby to house relics of her great hero, Napoléon I: his uniforms, robes, carriage of state, even the Sèvres cup from which he drank his morning coffee. She added a church dedicated to Saint Michael and had Napoléon III's remains and those of the Prince Imperial buried to right and left of the altar.

The English musician Ethel Smyth was a neighbor at Farnborough, and visited Eugénie frequently. Ethel detected in her character a "curious hardness," an "uncertain sense of humor," and "a lack of sensuality but not of romance." Ethel concluded that "love can never have played a great part in her life." Miss Smyth also noted in her memoir *Streaks of Life*: "I have seen her possessed by a passion of wrath and pouring forth a torrent of magnificent invective" in "swift, concentrated fury." (This was in 1918, when Eugénie was ninety-two.) Eugénie tried to calm her raging spirits not, as formerly, with other people's needlework, but with her own. A large, unfinished tapestry in a Farnborough convent, copied from Murillo's painting "The Assumption," still has its sharp, steel needle where her fingers last placed it; Notre Dame de France church in London's Leicester Square owns a set of vestments embroidered by the ex-empress.

Eugénie kept on the move. She bought a yacht she christened *Thistle* for cruising in the Mediterranean, and built a villa at Cap Martin, on a promontory near Monte Carlo, where, from her bedroom, she had a magnificent view of sea and shore and sky. When she stopped in Paris en route to Cap Martin she invariably stayed at a hotel whose windows overlooked the place where the Tuileries Palace had once stood. When asked if this upset her, she replied, "The Empress died in 1870."

She visited Scotland, Ireland, Scandinavia, Austria; she went frequently to Spain, and once to Ceylon for a six-week stay. In Egypt, at age eighty, she rode a donkey. Her face assumed the pallor of old ivory; her profile was still sharply etched, but her figure grew stout. She stopped dyeing her hair and let it go white. Her eyebrows went white too, but she made a slight concession to her flamboyant past, and blackened them, but only half the arc.

She welcomed all the latest inventions of the new century, bought a motor car, entertained Marconi and lent him her yacht for his experiments. When in 1901 his marvel, the telegraph, was inaugurated between Canada and England, the first message flashed to King Edward VII – and the second to Eugénie.

When her favorite man and mentor Charles Frederick Worth died on March 10, 1895, she sent his sons a long telegram which concluded: "In my prosperity and in my sorrows he was always my most faithful and devoted friend." (Worth had been working in his Paris salon until two days before he died. His sons Gaston and Jean-Philippe, and then grandson Jacques, kept the business going until 1956.)

By 1902, Eugénie had lost all interest in clothes. When Lady Airlie came to see her that year, she noted that Eugénie's skin was "wrinkled and uncared for, her figure heavy and shapeless. She wore an old black gown, a dingy woolen mantelet trimmed with a little black jet, and shabby big black garden hat." She looked, Lady Airlie decided, "like any old French peasant woman."

Was Eugénie's passion for clothes, in the final analysis, more political than personal, more the product of role than inclination? Was the whole mad clothes-circus one big put-on?

"I am now a very old bat," Eugénie told a guest in 1919, when she was ninety-four, "but like butterflies, I long for light; and before I die, I would like to see the sky of Castille," whose color was that amazing blue which had always been her favorite shade and which more than one nation called "Eugénie blue." She left for France and Spain in December 1919, stopping off as usual in Paris, and ending up in Madrid, at the Palacio de Liria where her nephew, the current Duke of Alba, lived. In her end was her beginning. She had gone to Spain because she wanted, one last time, to put on that perfectly fitting milieu.

Cataracts in her eyes made the sky look far too milky, so she underwent a successful cataract operation, and some days later went to a bullfight, searching for her former self. "I have returned home!" she declared exultantly.

She died peacefully on July 11, 1920, at age ninety-four, in her beloved sister Paca's bed, in Paca's room in the Palacio de Liria. Her body was dressed in the white robes of the Order of St. James, then shipped back to England in preparation for burial in the Farnborough Church of St. Michael. But there was one last comic-opera touch. Where was the granite sarcophagus which had been waiting, lo these many years, to receive the ex-empress' remains? Servants searched high and low but it was nowhere to be found. A replica was hastily made, and on July 18, 1920, Eugénie was laid to rest beside her husband and son.

Eugénie's mode of dress began as instinctively consonant with self. But her marriage and her crown forced her to bury her romantic sensibility deeply and silently inside her. Only through her clothes did it find a voice. The apparel of Eugénie de Montijo Bonaparte, Empress of France, declaimed a language full of sentiment, hyperbole, fanciful conceits, novelty and exaggeration almost to the point of self-parody. During her Second Empire days, her style was too frantic and too fevered. But the hectic flush of consumptive excess eventually cooled, and in her last days Eugénie returned to the pure and simple habit of her youth.

CHAPTER 2

Elinor Glyn

The most exciting day of the whole year – better than her birthday, better than Christmas – was the one on which *le tonneau bienvenu* – that was what everyone called it – arrived from the far-off paradise known as Paris. Once a year Elinor's rich relatives, the Fouquet Lemaîtres, took pity on their poor deprived cousins and dispatched a barrel joyously received by Elinor's grandparents, aunts and mother, living their frugal existence in the wilds of Canada. In the spring of 1870, when the big barrel was fetched as always from the Guelph, Ontario train station by Grandfather Saunders in his horse and wagon, Elinor was six, old enough for memory to paint the event vividly, permanently, in her mind.

The *tonneau* heralded the end of another stark, relentless winter, when every bit of color in the landscape vanished, leaving only black tree trunks, dead-white snow and lengthening shadows. All that winter Elinor had craved color, but had to settle for the few fuchsia plants and salvias in the "conservatory," Grandmother's word for the small, glassed-in room at Summerhill filled with plants. Elinor had used these flowers to people her fantasy world. "I wove [note her choice of word] fairy tales for myself in the conservatory which was my principal playground during the long cold winter. I lived in a fairy kingdom of my own and fancied myself its queen. I used to drape a tablecloth round my shoulders, and march about with measured tread, my head held high beneath an imaginary crown." She played with a "Salvia Prince and Fuchsia Princess," while beyond the windows everything was silent, white and cold. Most children outgrow their desire to inhabit a world of kings and castles; Elinor never would, and what is even more amazing, she would make her wish come true.

Summerhill, home of her maternal grandparents, had pretensions to grandeur, not only in its conservatory but in its pillared portico as well. The house was built on a hill, so that its residents could look down from their superior position on the town of Guelph, population 2000, a cluster of stores and modest houses, with nothing but endless fields and forests and rutted dirt roads fanning out around it.

Inside Summerhill's kitchen, on that special spring day in 1870, as soon as Grandfather pried the top off the rough, brown, very utilitarian barrel, the magic began. In a moment the plain pine table and chairs were covered with the most wondrous stuffs and colors, as if a cloud of giant butterflies had wafted into the room. There were silk stockings of fairy gossamer; dresses the color of lilacs or goldenrod, frothed with creamy lace at neck and sleeves; bonnets trimmed with birds' wings, whole wings, in subtle shades of teal blue or blackcurrent. There were gloves with gaily embroidered cuffs, skirts with so many flounces Elinor couldn't count that high, slippers in violet leather soft as Grandmother's pansies. There were wigs of hair dressed in elaborate hair-styles, and bolts of shimmering silks from which one could fashion anything one's heart desired, anything at all. Out of that humble barrel, into that modest room, flowed the very luster and imagery which Empress Eugénie and Charles Worth, in Second Empire France, had created together to form a garden of earthly delights. Someday, Elinor promised herself, tracing with one small finger round and round a curlicue of silk ribbon spiraling outward on a velvet ground, somewhere, she would find that world where high-born ladies danced in gowns like these across floors shining like slabs of cooling toffee.

Lucy, aged seven, Elinor and her mother and namesake, whom we shall call Elinor senior, had been living at Summerhill with her mother's parents, Thomas and Lucy Saunders, for the past five years. Thomas and Lucy had emigrated to Canada in 1833, bought farmland at Guelph, then a town of only a few cabins and one store, and endured the usual pioneer hardships. In 1840, after helping to build Guelph's jail and town hall, Thomas became Clerk of the Peace for Wellington District and built a farmhouse called Woodlands, where he and Lucy raised one son and eight daughters, the seventh being Elinor senior, who grew into a pretty girl with a cameo profile and long mahogany-brown hair. When she was sixteen, in 1858, she was courted by Douglas Sutherland, a twenty-year-old civil engineer working on the Grand Trunk Railway, son of Captain Edward Sutherland of Sydney, Nova Scotia. Like Elinor senior and her mother Lucy, who maintained rigid standards of gentility and never mixed with lower-class settlers, Douglas was a social snob, claiming to be the rightful heir to the Scottish Lord Duffus who had lost his estates by supporting the Jacobite cause.

Elinor senior and Douglas married in Guelph three years later, in January 1861, and lived there briefly before moving to Brazil, where Douglas worked on railroad construction and his bride tried to make a home of a back-country shanty with no water but plenty of snakes. His next job took them to Europe; Lucy was born in London in 1863 and Elinor on October 17, 1864 on the island of Jersey, where her mother had gone to stay with a half-French aunt to await the birth; husband Douglas was then working on the Mont Cenis tunnel at Turin. He caught typhoid fever there and died on January 30, 1865. His widow, only twenty-three, totally alone, distraught and penniless, returned to her parents' homestead in Guelph, arriving on August 25 in black dress and veil, a small daughter clutching each black-gloved hand. Little Elinor was a precocious, red-haired child of ten months, already able to walk, who had worn down the heels of her patent-leather shoes, just two inches long, by "determined tramping on the deck of the steamer which brought us to Canada." Elinor already knew that shoes were made for walking and that if she walked far enough, she would find an adventure.

During the next five years in Guelph, there were three stories of her mother's married life that Elinor listened to with rapt attention. Since they all centered on apparel, they made Elinor aware of the primary, and perilous, import of clothes in one's life. Elinor's green eyes would widen as her mother frequently recounted how she'd watched the pretty trousseau dresses and bonnets which she'd made herself go up in flames when fire destroyed the newlyweds' wooden home in Guelph, on a winter night when all sources of water were frozen solid; how she awoke one morning in her Brazilian shanty to find her lovely white-silk wedding shawl so chewed by rats that only a few threads remained; and finally, how her happiest moment in Brazil came when she opened a letter from sister Fanny and out fell a tissue-paper pattern showing an exciting new straight-from-Paris method of cutting a skirt!

"The years of my childhood," Elinor would write in her autobiography, "developed my character, moulded my tastes, and colored my point of view for life." Grandmother Saunders was a "frightening woman, proud, aloof, autocratic," who wore stiff, black silk dresses and snowy caps, whose only concession to tenderness was a pink velvet ribbon. Appearances counted: Grandmother dined every evening at Summerhill in a Paris gown from *le tonneau bienvenu* as if she were at Compiègne or the Tuileries Palace, and grieved for days when her last pair of silk stockings went to holes. Grandmother never allowed Lucy and Elinor to leave the grounds of Summerhill, and made them sit on hard, straight chairs for five minutes every day without making a single sound or movement. If one were upper class as they were, Grandmother would explain, one must never "be familiar with the wrong people," nor show the slightest emotion in public. In those first six years of her life, Elinor had great need of the colorful dream skeins with which she embroidered her drab, pinched frontier existence.

In her seventh year, Elinor's life suddenly took wing. Her mother married a sixty-four-year-old crusty, but well-to-do Scottish bachelor named David Kennedy. They wed in Guelph and went to live abroad, taking little Elinor and Lucy with them. Elinor senior was anxious to fulfill her first husband's dying request that his daughters be raised in Britain, and so used her second husband to achieve it.

Young Elinor's first real-life adventure began with a fine flourish which kept fantasy and fact as close as coat and lining. Mr. Kennedy took his bride and step-daughters to visit his elder brother at Balnegan Castle, in southern Scotland's Mull of Galloway. "It was dark when we arrived," writes Elinor, "and we were ushered by grand-looking footmen into a spacious, beautiful room with shaded lamps, filled with ladies and gentlemen in full evening dress." Sixty-four years after the event she could still recall that their host, Peter Kennedy, wore a brown evening coat and high stock collar. Balnegan had splendid suites of rooms, winding staircases, a gratifying number of turrets – and a lady guest called Mrs. Bovill, very beautiful of face and raiment, who made a lasting impression on the two little girls. She invited Elinor and Lucy into her bedroom, hung with cerise silk, and let them "play with the fascinating things on her lace dressing table. I was thrilled," remembers Elinor, "by her beautiful pink satin peignoir and quilted slippers, and longed most ardently to become a society lady just like her." Peignoir and slippers joined the Paris barrel's bounty in the closet permanently lit in Elinor's mind.

When Kennedy developed bronchitis, his doctor advised him to live in Jersey. Kennedy promptly installed his new wife and step-daughters in a furnished house called Richelieu on the outskirts of Jersey's capital, St. Helier. Elinor loathed her "crotchety, cranky, invalid" stepfather, who was impossibly miserly with his money. Her mother made the few clothes they were allowed to have, and taught both Elinor and Lucy to be skilled needlewomen. The social life of Jersey, home to retired British generals and colonial clerks, revolved around Government House, where its resident lieutenant-governor, Sir William Northcott, gave frequent elegant parties. Certainly young Elinor, thanks to her mother's skills and her own, was always well dressed, but her mother's new friends soon impressed on her that she suffered from a dreadful handicap: her bright red hair. In those days, red hair was considered unattractive, "common," and the property of "loose women" who could only come to bad ends. One lady who had perhaps heard of Empress Eugénie's remedy, advised Elinor to comb her flaming locks with a leaden comb to darken them. Elinor became obsessed with her appearance, a preoccupation which would last all her life, but felt encouraged when Sir William Northcott patted her head and told her not to worry; her dark eyelashes countered her red hair and guaranteed that she would not grow into complete ugliness and depravity. Her mother told Elinor never, ever to go out in the sun without a parasol. Elinor never did, and this preserved the stunning foil for red hair of unfreckled skin, white and smooth as gardenias.

All around the walls of their Jersey home were paintings of beautiful seventeenth- and eighteenth-century ladies by Lely, Gainsborough and Lawrence. These portraits, like those in London's National Gallery which had first inspired Worth, now inspired Lucy to start designing clothes, which she made, at this stage, to fit her dolls. Elinor, meanwhile, wove stories in her head about these ladies with high-piled, powdered curls and a look of rose-tinted hauteur.

Elinor and Lucy often spent the day at Government House with their new friend, Ada Northcott, Sir William's daughter. Ada would cut the outlines of dolls from paper; Elinor, skilled at drawing, would give them faces and Lucy would paint on dresses in the very latest fashion. One memorable evening when the three girls were together at Government House, they heard with excitement that Lily Langtry was coming to dine. Lily had grown up in Jersey, turned into a beauty, married nonentity Edward Langtry, gone to London with only one dress. In that simple black frock she caught the eye of Edward, Prince of Wales (later King Edward VII). She became his mistress, thereby gaining entrée to England's highest social circle and to a heady mix of basic black and pearls with everything. Her wardrobe and her fame grew ever bigger; other women copied her habit of wearing only black or white. Now here she was, expected any minute at Government House!

Elinor, Lucy and Ada hid beneath the dressing table in the room where Lily would have to leave her cloak. The table was covered with pink glazed calico and swagged with muslin; the three girls proceeded to cut peepholes in the calico so that they could see what Lily was wearing. Fifty-eight years later, Elinor could recall every detail of Lily's "white corded silk dress with a tight bodice and a puffed-up bustle at the back. The low neck was square cut, with a stitched pleating round the edge, and her elbow sleeves had lace frills." The only splash of color was a scarlet ribbon tying back her golden-brown hair. The next day, Lily switched to black, and strolled about St. Helier in svelte velvet and furs. She was still in black on her next visit to Jersey; Elinor sketched the arresting profile of her high-collared dress, whose ruffles cascaded down the back from bustle to hem. In dress, veiled bonnet and angle of parasol, Elinor caught Lily's saucy style, and years later would reproduce her drawing proudly in her autobiography.

In 1878, when she was fourteen, Lucy started going off for long visits to English relatives; Ada Northcott left Jersey; Kennedy dismissed the governess who had been teaching his step-daughters, and was too stingy, in spite of his wife's pleas, to hire a replacement. Elinor was thrown completely on her own resources, for both education and amusement, and rose to the challenge. When the Kennedys moved from Richelieu to 55 Colomberie, a larger, paneled stone house in St. Helier with a wonderful grape arbor for dreaming, Kennedy sent for his library of books from Scotland. For the next two years, Elinor read voraciously, all day and into the night. She devoured *Don Quixote*; Sir Walter Scott's romantic novels; Agnes Strickland's many volumes on *The Queens of England*; the poetry of Lord Byron; and Thackeray's collected novels, which had been prettily bound in old Chinese silk during Kennedy's stay in Peking. When she got to *Vanity Fair*, Elinor was particularly intrigued by its adventuress heroine, Becky Sharp, who whips up gowns from old brocade and who has, according to Thackeray, "as good taste as any milliner in Europe and such a clever way of doing things," but whose character he captures perfectly in one "ex-white satin shoe, down at heel." "It was impossible for me to live without a dream kingdom," writes Elinor, "but my new paradise was a much more realistic and worldly place than the old."

In the following year, 1879, Elinor began to keep a diary in penny notebooks; she would go on doing so for the rest of her life, but later volumes would be bound in purple velvet – purple for its royal connotations – and kept in canvas bags fastened with Bramah locks. She also filled sketchbooks with clever drawings of people she met, paying particular attention to what they wore. But her quintessential record, her autobiography in cloth, was her wardrobe book, in which she kept a detailed record, in both words and sketches, of her clothing acquisitions. Every new outfit was a milestone worth noting on her determined march to fame and fortune.

When Elinor learned in 1880 that Mlle. Duret, on holiday in Jersey, lived in Paris, she so charmed the elderly spinster that when Mademoiselle returned to her flat near the Boulevard Malesherbes, Elinor went with her. "Everything about Paris enchanted me," she remembers, and fulfilled the promise of the *tonneau bienvenu.* Taking in the well-dressed women, and the well-dressed windows of Paris' main shopping avenues, sixteen-year-old Elinor felt more strongly that "sudden awakening to the possibilities of life" which she'd first experienced at Summerhill ten years before. And she thrilled to her very first flirtation. At the Jardin des Plantes a young Frenchman whispered over and over into her shell-pink, highly receptive ear, "*belle tigresse*," giving Elinor an image which she would later make her own and exploit to the hilt.

In 1884, Lucy married a seemingly delightful, debonair Englishman called James Wallace, who, as the innocent young bride would all too soon discover, was in actual fact drunken and dissolute. The couple went to live in a cottage on the grounds of Cranford Park, the country estate near London, of Lord and Lady Fitzharding. Elinor soon ingratiated herself with Lady Fitzharding, too fat to be stylish. (Perhaps this was because their cook, eventually fired by his irate Lordship, used two thousand eggs a week in his cooking.) Lady Fitzharding introduced snobbish Elinor to England's most aristocratic and select society, launching her on a round of visits to England's country houses, the very best hunting-ground for husbands. It was the custom then for the owners of stately homes to fill them with houseguests for week-long stays during which the married male guests stalked grouse and pheasants by day and other men's wives up and down the creaking corridors by night. Single men and women settled for a little groping in the shrubbery or in the darkest corner of the library, and by the end of the week had aligned themselves into tentative pairs.

In this first stage of her tripartite life, Elinor was bent on raising her social status – and her clothes allowance – through the right marriage. She had turned into a real beauty by then; her unique coloring of white skin, emerald eyes and flaming hair made her stand out from all the other husband-hunting girls. One gentleman would recall years later that Elinor Sutherland was the most stunningly beautiful creature he had ever seen. To land a titled husband, however, Elinor lacked the one essential: a dowry. British aristocrats expected brides to come complete with cash settlement – which is how so many *nouveau-riche* American girls in the Gilded Age, whose fathers had made their pile in railroads or oil secured British dukes and earls for husbands.

Elinor, lacking a dowry, decided to compensate with another effective bait: her clothes. It was during these pre-nuptial years that Elinor's wardrobe first became a conscious marketing tool, a most effective soft sell. Later in life, clothes would help promote her creative products; in this first stage, she was selling herself. Act One of the drama of a red-haired adventuress reveals Elinor as an arch romantic and a feminine, passive, compliant creature – or so she took care to appear – twirling her parasol, batting her dark eyelashes, mincing about on high heels, confident that soon she would find Prince Charming and live happily ever after. At this point, she had no thoughts of any career beyond that of socialite.

"If it had not been for Lucy's genius for making smart clothes appear out of nowhere," declares Elinor, "we could not possibly have gone about in the Cranford society we did. Between us we made every one of the dresses we wore, even the tight, supposedly tailor-made garments of those days; and very chic we looked!" Elinor became obsessed with her attire, as a letter to her mother of May 18, 1883, while on a country-house visit, shows: "From what I have seen of this house I shall be bored to tears. When you send my blue dress send my velvet body with the cream lace, the one laced down the front. Though I may not want it in this benighted place, I may if something better turns up."

Current fashions played into Elinor's hands. The bustle was shrinking fast; skirts still came to the ankles by day and had languorous trains by night. However, it was impossible to cross a croquet lawn or ascend a curving stair without holding up one's skirt; petticoats beneath were well-laced with erotic appeal and Elinor made sure hers were seen. Sleeves were puffed and enormous from shoulder to elbow, making one look as if born with angels' wings. Day dresses had lace jabots cascading prettily and showily over the breasts, or one long ribbon, anchored to a rosette on the bosom with its other end waving about like a leash, begging for a strong manly hand to grab hold and command the creature attached. Day blouses of delicate muslin had high boned collars to just below the chin, with seductive little bands of see-through lace running up and down the body. Skirts fitted smoothly and snugly down to the hips, and then flared out like giant lilies to the hem. Capes were waist-length, with stand-up wired Medici collars which looked like calyxes drawing the eye upward to the gardenia-face above. One always wore a hat by day; Elinor's were small so as not to obscure her spectacular hair, and trimmed with a high-flying wing or two. Stockings were black silk or lisle; hers were silk as sheer as she could find it. Her shoes and boots – Elinor prided herself on her small Cinderella feet – were leather or cloth, laced or buttoned, always with high heels. Fashion decreed that "gaudy" colors were for matrons; single women wore white or pastels, but Elinor determined to stand out from the phalanx of maidens. In a letter to her mother, she describes one new dress in which she paraded before the females at a country-house gathering:

> Mrs. S. looked up. "Oh. An evening dress I suppose?" I said, "certainly not." "You are surely not going to wear it *in the street*?" I said, "Of course I was, it was for the park," and then she sniffed. "Silver is a great deal too gaudy for the daytime."

The total effect of all this silver and lace and lost ribbons looking for a good home spelled out a message, loud and clear. The medium was the message, which said: "I am all woman, helpless, soft, pliant as a flower, needing the love and protection (and bankroll) of a good man." In her first two seasons circulating prettily in the marriage market, Elinor had three proposals, all of which she rejected, holding out for something of greater worth. One was from a "bibulous peer" with a walrus moustache who spluttered all over her lace jabot as he proposed; the second was from the Duke of Newcastle, not at all interested in *her* wardrobe but only in "the details of ecclesiastical apparel"; and the third from a too-new millionaire with "a common voice and unfastidious manners."

In 1888, Elinor's rich cousins, Auguste and Margot Fouquet Lemaître, who owned a château in Normandy and a townhouse on the Champs Elysées, invited her to spend the social season with them in Paris. She packed up her come-hither wardrobe and went off with high hopes. When cousin Margot saw the contents of Elinor's trunk she added cast-offs from her own closet, elegant Doucet dresses – Jacques Doucet was then one of the top designers in Paris along with Worth and Paquin – which Elinor accepted with mixed feelings, ashamed to be the recipient of charity but delighted with the beautiful garments themselves. Someday, she vowed, she wouldn't have to rely on second-hand style.

The joys of Paris consoled her. "I went everywhere and met everyone." On one memorable evening, Elinor attended a ball at the American Embassy looking very *jeune fille* in a white tulle gown which Margot had given her. (In France, all single girls advertised their purity by wearing white to balls.) That afternoon, the hairdresser Marcel, famous for inventing the Marcel wave, had kept two well-known ladies waiting because he so admired Elinor's hair that "he had insisted on doing it himself, in order," as he said, "that he might have the pleasure of handling such a strange mop of fine spun copper." This compliment to her despised "carrots" combined with her French frock gave Elinor such confidence that she was "as gay as Cinderella at the Prince's ball," as she waltzed across the polished floor and dreamed of snaring a French comte or duc complete with ancient, moated château. Certainly she had plenty of partners. On succeeding days, she rode one of cousin Auguste's polo ponies in the Bois, in a "perfect English habit which I had saved up to buy," and which probably came from the House of Creed patronized by Empress Eugénie. Unlike the empress, however, Elinor was terrified of horses and a poor rider; that didn't really matter because what she was showing off was not her horsemanship but her figure. "I was very slim and had such small bones that I could easily achieve an eighteen-inch waist," she recalls proudly. (At age seventy-one, she still had that riding coat and notes that neither her daughters nor granddaughter could get it on after the age of seven.) As the days passed, Elinor began to realize, alas, that no well-born Frenchman would *ever* choose a bride with no dowry, no matter how many white-tulle ballgowns and skin-tight riding habits she paraded before him.

Mr. Kennedy died the following year, 1889; Elinor and her mother rented a London flat at 25 Davies Street, just off Berkeley Square, and were soon joined by Lucy and her five-year-old daughter Esmé. Lucy's drunken husband, she told them tearfully, had run off with a girl dancing in a pantomime. Lucy promptly divorced him – a daring thing to do at that time, in that society – and decided to earn her living making clothes. She cut them out on the dining table, and her mother helped her stitch them together.

For her first paying customer, the Honorable Mrs. Arthur Brand, Lucy made a teagown that was so successful that orders from other ladies wanting "teagies," as they called them, soon poured in. The teagown perfectly encapsulated the manners and morals of the Gay Nineties, that Edwardian period of luxe and indulgence which ended abruptly with World War I. At five o'clock each afternoon, when their current lovers came to call, married ladies took off their restricting whalebone corsets to make way for exploring male fingers, and donned semi-sheer, floating, ribbon-festooned teagowns. Elinor eyed those taking shape on the dining table with envy, for convention decreed that only married ladies could wear teagowns. Lucy made her sister plenty of other seductive garments, and Elinor cinched her eighteen-inch waist and continued on her country-house, husband-hunting round.

In the winter of 1890, after six unproductive years on the circuit, came the Hillersdon house party, assembled for duck-shooting, which changed Elinor's life. One evening, all the guests attended the nearby Exeter Ball where Elinor, as usual, moved in a flock of men. When four of them, after a great deal of champagne, returned to Hillersdon, arguing loudly over which of them Elinor preferred, they settled the argument by pushing each other into an ice-cold lake. The news of this event spread from country-house to country-house until it reached the Chisenhale-Marshes at Gaynes Park. They in turn passed it on to their Essex neighbor, Clayton Glyn, eligible bachelor and substantial landowner. He declared that, by Jove, he'd like to meet the girl who could persuade four chaps to dive into a lake at three a.m. on a cold winter's night. Such a girl must be well worth looking at! The obliging Chisenhale-Marshes invited Elinor to their shooting party the next fall and introduced her to Clayton.

Like her Grandmother Saunders, Elinor put great stock in appearances, and in appearance Clayton was exactly right. In addition to a tall figure and china-blue eyes, Clayton had a shock of white hair, as the result of a gas explosion at his boyhood school, which reminded Elinor "of the illustrations in my books of Cinderella's fairy prince, for his thick silver hair was like the powdered wigs of the eighteenth century, to which the story of Cinderella always seems to belong." He was the descendant, Elinor soon learned, of Sir Richard Carr Glyn, banker and Lord Mayor of London, and he owned a large Essex estate comprising a big Georgian house called Durrington, a medium-sized farmhouse called Sheering Hall and a little cottage called Lamberts. Clayton was the usual hunting, shooting country squire, quite unoriginal, and his passions ran mainly to food. But he had the right image and the social status Elinor craved. Besides, Elinor was twenty-eight and desperate. She narrowed her green eyes, and raised her skirts high enough to show Prince Charming her Cinderella-sized feet.

It took her just over a year to capture him. In February 1892, Elinor and her mother pursued him to one of his favorite haunts:

Monte Carlo, and there, at last, Clayton took the big gamble and proposed. Elinor said yes at once. She wasn't in love, but, as one of her fictional heroines would later put it, "It is wiser to marry the life you like because after a little the man doesn't matter." They set the wedding date for April 27, only two months away. Clayton came through with an impressive diamond engagement ring from Cartier, and then suddenly announced that he had to return at once to England, "to see how the young pheasants were doing." Between that time and the wedding, Elinor hardly saw him, and "but for the ring I should have imagined that I had dreamt the whole incident." She and her mother went straight from Monte Carlo to Paris to buy a few choice items for her trousseau, the bulk of which Lucy would make, including the wedding dress. Now at last, Elinor could indulge her taste for dramatic lines, showy colors and plenty of jewelry. Single girls adorned their sweet-pea colors with one bangle and a velvet choker, trying to look as young and virginal as possible. After they married, women were expected to show off a husband's wealth and status by switching to prominent colors and as much jewelry as they could muster.

The wedding took place at one of London's most fashionable churches: St. George's in Hanover Square, with Auguste Fouquet Lemaître imported from Paris to give Elinor away. Her wedding dress of very heavy white satin had a bodice cleverly cut on the bias to hide mundane seams and side closing, and elbow-length sleeves of old Honiton lace. From the shoulders fell a stately train of heavy brocade, lined and ruched with satin. Did Elinor recall, as she walked slowly towards Prince Charming, the tablecloth draped round her shoulders in the Summerhill conservatory twenty-odd years before? Like Empress Eugénie, Elinor got a lot of mileage from orange blossoms and wore an aigrette of them on her head, a spray at her waist and plenty more in her bouquet.

Her veil was held in place by a diamond tiara, gift of the groom. Clayton pronounced his bride "so like a Fairy Queen" – exactly the effect Elinor had been aiming for.

She made a detailed drawing of her going-away dress in her wardrobe book, and labeled it, triumphantly: "For E. Glyn not Sutherland any more." The newlyweds spent their honeymoon at Brighton, where Clayton made his first and last romantic gesture. He hired the public baths for two days so that Elinor could swim in them naked, her long red hair, which, of course, had never been cut, undulating slowly behind her. Since her later fiction frequently depicts the raw lust of gentlemen on their honeymoons, one can only presume that Elinor, like Empress Eugénie, was put off sex – but not, as with Eugénie, for life. One Glyn heroine declares that "no one can possibly imagine the unpleasantness of a honeymoon until they have tried it," and another, to her husband's suggestion of a second honeymoon, replies: "The first was a horrible, fearsome memory which was over long ago, but the thought of a second. Oh, it was unbearable – terrible – impossible!"

The second shock of Elinor's marriage came on her arrival in Essex when she learned that she and Clayton weren't going to live in the great house, Durrington, with its splendid Palladian façade, because it was rented to tenants; the newlyweds moved instead into the modest farmhouse, Sheering Hall. The ruddy-faced county wives who wore sturdy tweeds and stout boots by day looked askance at the new Mrs. Glyn, for Elinor was continuing to flout convention and to find her distinctive style. She owned one tweed suit but never wore it, preferring smart daytime costumes in liquid, languorous fabrics worn with high-heeled shoes. When the county wives turned their backs on her, Elinor merely shrugged her shoulders and instead sought out the most sophisticated, high-born women in the neighborhood. One of these was Daisy, Countess of Warwick, who lived ten miles away at imposing Easton Lodge and who had succeeded Lily Langtry in the Prince of Wales' affections. Soon Elinor and Clayton were being invited to the Warwicks' select house parties for twenty-odd guests, composed in Elinor's words of "the *crème de la crème* of English aristocracy." In her memoir, she lingers lovingly over every luxurious detail of these visits, beginning with one's arrival at tea-time:

> After helping to remove your furs, Hall [the butler] would usher you into the salon, where the hostess and any lady guests were to be found, arrayed in the most exquisite teagowns of sable-trimmed velvet or satin brocade. They showed low V-necks, and had elbow or open sleeves and were of splendid materials, or else of seductive silk gauzes and lace, in either case terribly expensive and very luxurious. There would be every kind of lovely muffin, crumpet, scone, cake, sandwich, jam, honey and Devonshire cream.

The bedrooms at Easton Lodge had "exquisite furniture and hangings, big comfortable armchairs, heaps of down cushions, great white bear hearthrugs" and fresh flowers on one's dressing table. Just before dinner, as Elinor put on her twenty-button kid gloves and chose from her collection of big ostrich-feather fans, Guy, Lord Brooke, the Warwicks' eleven-year-old son, on his rounds to each lady's room, would come in with a spray of orchids or gardenias. Elinor would pin them onto her gown, at just the right spot, just the right angle, reflecting as she did so that she had come a long way from the Spartan rigors of her Guelph childhood.

Elinor became pregnant five months into her marriage, and "gladly gave up the struggle" of playing the role of sporty, outdoor country wife. She wore beautiful indoor clothes and sat by the fire for hours happily sewing "the large wardrobe considered necessary for baby girls in those days," including "corded silk pelisses and adorable muslin caps and little satin coats." It was fortunate that the baby was, in fact, female; Margot was born in June 1893, and while Clayton was disappointed not to have a son and heir, Elinor was "secretly delighted." Having launched her daughter on the right road to fashion, Elinor left Margot's care to a most efficient nanny "who took all maternal responsibilities off my shoulders from the start."

Clayton took Elinor to Paris two or three times a year so that she could buy herself more chic apparel; he liked her to be smartly dressed and paid her enormous clothes bills without even reading them. To escape the gray chill of an English winter, Clayton and Elinor usually holidayed for several months in some sunny Mediterranean resort. It was a good life, an easy one, but its rose tints faded fast.

In 1894, Elinor was shocked when one of her friends came to stay at Sheering Hall and Clayton promptly took her to bed. When Elinor tried to retaliate one evening while dressing for dinner by telling her husband that one of *his* friends wanted to become *her* lover, Clayton merely mumbled "dear old Bob" and went on tying his tie, intent on his silver-haired reflection in the mirror. "My romance," declared Elinor dramatically, "was over, after only two years of marriage. It was a bitter blow." She stayed chaste, but her clothes buying accelerated; she ordered frock after frock, mainly from sister Lucy, and drew and described them in her wardrobe book.

Lucy's business was thriving. The Maison Lucile opened that year in Old Burlington Street, turning out twice-yearly collections, and would move twice before settling into 23 Hanover Square in 1897. Eventually Lucy would find herself dressing Lily Langtry,

Irene Castle, Isadora Duncan, Norma Talmadge, Fanny Brice and assorted Astors and Vanderbilts. In addition to day-clothes, "teagies" and evening gowns, Maison Lucile made delectable lingerie, displayed in the Rose Room, its walls and daybed hung with pale pink taffeta overlaid with lace. Women had always worn white underclothes and nightgowns; Lucy put them into pale mauve, pink or blue fabrics so sheer and lacy that garments were often returned by irate husbands.

Following Worth's lead, Lucy was the first designer in England to show her clothes on live models. She also used them for creating her designs. A model would stand stock still wearing a flesh-colored satin underdress while Lucy, using it as permanent foundation, pinned and draped her pale silks and chiffons over it. She would then sketch the result, and hand it to her seamstresses to be made up. Lucile designs were noteworthy not for line or cut but for detail: minute buttons, silk flowers tucked into a sash, tiny lace frills. Lucy herself was hard-headed and practical, but her designs were vague and ethereal: palest pink ribbons threaded through silver lace; wind-gray tulle combined with silver fox; gold lamé with rose chiffon.

Elinor packed plenty of Lucile creations for an 1895 house party in Scotland, at Dysart House, home of the fourth Lord Rosslyn, the Countess of Warwick's half brother. His wife Blanche routinely ran up exorbitant dressmaking bills, and when his Lordship reproved her, she always replied that she "dressed only to please him." Their daughter Millicent, Duchess of Sutherland, a great beauty and one of Elinor's friends, used to stand on the top stair at London's Stafford House, greeting her guests while her gold lamé train flowed halfway down the stairs. At Dysart, Elinor played a starring role in an amateur production for charity of the play *Diplomacy*. A review of it in the local paper gave full details of Elinor's two Lucile gowns – details she herself had given to the reporter. One outfit showed Elinor in her dreamy, maidenly, premarital mood: a teagown of white chiné silk, edged with gold and jeweled dragons. The other teagown hinted at the highly focused, consciously flamboyant Elinor to come: a bright magenta silk, edged with narrow bands of white satin, and narrower yellow insertions, buttoned in diamonds.

She reverted completely to fairy tales for her court dress and presentation to the British Royals at a Buckingham Palace Drawing Room ceremony in May 1896. In lieu of Queen Victoria, Princess Alexandra, long-suffering wife of the playboy Prince of Wales, presided, her beautiful long neck adorned with its usual dog-collar of diamonds and pearls. Elinor described her Lucile gown in fulsome detail in her wardrobe book: white satin peau de soie, with silver gauze ribbon ("very bright silver" writes Elinor) applied everywhere, in edgings or large bows, to bodice, skirt and four-yard train. "The best old Buckingham lace" formed angelic sleeves (three yards in each) and made generous festoons on the train, held on by silver-pink bows. Elinor was gratified to note the "numbers of hideous women" being presented "with – Ye Gods – what skins. Brown or pimply, red or coarse." She had to admit that Lady de Grey, the Earl of Pembroke's sister, looked "quite splendid in cloth of gold and mauve velvet," but felt cheered by another lady in "shabby black dress and rather dirty feathers in her hair," only partially redeemed by spectacular diamonds.

Elinor's life took an exciting new turn in the spring of 1898, and style was the catalyst. Lord Rosslyn, recalling the well-dressed actress at his theatricals, hired her to write fashion articles for his newly-launched magazine *Scottish Life*. Her column, "*Les Coulisses de l'élégance* by Mrs. Glyn" first appeared on May 14, 1898, and was sometimes illustrated with Elinor's own pen-and-ink sketches. Her drawings of the new Paris hats for fall were particularly fetching, perhaps because, being pregnant again and forced into tents, her own style had gone to her head. Lord Rosslyn, however, soon ran out of money and the magazine, much to Elinor's regret, folded before daughter Juliet was born on December 15 of that year. After a difficult delivery, Elinor's doctor told her she could never have another child. She didn't mind at all, but Clayton was so distressed to think he'd never have an heir that he had to console himself at Monte Carlo, where he gambled away a great deal of money.

Elinor consigned Juliet to Nanny Dawson's care, fell ill with rheumatic fever, and hastened her recovery by scribbling a slightly naughty novel in letter form, based on all those husband-hunting years of country-house visits. She took the finished manuscript round to the Countess of Warwick. Daisy laughed heartily at every page, and used her connections in the publishing world to help Elinor sell her manuscript to *The World*, a paper, as the Countess recalls, "that touched the very centre of fashion." When "The Letters of Elizabeth" was serialized in the fall of 1899, to instant acclaim, Elinor's writing career was launched.

Six months later, the curtain went up on Act Two of Elinor's life as she stood on stage posing in a charity *tableau vivant* with four other redheads, imitating Titian's painting of *The Five Senses*. She looked, according to *The Ladies' Field*, "superbly handsome in a dress of bright purple velvet trimmed with sable," its skirt "studded with pearls and emeralds." The young woman, innocent, dreaming and playful, formerly wrapped in a pale gauze chrysalis, metamorphosed that day into a sophisticated, focused, hardworking professional, spreading her wings proudly in velvet and sable paid for with money she'd earned herself by her writing. Elinor had found her midlife style. Her habitual costume from now on would be born to the purple, with a conscious touch of class. But it was not just dignified and regal; it was also strut-my-stuff, opening number, show-biz flash.

In August, publisher Gerald Duckworth – best known to posterity as the rogue who fondled a young Virginia Woolf and turned her off sex for life – asked to publish the Elizabeth letters in book form. In the spring of 1901, Elinor was thrilled to see, piled high in every London bookstore window, *The Visits of Elizabeth* looking splendid in apple-green cover and gold lettering. The novel sold extremely well. One reviewer boosted sales by calling it "shockingly immoral" (it wasn't). The book had been published anonymously, but Elinor, eager to cash in on her new celebrity, soon stepped forward as its author.

One night she dined with all the smartest people at the London home of Sir Francis and Lady St. Helier. Another guest was the California novelist Gertrude Atherton, who has left us a vivid account:

> My attention was immediately attracted by a woman standing alone by the hearth: the other women were grouped together on the opposite side of the room and evidently discussing her. She was rather tall, slender, very smartly gowned in black, and remarkably striking in appearance. Her skin had the white translucence of alabaster; the only color in her face was in the lips of a well-formed mouth. An immense amount of blood-red hair was wound about her head in massive braids, and small dark-green eyes with thick, short black lashes gave the final touch to a countenance of singular individuality.

For a *lady*, a member of high society, to write a novel was considered shocking, which is why the female guests were looking askance at Elinor. They sent Gertrude across the room to find out what kind of make-up Mrs. Glyn had on her face. When

Gertrude reported back "there's nothing on her skin, not even a light coat of powder," they envied and felt threatened by Elinor even more. By their actions, they were doing Elinor a favor, pushing her towards full expression of her extreme, idiosyncratic individuality. Thus far she had moved more or less in the protective coloring of the flock; now she stood out, and apart.

She persevered at her writing, loving the income it brought her, and the fame. Her complete canon of works would eventually number thirty-nine: fourteen books of non-fiction and twenty-five novels, whose contents reveal their author well-veiled in romantic, rosy gauze, the Danielle Steel of her day. Her heroines, with names like Amaryllis and Ambrosine, are occasionally low-born, with butchers and chauffeurs on the family tree, but more often aristocratic – including one queen, one granddaughter of an empress, and one peeress in her own right. But whatever their status, they marry above themselves. The husband tally stands at two dukes, one marquis, one earl, three barons, five baronets, two Russian princes, a Scottish laird and a Hungarian count. To be sure, five are commoners, but of ancient stock. A heroine's clothes and jewels get full coverage on every page. Ambrosine in *The Reflections of Ambrosine* (1902) owns "a diamond necklace and three yards of pearls." Zara in *The Reason Why* (1911) appears at dinner in "deep sapphire-blue gauze" and "the Duke's splendid brooch." Henrietta in *The Price of Things* (1919) is "resplendent in yellow brocade and gardenias." This ongoing clothes rhapsody would inspire Hollywood costume designer Helen Rose, who recalls in her autobiography *Just Make Them Beautiful* how Elinor Glyn heroines are "still burned indelibly in my memory." She used to devour Glyn novels as a girl, and "in my imagination I would see these heroines in my gorgeous creations."

Elinor's fictional love scenes acquired a new resonance in 1901 when, for the first time, Elinor herself fell madly in love, seduced, as one might expect, by appearances. She had first met Guards officer Major Seymour Wynne Finch at Easton Lodge parties where the male equivalent of the teagown was a velvet smoking-suit. Clayton's was sapphire blue; Lord Cairns' emerald green; Grand Duke Michael of Russia was resplendent in rich crimson. But Seymour Wynne Finch showed originality and taste by having his smoking-suit made from a beautiful Paisley silk shawl, with black facings. Elinor claims in her memoir that she and Wynne Finch never consummated their affair, but one suspects that this is just one more of her strategically placed veils.

She and Clayton went to Cairo that winter, where Elinor shopped in the *mouski* for cheap emeralds, worn to good effect when she appeared in a charity *tableau vivant* as Lorelei, clad only in tights, yards of green gauze and her hair, which she'd combed out to full length and sprinkled with emeralds. The exhibitionist in her which had first surfaced in the *tableau* for Titian's *Five Senses* was definitely triumphing over the genteel wife raised to Grandmother Saunders' correct standards. Elinor was flattered when the Sultan of Turkey, having seen her on stage, offered to buy her, for she was thirty-seven at the time. After Cairo, Elinor and Clayton toured about Italy in a twelve-horse-power Panhard auto, with Elinor in an enormous flat hat made like a man's tweed cap, tied on with voluminous chiffon veils: an apt symbol for her half down-to-earth, half dreamy self.

It was in Lucerne, their next stop, in the spring of 1902, that the exhibitionist in her took the next step. In a shop near the Hotel National where they were staying, Elinor spied a magnificent tiger skin; that very morning she'd received a large royalty check from Duckworth for *The Visits of Elizabeth.* She bought the tiger skin for "a fabulous sum," far more than it was worth, realizing, with the most real and least romantic part of her dual, warring nature, that she'd found a startling, original sex symbol and an ambitious author's highly effective and memorable prop. Clayton exploded when he heard what the damn thing cost; he was already weighed down with luggage containing the thirty-seven new dresses and countless hats which Elinor had bought along the way. Now he had to lug about a great big trunk full of tiger!

The tiger henceforth would be Elinor's signature, logo and main tool for self-promotion. But her choice was more than just a calculated marketing ploy. On an unconscious level, the tiger signified passions, animal, crude and violent, which Elinor had long repressed. "The touch of the tiger," she would write, "awakens some far-off savagery in me," and it would be the tiger who would lead her to at least partial expression. Then, too, the tiger, by stealth and patience and cunning, always gets its prey. With the first payment from her writing, Elinor had purchased a purple velvet gown. With the second, she bought a tiger skin. Both were magic carpets to take her, in the real, everyday world, exactly where she wanted to go.

While Elinor indulged herself with emeralds and tiger skins, gourmet Clayton was drinking cases of champagne brandy, sitting up all night to catch a pear at the precise peak of perfection, and sinking deeper into a morass of debt. The Glyn household had to move in 1903 from Sheering House to much smaller Lamberts, a mere cottage. Elinor, feeling humiliated, used her income to pay some of Clayton's creditors, and to build her own wing onto Lamberts. With her usual royal aspirations, Elinor called it Le Petit Trianon, remembering Marie Antoinette in her days of opulence. It contained sitting room, bedroom, personal maid's room and a room for Elinor's extensive wardrobe. Le Petit Trianon was a fit setting for a romance novelist on the make, filled with French period furniture, a sunken marble bath, and bed canopy, curtains and bedspread covered with hundreds of pink silk roses handmade by Elinor and her daughters' governess, Dixie.

Mrs. Glyn curled up in her rose bower, seized a block of paper and stylo pen, and scribbled *The Vicissitudes of Evangeline* (1905). "What a mercy black suits me! My skin is ridiculously white" writes its red-haired heroine, whose eyelashes, fortunately, aren't white but "by some freak of nature black and thick." Evangeline is not the only Glyn heroine to have the Glyn coloring and to become one more vehicle for Glyn self-promotion. Evangeline marries Lord Robert Vavasour because he's the son of a duke, because "he does have such lovely clothes and ties" and because he whispers "beautiful tiger cat" into her ear. Elinor may be paying the bills, but she's also sinking fast, there among the pink silk roses, into a combination, fatal to creativity, of soft sell and solipsism.

Elinor herself took a lover, Alastair Innes-Ker, of the Royal Horse Guards, younger brother of the Duke of Roxburghe, about this time. He provided the prototype for Paul, "splendid young English animal of the best class," as she puts it, hero of Elinor's most famous novel, the sex-sizzler *Three Weeks*, written at a white heat in six, straight from the subconscious. It was published in 1907, with a purple cover to match its purple prose. The story centers on bachelor Paul and his tempestuous three-week affair with an older, mysterious lady (never named, but queen of some Balkan country, married to a cruel old king). *Three Weeks* created a sensation, and a whole new genre, the sex novel. The book was years ahead of its time. A new balance of sexual power emerged wherein an older woman initiates the affair and dominates a younger man. There is also adultery and an out-of-wedlock birth; a union which is purely physical; a twenty-one-night stand with no follow-up; and the kind of man-woman coupling which Erica Jong celebrates in *Fear of Flying* (1973) and Robert James Waller, more sentimentally, in *The Bridges of Madison County* (1993). *Three Weeks* has oblique eroticism on every page, and lots of purposeful lounging on couches draped in tiger skins. The queen is costumed for passion in a "strange clinging garment of heavy purple crepe, its hem embroidered with gold" and in "a marvelous garment of shimmering purple, while round her shoulders a scarf of brilliant emerald gauze, all fringed with gold, fell in two long ends, and on her neck and in her ears great emeralds gleamed." *Three Weeks* created a furor in the press, and sold 50,000 copies in a single month. Nine years after publication it had sold two million copies and been translated into most European languages, with particularly heavy sales in Spain and Scandinavia.

Among her own social set, Elinor was instantly ostracized. King Edward VII declared that no one must mention the book in his hearing – and sales boomed higher. Round two continents flew the verse some wag invented:

Would you like to sin
With Elinor Glyn
On a tiger skin?
Or would you prefer
To err
With her
On some other fur?

The book was banned in Boston, and for a time in Canada. As late as 1932, a Mickey Mouse cartoon which showed a cow reclining in a field reading *Three Weeks* was banned in the state of Ohio. By that time the novel had sold five million copies worldwide.

If Elinor's social reputation was in tatters in English society, her celebrity status had taken a huge leap forward. *Three Weeks* made her rich as well as famous, opening wide the door to the luxe life she'd first glimpsed in the Paris barrel of her childhood. The book also pushed her personality much farther than *The Visits of Elizabeth* had towards free-standing eccentricity, towards her own unique blend of high-flying romance and down-to-earth realism. Full flowering, however, was still thirteen years and an ocean away.

In the autumn of 1907, Elinor sailed for America on the White Star liner *Cedric*, chasing her fame to the country where selling and promotion were a way of life. Elinor had packed her many bags with appropriate costumes for a celebrity novelist. Since *Three Weeks* had turned her, in the eyes of the public, into a sex goddess (the first of a long line stretching all the way to Marilyn Monroe and Madonna), she vowed to dress the part and play the role to the hilt, consciously constructing a public persona guaranteed to sell books and to keep her name and likeness appearing in newspapers and magazines. In this, as in the contents of *Three Weeks*, Elinor was years ahead of her time, presaging, for example, romance novelist Barbara Cartland, who has enhanced her reputation with pink tulle, blonde wigs, diamonds galore and fake eyelashes longer than Bambi's. From now on, Elinor would be a superb, single-minded public relations expert for one product: herself. Sister Lucy, who seven years before had raised herself socially by marrying Sir Cosmo Duff Gordon, was cut from the same cloth as her sister and knew how to cash in on Elinor's sudden notoriety. A sexy dress called "the Elinor Glyn" would be featured from now on in every Lucile couture collection.

When the liner *Cedric* docked in New York on October 5, Elinor came slowly down the gangplank ready for the scrum of reporters awaiting her. Skirts were still ankle-length in 1907 and the female figure in profile still formed an S-for-Sex curve, with pushed-out bust, cinched waist, and padded posterior. Elinor wore a purple Lucile costume, an enormous purple hat and yards and yards of chiffon veiling – her second-best prop after tiger skins – swathed round the hat, thinly across her face and wafting long purple ends in all possible directions. ("Mrs. Glyn is a handsome woman about thirty-five years old," scribbled the dazzled *New York Times* reporter into his notebook. She was in fact forty-three.) Veils suggested a sex goddess' essential mystery by illustrating the fact that the most precious parts of a woman, her biological center, unlike a man's, are hidden and therefore unknowable. Elinor knew in 1907 what Camille Paglia pointed out in 1990 in *Sexual Personae*, that mystery is "woman's basic metaphor" – a fact which present-day sex goddesses, baring their bodies to almost total nudity, might do well to remember.

Several days later, Elinor went off with a friend made on the crossing from England: American heiress Consuelo, Duchess of Manchester, a real-life heroine who had snared the doubtful prize of an English duke. Consuelo preferred comfort to style and had once removed her constricting corset on the way to a ball, tossing it, hard, into a corner of her carriage. She and Elinor stayed for several days with Frederick and Louise ("Lulu") Vanderbilt at their Hyde Park estate on the Hudson River. They arrived at teatime to find Lulu ostentatiously wearing long white gloves and $250,000 worth of pearls, while powdered footmen passed the cakes.

Back in New York City, Elinor moved up market to the Plaza Hotel. She was out when Samuel Clemens, known to the reading public as Mark Twain, came to pay his respects, so the next day she went to see him at his house near Washington Square. He was dressed in "putty-white broadcloth" and she thought him "the wittiest creature imaginable." He, in turn, found Elinor "slender, young, faultlessly formed and incontestably beautiful, crowned with a glory of red hair of a very peculiar, most rare and quite ravishing tint. She was clad in the choicest stuffs and in the most perfect taste. There she is, just a beautiful girl; yet she has a daughter fourteen years old." But, in the final analysis, Twain saw through the sex-goddess veils: "She *acts* charm and does it well, exceedingly well in fact, but it does not convince, it doesn't stir the pulse," and decided that if the hero of *Three Weeks* had met Elinor, he would have been able "to get away with his purity in good repair."

Elinor used her charm to try to persuade Twain to publicly endorse her naughty novel in still-Puritan America, but he politely refused, clothed in the purity of his white broadcloth, calling the book "an assault upon certain old, well-established and wise conventions."

When Elinor turned up in eye-catching attire at a Waldorf luncheon where the Pilgrim Mothers had asked her to speak, still ignorant of the contents of *Three Weeks*, they refused to seat her at the head table or allow her to deliver her speech, having read the book in the interim. Elinor stomped out and took a typical revenge, telling a *New York Times* reporter that one Pilgrim Mother "looked like a man, except her hat. That was a funny little bonnet."

Elinor's vanity was mollified by a visitor to her Plaza suite, a "crass millionaire" admirer who had sent her masses of gardenias because, as he told her, "they are a darned sight the most expensive." When Elinor swept into her sitting room to meet him, she found him standing in awe before the glass-fronted bookcase which advertised her small feet by showing, neatly arranged on its shelves, the sixty pairs of shoes and slippers she'd brought to America. The millionaire was holding in his big rough palm one tiny blue-satin mule. "In those days," explains Elinor, "one wore negligées of lovely satins, with little mule slippers which had Lucile silk roses as buckles, deliciously feminine and alluring" – and very like those which little Elinor and Lucy had admired on Mrs. Bovill's feet at Balnegan Castle thirty-six years before. The millionaire cradled the Cinderella slipper and promptly offered marriage. When Elinor declined, he reluctantly let go the mule, saying: "Well, I'd like you to know, Ma'am, the love wouldn't be wanting on my side."

Back in England, Elinor, as she always would, turned her travels into a novel (this one was *Elizabeth Visits America*) and told Lucy exactly what the women of America were buying and wearing. Lucy listened closely, and after a Christmas visit to New York in 1910, opened a branch of Maison Lucile in 1911 on West 36th Street, where fashionable shops were then situated.

But all was not well with Clayton. He'd grown very stout and had a "pathetic look"; Elinor thought his cheeks had "the violet tinge one associates with serious heart trouble." Reluctantly, he told a shocked Elinor his tale of woe. He'd been living on his capital for some time, had mortgaged his estate heavily, was in debt to the bank, to friends, to money-lenders, all of whom were demanding payment. Elinor realized that henceforth she'd have to support not only her clothes habit but also the Glyn household: Clayton, her two daughters, her mother, and the usual complement of servants. She became a totally focused career woman, frantically scribbling book after book there in her bower of silk roses. For the next five years, the black clouds of "recurring financial crises" were always there – but there was one shining scrap of silver lining.

On July 23, 1908, *Three Weeks* was dramatized at London's Adelphi Theatre, with Elinor, in slinky Lucile gowns, playing the queen. Lord Curzon, who was in the audience, fell under Elinor's spell and arranged to meet her. He was a former Viceroy of India who, like Elinor, was permanently tagged with a verse:

My name is George Nathaniel Curzon.
I am a most superior person.
My cheek is pink, my hair is sleek,
I dine at Blenheim once a week.

George Nathaniel was a proud, pompous man, always formally dressed in frock coat and stiff collar, who knew how to charm the ladies. He'd been a widower for two years. His deceased wife Mary (née Leiter), whose greatest claim to fame was the peacock-feather and emerald ballgown she'd worn to the Delhi Durbar ball in 1903, had been an American heiress whose father co-owned Marshall Fields department store in Chicago. Mary's greatest attraction for impecunious George Nathaniel had been her money. She had succumbed to the overwhelming combination of his Lordship's ego and India's climate, and died at age thirty-six. For Elinor, Curzon was the one grand passion of her life. For Curzon, Elinor was mere diversion; he gave her a tiger skin and some jewels, and enjoyed her quick wit. When asked why her daughters were so much more intelligent than his, Elinor replied: "Well, the mother does make a difference!"

Elinor and Curzon began their affair with clandestine meetings over luncheons at a hotel in London's Jermyn Street. They met so often that the hotel would later christen the dining spot "The Elinor Glyn Room." The lovers first went to bed on a prearranged tryst in Heidelberg. One wonders how much pleasure Elinor could enjoy with a man who once declared to his wife that, when making love, "ladies never move."

Curzon commissioned a portrait of his new love from French painter Jacques Emile Blanche, and instructed him, after it was finished, to change Elinor's hair ribbon from pink to blue. Elinor was thrilled that her lover, like herself, understood the importance of appearances. She found herself in the grip of a compelling passion, and fought a losing battle against it. "Your duty lies in using your brain and force for your sweet ones and your family," she told herself sternly in her diary. "It does not lie in undesired and idolatrous obsession over the sun, moon and stars." But such words were useless; the tiger called sexual love had her by the throat.

She diverted herself with a trip to Russia in 1909, invited by Grand Duchess Kiril to come spend a winter in St. Petersburg and write a novel showing the extreme luxury of the Russian court, then under heavy attack in the press, in a favorable light. Elinor bought a whole new Lucile wardrobe and added hats from the best Parisian milliner, Réboux. Having a hat made at Réboux was serious business. First the hatter made a form of white muslin, fitted it to Elinor's head, then remade the form in fabric, and fitted it once or twice more. At the final fitting, Réboux's chief designer, Madame Lucienne, was sent for to give her approval. If she didn't approve, the hat with which Elinor had already fallen in love was torn from her head, cut into ribbons and the whole process started all over again.

When Elinor arrived in St. Petersburg on December 28 and checked into the Hotel de l'Europe, she was devastated to learn that her finery couldn't be worn. The whole court had gone into mourning for recently deceased Grand Duke Michael. Elinor couldn't even wear her few black Réboux hats, but had to don the regulation mourning bonnet of black crêpe with long veil. However, as Elinor tells us in her memoir, she was "somewhat consoled, on trying it on, to discover that it was really very becoming!" One month later, she could "fetch out of their cupboards my lovely Lucile dresses which had been so long put away and neglected." The wildest Cinderella dreams of her Guelph childhood then materialized before her appreciative eyes, as women in splendid raiment and jewels and men in peacock-bright uniforms danced every February and March night away at magnificent balls. Around five a.m., everyone would wrap themselves in sables, pile into troikas and glide swiftly and silently across the frozen Neva to some dark little gypsy café. Elinor caught this world in her Russian novel *His Hour*, published in 1910.

Lucy opened a Paris branch of Maison Lucile in 1912, but faced stiff competition from the newly popular Paul Poiret, apprenticed to Worth before opening his own couture house. Poiret had introduced a brand new silhouette in 1908; instead of the usual S-curve, he put women into slender tubes, sometimes narrowed at the hem. Inspired by Leon Bakst's costumes for the Ballet Russe, Poiret, in 1912, designed harem skirts, tunics slit over harem pants and lamé turbans. Instead of Lucile's pale pinks and orchids, he favored vivid purples and oranges, colors Elinor loved. Publicly she stayed loyal to her sister, declaring that "no lady should ever dress at Poiret, his clothes are too showy," but her own closet began to exhibit Poiret shapes and colors.

Clayton, meanwhile, was looking ever more doleful as debts and empty brandy cases piled up in tandem. One day, he fled. Elinor had no idea where he'd gone until a letter to Dixie, the governess, asking for his clothes, showed him to be resident in Constantinople. He and Elinor permanently separated; she took a long lease on No. 5 Avenue Victor Hugo, Parc des Princes, outside Paris, redecorated it with specially woven, glorious brocades and installed a secret staircase so Curzon could come and go discreetly. He commissioned another portrait, this one by Philip de Laszlo, and ordered Elinor, in his imperious way, to wear the sapphire earrings he'd given her.

De Laszlo was a forty-four-year-old Paris-based Hungarian who looked like a dashing cavalry officer. Before her sittings began, Elinor wrote him a revealing letter which shows how very assured her style had become:

> Although I am so fond of my sapphires, still I realize that emeralds are really more in keeping with my character. I have always visualized a portrait of me, [with]

> a black mysterious background – some kind of a seat over which is thrown one of those tiger skins with the very long orange hair (from Manchuria, I think).... Seated on this – ME! in some transparent black drapery, no particular fashion, my orange head against the black of the background, and the same strange tones repeated in what shows of the tiger skin – no other colour at all, except the huge emerald earrings and the jewel on the forehead, and nothing round the neck or on the arms. An effect of lighting so that the woman appears to be coming right out of the picture, startling and real, so that one holds the breath.

Even though Curzon insisted on the sapphires, Elinor was pleased with the result. "It is the living, breathing portrait of Elinor Glyn in the mood which is most often there," she told de Laszlo, and added that he had captured her soul, "two thousand years old and more." "I was very happy in painting Glyn," de Laszlo told his wife. "The picture will be diabolic – she feels it, and I see it."

When the Great War broke out in 1914, Elinor got a job as war correspondent for Lord Riddell's *News of the World*, had a smart khaki uniform custom tailored, wore it with black and white chiffon veils, and when she was inexplicably arrested one night for being a spy, proved her innocence by pointing to the pretty pink satin nightgown in her traveling bag. Would any real spy, she asked the suspicious officers indignantly, sleep in such frivolity? They let her go at once.

Clayton died in November 1915, and Elinor nursed a secret hope that now Curzon would ask her to marry him. She pictured herself as Lady Curzon sweeping through the lofty rooms of Montacute, his Jacobean country house, wearing something regal. Her hopes soared higher when Curzon asked her to completely redecorate it to her taste. She slaved for weeks, in coveralls and choking clouds of plaster dust. She was hard at it on the morning of December 17, 1916, when she opened a week-old copy of the *Times* to read that Lord Curzon was about to marry Grace Duggan, an American quite as wealthy as his first wife. Elinor never saw Curzon or spoke to him again. She threw his five hundred love letters into a bonfire, but hung onto his gifts: one tiger skin; one antique brocade train; one pair of sapphire earrings; one pair of emerald ones; one large sapphire and diamond ring.

Elinor was in Paris through 1917, describing its devastated areas for William Randolph Hearst's American newspapers, and living at the Ritz. To Elinor's surprise, Paris showed few signs of being at war. The women were as elegantly dressed as ever, draped in silver fox furs costing the equivalent of $500 each, "looking brushed and groomed and scented." By war's end, however, fabric was in short supply; designers were instructed to use no more than four and a half yards for any suit, dress or coat, so that skirts began to creep slowly upward from the ankles – and for daytime would never descend again. Lucy teamed up with Florenz Ziegfeld, who bought her entire collection and whisked away four of her best models, including six-foot-tall Dolores and Hebe, to star in the Ziegfeld Follies, which included such production numbers as "Furs," "The Legend of Pearls," "Laces of the World" and "The Episode of Chiffon."

By 1919 Elinor was ensconced in a rented apartment near Versailles, in the middle of having her salon walls painted purple, when she had an unexpected visitor, friend King Alfonso XIII of Spain. Alfonso was not handsome, for he had the long Hapsburg nose and the long Hapsburg chin, but he was a charmer where ladies were concerned. He made his attendants wait for him in another room while he tried to seduce Elinor; she told him that she wanted only his friendship – and would just *love* to come to Spain, meet his wife Queen Ena and see the splendors of the Spanish court. Elinor was busy that year collecting her thoughts for *The Philosophy of Love* (1920), which told women how to get and keep their man, and which would sell a quarter of a million copies in its first six months. Elinor also entertained friend Queen Marie of Roumania, whose flamboyant style had influenced her own and given her inspiration for the heroine of *Three Weeks.* Queen Marie, like Queen Ena, was a granddaughter of Queen Victoria; Marie was an extremely beautiful woman who adored being photographed, preferably amid huge bronze urns of lilies, leopard skins and purple velvet cushions. Like Elinor, she knew how to market a product, namely herself, keeping her name in the international press and making it onto the cover of *Time* magazine, the number one celebrity feat in America, in 1924.

Elinor went to Spain for Easter, 1920, to deal diplomatically with the hot hands of King Alfonso trying to explore her chiffon draperies and to ingratiate herself with Queen Ena, a lovely woman whose style ran to yards-long pearls and fur boas. Here, as in Russia, Elinor achieved her childhood dream: she was close enough to touch the Royal velvet, and the lives of those who wore it. *Letters from Spain*, set in the sumptuous Spanish court, would appear in 1924.

It was in the autumn of 1920 that Elinor began the momentous, exciting, far-reaching third and final act of her life. In Act One, style had been her ladder to marriage and higher social status; in Act Two, style was her tool of self-promotion aimed at selling books. In Act Three, style would still be a selling tool, but now she would be marketing a brand new medium and influencing a whole continent of women to change their conventions of dress and behavior.

Jesse L. Lasky of Famous Players-Lasky invited Elinor to come to Hollywood to write scenarios for his silent films and supervise their productions. He offered her $10,000 per picture, plus travel expenses. Elinor would have to uproot herself from family and friends, live in a strange milieu where she knew no one, and work in a new medium about which she knew nothing. But, as she says, "it was just such an adventure as I had always loved" and she "felt certain that a great new art was being born which would profoundly influence the whole world." She sailed on the *Mauretania*, telling her mother that she was going "full of hope and confidence, with the spirit free and strong." Somewhere in mid-Atlantic, she put on her new persona: that of "Madame Glyn": haughty, aristocratic, sultry, autocratic – and destined for a long, successful run.

She had very few Lucile garments in her many trunks. Lucy and Elinor, always highly competitive in their race for fame and fortune, had had a temporary falling out, their acrimony surfacing in a heated exchange over which of them was wearing the correct skirt length. Poor Lucy's star was sinking just as Elinor's was about to rise. Maison Lucile was foundering; Lucy's ultra-feminine, hot-house designs looked old-hat at a time when women were climbing into tan leather aviator suits or dashing around town in jersey suits and navy serge military greatcoats. Lucy sold her shares in the American branch of Lucile and closed the London one in 1919; the Paris house would close in 1923.

At fifty-six, Elinor had supreme self-confidence and sure sense of identity. She knew that hers was a baroque personality, one which was over-the-top and one-of-a-kind. This sureness of self meant that she knew exactly what image she wished to project and exactly what clothes to wear to achieve it. She had put on her mature style and would keep it, with only minor variations, for the rest of her life.

She had hired a talented dressmaker named Ann Morgan, a small, compliant woman with an angelic little face, to make the Madame Glyn wardrobe. To keep production rolling, Elinor persuaded Ann to accompany her to Hollywood. Ann made Elinor dresses in slinky, bias-cut crêpe de Chine or silk velvet in three colors: purple, emerald and black. These dramatic choices were not the popular ones of the early 1920s, when the most fashionable color schemes were muted: brown with grey, or silver with rose-pink. Black as a favorite for evening – in satin or lace, not velvet – wouldn't catch on for another six years. With her black garments, Elinor often wore touches of white: a consonant choice for a woman about to promote her second black-and-white medium, the first being print. At other times, she accented black with scarves or furs in the exact orange-red shade of her hair.

Elinor's clothes now had a classic cut beyond fashion's frequent changes, since this timeless quality suited one who considered her soul two thousand years old. Some of her dresses had matching waist-length capes trimmed with fur. Her long-standing interest in the exotic East, whose inhabitants shared her beliefs in reincarnation and an intuitive, non-rational approach to life, led Elinor into floating scarves and veils to suggest the ultimate mystery of the female, and of the universe itself; into long, dangling earrings; armloads of bangle bracelets; and elaborately draped turbans. Sometimes instead of a real turban, Elinor wound thick braids of false red hair around her head. The turbans expressed the dreamy, romantic side of Elinor's nature; her practical, realistic side surfaced in Réboux cloche hats for daytime, all the same shape, with a diagonal crease in the felt from crown to edge, all of them shaped to her head by Madame Lucienne, who snipped away at the brim and carefully moulded the crown (*la calotte*).

Elinor's confident chic, packed into trunks and hatboxes in the hold of the *Mauretania*, can encourage and hearten women readers of the baby-boom or an earlier generation who are tired of flipping through fashion magazines showing nothing but scanty designs suitable for sixteen-year-olds. Elinor Glyn had felt her first grand passion at age forty-four, become a war correspondent at fifty-three, and now here she was, three years later, in total, memorable elegance, getting ready to storm Hollywood.

Jesse Lasky himself met her when the ship docked in New York, and was bowled over. "Madame Glyn," he writes in his memoirs, "was as adept as Salvador Dali at drawing attention to herself. From the moment she stepped off the *Mauretania* in New York and proceeded to a press reception at the apartment we had arranged for her to live in, she made 'good copy.'"

After a successful press conference, Lasky took Madame to the photographer's. As they exited the apartment, Elinor snatched up her tiger skin (this one was geared to Hollywood, being fake), declared that they mustn't go in his car, they must walk, and gave him the tiger skin to carry. "My promenade down Fifth Avenue with the garish rug on one arm and the garish Glyn on the other was like a nightmare," writes Lasky, as everyone turned and gawked at "Madame Glyn's flamboyant taste in clothes and her flaming red hair." Elinor's effect on New Yorkers was, of course, exactly the one she'd been aiming at.

Elinor didn't stay in New York long, and when she descended from the train some days later at Pasadena, she saw a small town of one or two-story pepper-pot Spanish houses surrounded by orange groves. She was surprised to note that Hollywood's few shop windows displayed Paris dresses and hats – with exorbitant price tags. (America's fashion industry was just beginning, with the first manufacturers having set up shop on New York City's Seventh Avenue two years before, in 1918.)

Elinor checked into the Hollywood Hotel, a sprawling building with wrap-around veranda, run by eighty-year-old Miss

Hershey. The pink Beverly Hills Hotel, opened eight years before, was more luxurious, but it was too far from the studios for a daily commute over bad roads. Madame Glyn took two adjoining rooms at the Hollywood, since other guests had only one, and proceeded to turn them into a suitable setting for herself.

In décor, Elinor's mature style focused on those colors which she loved and needed, not so much for their impact on others as for their positive effects on her own sense of well-being. She had to have blue of a particular azure hue, for, as she told one journalist, blue "is the color of thought. It is like a current flowing through me. I try to mould myself and my life by thought; to use blue as imagination's parachute." She had to have orchid and royal purple, to energize and inspire her "strength of brain and body." Touches of green suggested nature's leaves and grasses and ongoing growth. Accents in décor, there at the Hollywood Hotel and all future establishments, included the inevitable tiger skins, oriental rugs, purple velvet cushions, Buddhas, gongs, crystal balls and incense-burners.

Having settled in, Elinor met the other novelists staying at the hotel whom Lasky had lured there as scriptwriters: Maurice Maeterlinck, Edward Knoblock, Somerset Maugham and Gilbert Parker. None of them could adjust to the demands of film production. Maugham lasted seven days before he fled; the others gradually followed, all but Elinor. She had, at long last, found her natural milieu; her whole life had been a dress rehearsal for the Hollywood experience. "If Hollywood hadn't existed, Elinor Glyn would have had to invent it," wrote fellow scriptwriter Anita Loos. Elinor loved Hollywood and Hollywood loved her, because, long before she got there, she already had the Hollywood state of mind, a combination of a dreaming optimism, a race for power and wealth, a talent for hype, an obsessive attention to appearances, and a zany belief, exemplified today by such figures as Shirley Maclaine, in astrology, the supernatural and reincarnation.

Elinor would prove to be a brilliant prophet at predicting audience tastes, and a supreme creator of images and stars. A journalist who interviewed Elinor after she had been in Hollywood for six years declared her "trusted and respected as a director. The girl stars whom she moulds for their parts in her pictures feel her fascination and believe that her influence upon them doesn't end when their work together is finished."

Elinor reached her creative heights in Hollywood partly because film was the logical synthesis of the two previous stages of her life. In the first, image alone dominated as she concentrated on clothes to get her man and the right social status. In the second, story reigned supreme as she scribbled her novels; now, in the third stage, image and story would combine into full creative flowering.

The first "Elinor Glyn Production" was *The Great Moment* (1921). Elinor wrote the scenario and dictated costumes and settings. The film was directed by Sam Wood, a practical man who'd made his money in real estate, and starred Murray Stills and Gloria Swanson. Elinor's first meeting with Gloria is described in the latter's autobiography. Gloria thought her "something from another world." "She was the first woman I'd ever seen wearing false eyelashes," remembers Gloria, "and although she was old enough to be my grandmother [Gloria was twenty-two] she got away with it." Miss Swanson adds that Elinor walked with tiny steps; had teeth "too even and white to be real"; hair braids "the color of red ink"; smelled of incense and "talked a blue streak." Elinor told Gloria that since her arrival in the United States, she'd had forty proposals of marriage, most of them by mail from men who sent their bank statements along with their photos. "You're the new kind of woman altogether," Elinor enthused, "daring, provocative, sensuous." Elinor gazed at Gloria intently. "Egyptian!" she exclaimed, pointing at her new star with a ringed hand, clanking her bangle bracelets. "Your proportions are Egyptian; anyone can see that when you turn your head." Elinor went on to say that her friend the Prince of Wales (later King Edward VIII and then Duke of Windsor) had loved Gloria in *Male and Female* (1918), her first film. "You children don't realize yet what has happened," Elinor told her. "But you will. Motion pictures are going to change everything. They're the most important thing that's come along since the printing press. People don't care about royalty anymore. They're much more interested in queens of the screen, like you, my dear."

Elinor understood that because film submits to the eye's dominance, it prefers surfaces to essences and types to individuals; film is always allegorical. Silent film, even more than sound, was allegorical because it dealt *only* with surfaces and types. Women in silent films could be seen but not heard. Time turned backward as words dissolved once more into images, the post-Gutenberg age of print reverted to icons which carried the same magic and power as the ancient icons of pre-literate eras. The new images went straight to the subconscious in a way that words never could, stayed there much longer, and exerted a stupendous influence on the movie-going public. It is no accident that Hollywood's first producers had been in fashion, making images not in celluloid but in fur and leather. Adolph Zukor, who co-owned Famous Players with Jesse Lasky, had been in furs. Sam Goldwyn had manufactured gloves before he teamed up with shoemaker Louis B. Mayer to form Metro-Goldwyn-Mayer. During her Hollywood years, Elinor would work hand-in-glove with all four of them. In silent films, dressing the part and playing the part were one and the same, as Elinor and the other members of Hollywood's pioneer film industry instantly understood. A February 1916 article in *Photoplay* by actress Louise Howard is called "How I Teach My Gowns to Act." Dress had to place a character quickly and efficiently in one symbolic sweep. Frederick Palmer, in his chapter called "Visualization" in his 1922 screenwriting manual, tells aspiring screenwriters to study character by observing gloves, shoes and jewelry, because "so much of character is told in one's manner of wearing clothes." Elinor had known this ever since she went from sketching her acquaintances in girlhood journals to describing her heroine's clothes in her novels. Before she left Hollywood, she would create two long-lasting and highly influential types, of which Gloria Swanson would be the first, each springing from one side of Elinor's own dual personality. Both types would teach American women, in their presentation of self, to submit to the tyranny of stereotype. It is ironic that a woman like Elinor who was so markedly individual would be instrumental in turning other women into look-alikes of their favorite film star.

The Great Moment shows Gloria, daughter of an English aristocrat, wandering into the sagebrush, being bitten by a rattlesnake, then rescued by the hero, who appears most opportunely, picks her up, tears at her blouse, bares her bosom, turns her from the camera's vulgar stare, bends over and sucks out the poison. The climactic love scene which follows in due course takes place – where else? – on a tiger skin. While writing this particular scenario, Elinor realized that she couldn't adequately convey in words what she wanted, so she merely wrote: "Rather than describe this scene, Madame Glyn will personally enact it on the set."

Elinor completely recreated Gloria's screen image. In all her earlier films, Gloria had looked like an expensive doll, with blonde hair curled into an aureole which made her head look far too big. She wore elaborate French frocks dripping with too much detail in the form of beaded fringes and curlicues of crystals. With

Elinor's guiding hand, fussy dresses gave way to slinky, elegant simplicity and fluffy hair to the dark, satin sleekness of a new chestnut. Gloria's small, exquisitely shaped head and long neck were two of her chief charms; her new glamour in *The Great Moment* lit up the whole screen. In one scene, Gloria wears an evening dress, conceived by Elinor, that has a four-foot train composed entirely of pearls and ermine tails. Realizing that a star's image off screen had to be consistent with her on-screen one, Elinor enlisted her dressmaker Ann Morgan to help turn Gloria into the screen's first glamour goddess, a type which would reach full flower in another nine years with Marlene Dietrich. Just as Elinor's fictional heroines bore a remarkable resemblance to their creator, so did her film ones. We can directly link Elinor Glyn as she appeared in real life to Gloria Swanson as she appeared in all her films after 1921, including her role as Norma Desmond in Billy Wilder's masterpiece *Sunset Boulevard* (1950). As Norma, Gloria sweeps through her scenes in Glyn-like floating draperies, multiple bracelets, lamé turbans and leopard-skin hats.

Being herself part doer and part dreamer, Elinor knew that films demanded their own special mix of realism and romance, knew that if one rolled up the real world on a spool, with plenty of accurate detail, somehow one could unroll it as a magic carpet to dreamland, just as the Paris barrel of her childhood, full of real clothes, had sparked her own high-life fantasies. Elinor felt, first of all, "a passionate longing to bring reality" to the silver screen. Before she arrived in Hollywood, aspidistras and spittoons proliferated in sets supposed to depict old English castles. Elinor changed all that; she insisted both on total accuracy and high aesthetic standards. She complained in letters to her mother of "vulgar plush curtains" and "vile bad taste" and "Miss Swanson's awful hair, with two Chinese fans in it." Directors groaned at her demands; Elinor refused to compromise her ideals.

Secondly, to help the audience dream, Elinor had her films photographed in soft-focus; she had her heroines back-lit so that their hair looked like spun-sugar, and their champagne glasses sparkled like stars. Typical Glyn settings had silvery-white highlights flashing from marble floors and marble columns, with hothouse flowers in huge alabaster urns, and plenty of chaise longues for the heroine and hero to recline on.

When *The Great Moment* was released in 1921 it made money at the box office, and Lasky signed Elinor on for more pictures at a higher salary. Both Elinor's daughters got married that year in England, both to baronets, which pleased their snobbish mother, but Madame Glyn was having far too much fun in Hollywood to go back for the weddings.

At the end of a working day, she would put on one of her slinky black, purple or emerald gowns, don a matching turban, and head for yet another party. Gloria, who frequently went with her, recalls that "going places with Elinor was never dull." Madame Glyn would baby-step her way across a room or round a swimming pool, pronouncing her aesthetic verdicts as she went. "This is hideous," she would say, as people got out of her way, "as if she were a sorceress on fire." She soon acquired half a dozen young men, who swam in her wake like a school of eager dolphins. They taught Elinor the newest dances: the Charleston, the Black Bottom, the Cakewalk, and she began to dance the nights away in the Patent Leather Room of the Ambassador Hotel in Los Angeles, or at the Vernon Country Club, where she could happily face a newspaper camera at every turn. Elinor was amazingly supple, having taken lessons in Egyptian belly-dancing during her Cairo days. "Eat what you like, drink what you like," Madame Glyn told Hollywood, "so long as you dance every night."

On Sunday afternoons Elinor entertained at tea in her Hollywood Hotel suite, where she lay on a tiger skin, wearing harem pyjamas in orchid silk, reciting the poetry of Swinburne or Shelley in a sultry voice.

At dinner parties, Elinor could keep a whole table spellbound. Whereas other women tried to get attention by out-screaming each other, Elinor did it by speaking in a quiet, contralto voice which Sam Goldwyn thought sounded like "the lonely wind soughing through pine trees." Another guest commented on "its strange composure and quietness which makes everyone want to listen and hear what that voice is going to say." Goldwyn recalls the party where Elinor told each guest their identity in their previous existence. "No one ever laughed at Chaplin quite as hard as Chaplin laughed that evening at Elinor Glyn," concludes Goldwyn.

Elinor and Charlie Chaplin soon became great friends and often made a spectacular team on the dance floor. He found her "a little overwhelming at first" but soon warmed to her. They had first met when she invited him to dinner at the Hollywood Hotel with nine other guests, with cocktails first in her rooms. There Elinor cupped Charlie's face in her ringed hands, gazed at him intently and said: "Dear, dear, so this is Charlie Chaplin! Do you know, you don't look nearly so funny as I thought you would?" To this Charlie promptly replied: "Neither do you." She then led him by the elbow into her bedroom, where framed on the walls were photos of Seymour Wynne Finch, Alastair Innes-Ker and her other English conquests. "These are all my Pauls," said Elinor, referring to the hero of *Three Weeks*, making a dramatic sweep with one wide velvet sleeve.

Naturally, Elinor gravitated to Hollywood's king and queen, Douglas Fairbanks and Mary Pickford, who entertained at Pickfair, their pseudo-English stately home. Elinor would arrive accompanied by her personal maid Blinky and dressmaker Ann Morgan in case she needed touch-ups. Often dressed in black silk velvet with furs to match her red hair, Elinor stood out among the peroxide blondes in their pink or powder-blue frills.

Douglas and Mary had recently married – in March 1920. Other women were cutting their hair short; Douglas made Mary promise she wouldn't; he wanted a long-haired, old-fashioned girl. At parties, his eyes kept straying to his new wife. "Doesn't she look sweet?" he would ask. "I helped her choose that dress." Mary, who had once been paid $1000 by Lucy to advertise a Lucile gown, favored pastel shades, particularly pale pink or pale green, perhaps taking her cue from the real Queen Mary, she who shared the English throne with George V. At one Pickfair luncheon party which Elinor attended, everyone gazed in consternation at Mary Astor, who was to play Dolores De Muroz opposite Douglas Fairbanks in *Don Quixote, Son of Zorro* (1925). Mary's light hair didn't look at all Spanish, and Douglas vetoed a wig. Elinor solved the problem. She smeared Mary's hair with butter, parted it in the centre, combed it into a bun at the back and declared in her voice of authority: "That's the way she should look!" And that is exactly how Mary did look when the film was made.

In 1922, Elinor adapted her novel *Beyond the Rocks* (1906) into her second film, again directed by Sam Wood and starring Gloria Swanson, who this time was paired with Rudolph Valentino. Rudy brought a Latin sizzle to the role of an English lord; he had already made twenty-one feature films, but looked to Elinor to improve his on-screen love techniques. She showed him, among other things, how to kiss the palm of a woman's hand, rather than the back. In *Beyond the Rocks*, a poor but aristocratic English girl, Theodora, is married off to an elderly millionaire, only to meet the love of her life, Lord Bracondale, on her honeymoon.

The Hays office had recently come into being, wherein the studio heads hired Will H. Hays to keep movies clean enough for still-Puritan America. "But what will happen now?" someone asked Elinor. "What will happen now," she replied, already wise in the ways of movie moguls, "is whatever will bring in the most money." Sam Wood had to shoot each kiss in *Beyond the Rocks* twice: once for the American version, where Hays ruled that no kiss could last for more than ten feet of film; once for the European market where kisses could be more prolonged. In the movie's sexiest scene, Gloria and Rudolph dance a tango, Gloria in a slithering, shimmering gown dreamed up by Elinor of lace and gold beading which presages the gowns Marlene Dietrich would wear in the 1960s for her one-woman stage shows. Gloria also wore, as she tells it, "a king's ransom in velvet, silk ruffles, sable and chinchilla, all dripping from shoulders to floor with a million dollars' worth of jewels," all designed by Madame Glyn, who was now having lots of fun playing with jewels rather than tablecloths, and who, like Empress Eugénie, knew all about putting on the Ritz. Empress Eugénie's fashionable image had influenced the female world through photos or sketches in newspapers and fashion journals. Now the most influential images were appearing on the screens of America's cinemas, telling women who they were and how to dress, with Elinor Glyn as foremost fashion pundit. She began writing a column for *Photoplay* largely concerned with the inadequate dress sense of Hollywood's stars, declaring that "a woman should look straight as a dart, supple as a snake and proud as a tiger lily."

Elinor helped launch the make-up revolution too. Empress Eugénie and other nineteenth-century women had rouged their cheeks to give them a healthy glow, to improve a little on nature. With the advent of movies, modern make-up came of age, threw off its apprenticeship as nature's handmaiden and took up an artist's purposeful brush instead. Women began to paint their faces with such bold designs as Gloria Swanson's penciled eyebrows – or, later, Clara Bow's bee-stung lips.

Elinor was lured away from Lasky's Famous Players to Metro-Goldwyn-Mayer for her next six films. She moved from the shabby Hollywood Hotel to the more luxurious Ambassador, mid-way between Hollywood and Los Angeles. The Ambassador had dozens of shops selling candies, flowers, hats, even jewels, as well as its own film theater, art gallery and fortune-teller.

Elinor took a suite of five rooms on the top floor, with a view of the blue Pacific. She decorated her rooms with the blues and greens and orchids that she needed around her. She found a clever Chinese cabinetmaker to make her chairs, desks and tables in green or orchid lacquer. She slept in her bedroom only when it rained, which was seldom. The rest of the time she slept in an open sleeping porch where she could see the deep-azure sky above her. "I love to lie there for hours – not asleep but thinking," she told journalist Alice Williamson; "thoughts come to me there which never come anywhere else."

Elinor's film *Six Days* was made in 1923, directed by Charles Brabin; in it the hero and heroine, trapped for six days in a dug-out in wartime France, alternately make love and dig themselves out. *Three Weeks* followed in 1924, with Aileen Pringle, an Elinor Glyn look-alike who was the wife of a British diplomat, playing the queen and Conrad Nagle playing Paul. *Three Weeks* was directed by Alan Crosland, whose subsequent claim to fame was directing the first talkie.

Later that year, Elinor went on New York's vaudeville circuit, giving ten-minute talks on love and earning $2500 a week. Elinor was getting rich; this engagement lasted all through the winter of 1923. During her Hollywood years, Elinor hyped herself into such consummate celebrity status that when each new "Elinor

Glyn Production" was about to hit the screen, cinema managers across America were told by her studio to "boom the author." She also made cameo appearances as herself in such films as King Vidor's *Show People.*

In 1924, Elinor added actress Marion Davies and her lover, newspaper magnate William Randolph Hearst, to her list of friends. Marion was a born comedienne and former Ziegfeld girl whom Hearst was bankrolling to movie stardom. For the premiere of her first film for Hearst's Cosmopolitan Films, *Cecilia in Pink Roses,* Hearst came up with a publicity stunt which appealed to Elinor's romantic side: he surrounded the screen with thousands of pink roses whose fragrance wafted through the audience via discreetly placed fans.

Elinor often stayed with Marion at Ocean House, on the beach at Santa Monica, a 110-room Georgian-style mansion with gilded ballroom and oak-paneled library where, when Marion pressed a button, a movie screen rose up from the floor. Elinor also went for weekends to San Simeon, Hearst's incredible Gothic-Disney villa, boarding his private train at Los Angeles, which was complete with chef, kitchen and clubcar for the 248-mile ride north along the coast. At San Simeon, Elinor thrilled to the lions and tigers kept in a private zoo on the 350,000-acre grounds.

Elinor's next movie was *His Hour* (1924), adapted from her Russian novel, starring Aileen Pringle and John Gilbert, whom Elinor had discovered working as assistant director on the MGM lot and launched into stardom. Gilbert found Madame Glyn's hauteur a little excessive and once, when they were both staying at Ocean House, he decided to humble her by taking her to nearby Venice Amusement Park. But when Elinor's skirts blew over her head with a sudden jet of air in the funhouse, John could only exclaim: "What lovely legs you have!"

His Hour was directed by King Vidor, who recounts his first meeting with Elinor in his memoirs. When he said he'd never read *His Hour*, she offered to read it to him that night in her hotel suite. She did so reclining on her tiger skin, doing all the voices in suitable tones, while Vidor had to be stoked with three large pots of black coffee to keep himself awake. At 4:45 a.m. Elinor sighed "Fini" and Vidor staggered off into the dawn.

After three more forgettable films for MGM, *Man and Maid* (1925), *Love's Blindness* (1925) and *The Only Thing* (1926), Elinor returned to Famous Players-Lasky, now renamed Paramount, for her last three Hollywood pictures. First came *Ritzy* (1927), a rather silly story of an American girl in Paris, then the film that made her really famous: *It* (1927).

Elinor had written a two-part novella in 1926 for Hearst's *Cosmopolitan* magazine entitled "It," in which the possessor of this rare quality was male. B.P. Schulberg at Paramount offered Elinor $50,000 for the film rights (which led the Hollywood wags to declare that Madame Glyn got $50,000 for one word), and told her to write a script around a female heroine with "It." In her *Cosmopolitan* story and later in *Photoplay* magazine, Elinor defined "It" as that "strange magnetism, mysterious and quite unbiddable," possessed by tigers, cats and some humans. According to Elinor, "It" was unselfconscious and yet self-confident, and couldn't be acquired; one had to be born with "It." She once told a crushed Douglas Fairbanks Jr. that he certainly didn't have "It" because his ears stuck out too much.

Elinor had trouble writing her scenario around a female possessor of "It" until she met Clara Bow. The historic meeting took place in 1926 and like everyone who wrote about Elinor, Clara remembers what she wore: a dress of purple chiffon, with a great many purple veils around her face. Elinor was wearing more than the usual number that day, because she was recovering from cosmetic facial surgery so painful that her arms had been strapped to her sides for ten days while she lay immobile and suffered. The operation had fixed her jaw in a forward position so that as she aged she would never have wrinkles around her mouth. Elinor was in the vanguard of Hollywood's ongoing obsession with beautiful youth. She would publish her beauty secrets in *The Wrinkle Book or How to Keep Looking Young* (1927), in which she advised female readers to scrub their faces hard with a dry nail brush until the skin glowed red; and to sleep always with one's head pointing to the magnetic north.

Elinor gazed through her purple veils at Clara, and knew, with growing excitement, that she'd found the perfect "It" girl. Clara had a piquant, vital little face; amazing red hair, obviously but effectively dyed; brilliant, arresting black eyes; hot little hands, soft as a baby's; and loads of raw, primitive, uncontrolled sex appeal. She also – Elinor shuddered inwardly – chewed gum, dropped her g's and spoke with a Brooklyn accent. She'd been raised there in the slums by a mother who went mad and tried to kill Clara before being carted off to an asylum and a father who accompanied Clara to Hollywood and who probably sexually abused her. The Paramount studio worked Clara far too hard; in the year before she met Elinor she'd made fourteen films, more than one a month.

Once Clara and Elinor had clicked, the Paramount publicity department swung into action: Hollywood's oracle, Madame Glyn, had spoken: Clara Bow had "It." ("'It,' hell," sneered Dorothy Parker, "Clara Bow has Those.") The only other possessors of "It" in Hollywood, Elinor informed the press, were the movie's male star, Tony Moreno, the Ambassador Hotel doorman, and the equine star, Rex, the wild stallion. Paramount decreed that Madame Glyn and her newest protégé must be seen everywhere together. Elinor and Clara went for wild rides around town in Clara's bright red Kissel convertible, taking with them her two chow dogs, whose hair had been dyed red to match their owner's. Four red-haired creatures in a red car must have been quite a sight. Clara gave Elinor full details of her affair with Gary Cooper, then a stunt rider at Paramount, while Elinor tried to rid Clara of her sleazy off-screen clothes and her four-letter words. Clara resisted and sometimes referred to Madame Glyn behind her back as "that shithead."

Clarence Badger directed *It*, with Marlene Dietrich's magic-maker, Josef von Sternberg, pinch-hitting when Badger fell ill. *It* tells the story of a practical and single-minded lingerie salesgirl who uses her sex appeal to get herself married to her boss, and launched into a life of luxury. Elinor hyped herself by writing into her script a brief scene wherein she describes "It" for the audience, with one eye on the Hays Office, as merely "not at all cold."

In *It*, Elinor helped to create the film stereotype of the flapper, exactly right for the twenties, not too wild and not too tame. In earlier silent films, two stereotypes had emerged: Theda Bara's vamp, in jeweled headdress and zigzag hem, a wanton, depraved creature too exaggerated to serve as role model for women in the audience, and Mary Pickford's virgin, the little girl who never grows up, in ringlets and gingham shifts. The flapper cleverly combined vamp and virgin; she was real enough to serve as role model, naughty enough to hint at the vamp, girlish enough to hint at the virgin. The flapper shows her wildness in midnight joy rides, and stabbing cigarette holders, but ultimately settles for social and sexual power, rather than political or intellectual, and ends in the safe haven of marriage. Because the flapper expressed where they wanted to be on the road to liberation, American women, just then acquiring their movie-going habit, flocked to see her. By 1925, 113 million Americans were going to the cinema every week. In 1926, 800 films were produced to be shown in

20,000 theaters across the country. Five hundred of the movie theaters built during the twenties cost a million dollars or more to construct and had organ consoles, string orchestras and ushers whose uniforms bore a remarkable resemblance to those of Empress Eugénie's liveried servants at the Tuileries.

Populations have always been controlled far more by images than by laws and regulations, so the influence of the flapper – the other type Elinor had helped to create after Gloria Swanson's glamour queen – was enormous, and spread beyond America. Women copied Clara Bow's hairstyle, Cupid's bow lips, short skirts and brassy manner. When the "It" girl got as far as France, she metamorphosed into Coco Chanel, who was still "Mademoiselle," a slim, short-skirted girl, independent and sassy, until the day she died at age eighty-eight.

The film *It* not only ushered in the flapper but also heralded a shift in women's erogenous zone, which tends to move about as male eyes grow bored and sated. In Empress Eugénie's era, the female area considered to have the most sex appeal was the torso: bared bosom and cinched waist. In the 1920s, due mainly to the new medium of movies, the erogenous zone shifted to the wildness of legs and knees, where tensions find release.

If the erogenous zone changed, so did female consciousness. Until the 1920s, clothed female figures which influenced women were always stiff and static in paintings, drawings or photos; now, on the silver screen, they began to walk and dance and leap about. Style suddenly acquired legs, and life, and the consciousness of wearing and viewing clothes, for all women, changed forever. Since the end of World War I, skirt hems had continued to rise. By 1927, they had reached the knee, and American women, both metaphorically and literally, were on the move, and seen to be so. They'd finally got the vote in 1920, and they were striding, in skirts that clearly showed their forward progress, straight into an empowered future. Their bodies were now stripped of the weight and constriction of about fifteen pounds of clothing, part of the conspiracy of patriarchal society to keep women such as Eugénie and Elinor in her youth passive, dependent and more or less stationary. Perhaps as Elinor watched Clara Bow's legs scissoring across the set or screen, bound for adventure, she recalled her own, at age ten months, tramping ever forward on the deck of the steamer which brought her to Canada.

Since *It* and other late-twenties films highlighted the new power and sexiness of legs, it was probably inevitable that Elinor's original definition of "It" as a combination of eroticism and mystery, as a kind of charm comprising far more than sex, would become simplified and one-sided. As always, image triumphed over words. Webster's Dictionary, when Elinor's coined word got between its covers, would correctly define "It" as "personal magnetism," but for the rest of the world, "It" soon came to mean mere sex appeal. Following Hollywood's lead, women in the general population kept the tiger and dropped the veils.

When the April 1994 issue of *Vanity Fair* magazine headlined the newest crop of young Hollywood beauties "The It Girls," it showed full-page photos of Sofia Coppola, Zoe Cassavetes and three others in slivers of silk or maribou which bared a lot of skin. They are reduced on the page to commercially presented sex objects, with not a hint of mystery to challenge the imagination. One feels that Elinor would not have approved. But all was not yet lost. Building on Gloria Swanson's glamour-queen type, woman's essential magic and mystery would, in another four years, appear on screen in its finest image, as Marlene Dietrich made her Hollywood debut. But after that, mystery would wane and sex would triumph.

Having made the movie, Elinor was far from finished with "It." She produced a book entitled *It and Other Stories* (1927), did a coast-to-coast tour lecturing on that quality, and answered huge stacks of letters from young women asking how they could acquire "It." Elinor also added three more men to her public pronouncement of who had this personal magnetism: Gary Cooper (Clara had convinced her), Lord Beaverbrook and the Prince of Wales, who would use his "It" to good advantage on a later woman of style: Wallis Warfield Simpson.

The film *It* grossed more than a million dollars at the box office, a prodigious amount for that time. Hoping for another such hit, Paramount bought the rights to *The Vicissitudes of Evangeline* (1905) from Elinor for $50,000 as another vehicle for Clara Bow and turned it into *Red Hair* (1928). Paramount had altered Elinor's script for *It*, calling in Louis Lighton and Hope Loring to make Clara Bow's role more important. With *Red Hair*, Paramount scrapped Elinor's screenplay entirely, including the small part she had written in for herself. Elinor merely smiled, shrugged, and pocketed her $50,000. The High Priestess of Hype had done her work so well that her name alone now made her rich. *Red Hair* cost $340,000 to make and would gross $900,000. Its plot turns Edwardian heroine Evangeline into flapper and manicurist Bubbles McCoy, whose image on screen put women into sexy nightgowns with the same impact with which Marlene Dietrich's would put them into trousers.

Sound films were making their debut; Warner Brothers had produced *The Jazz Singer* with Al Jolson in 1927; by 1931, there would be only two silent films on the commercial market. Clara Bow lost out; the nasal twang of her Brooklyn accent had no "It." She retired from films completely in 1933. Elinor, too, found herself suddenly out-of-date, although she did appear in a two-reel talkie lecturing on "It." "I wore the magenta Lucile teagown," she wrote to her mother, "which Lucy had made years before." This, in all likelihood, was the same magenta teagown with yellow insertions and diamond buttons which Elinor wore on stage in *Diplomacy* in 1895, and which heralded the exhibitionist to come.

Cult figures and celebrities eventually become prisoners of their own symbolic inflation, and this is what happened to Elinor. To keep the Glyn image, the natural red hair, starting to grey, had to be dyed; the naturally white skin, once translucent as alabaster, had to be covered with thick make-up which Anita Loos thought looked as if "scraped off the white cliffs of Dover"; the once-rosy mouth had to be painted vivid crimson.

At parties, Chaplin did his Elinor Glyn imitation, demonstrating how, since her facial surgery, she couldn't close her jaw easily, but only with a loud click. As late as 1948, Chaplin was still dining out on his Elinor Glyn stories, including the one in which he'd come across her on the set with her white-painted face, which, due to the weird lights cast by the Cooper-Hewitt mercury vapor lamps, turned green and her false teeth, mauve.

Hollywood was patently rejecting her; Elinor fled to New York, took a suite on the top floor of the Ritz Tower and stayed for nearly a year, writing articles for Hearst's newspapers with such titles as "It Isn't Sex – It's Good Pictures" and "How to Get a Man and How to Hold Him." She also wrote a story called "Such Men Are Dangerous," which she sold to Twentieth Century Fox for $30,000, and which was produced as a talking picture.

Elinor returned to England in the spring of 1929, and since she'd left behind her in the United States a large unpaid tax bill, she wisely stayed abroad for the rest of her life. She lost most of her Hollywood wealth by forming a disastrous British film company called "Elinor Glyn Productions" and renting studio space at Elstree. Her first film was *Knowing Men* (1929), directed by Elinor, costumed by Lucy, with whom she had reconciled, and featuring a supporting actor, the Honorable David Herbert, who wasn't a professional, but *was* the son of an Earl (Lord Pembroke).

Knowing Men opened with Elinor, in Addams-family black velvet and pearls, analyzing the various shortcomings of men. The inferior film had only one showing and Elinor's second film, *The Price of Things*, had none at all, for it was never released. Elinor was reduced once more to writing fiction-by-the-yard to pay off her debts, just as she had many years before. She took a modest flat in London's Hertford Street and in four years, churned out four novels and a book of short stories.

She went to Hungary in 1931, invited there by friends Baron and Baroness Rubido-Zichy, and turned her visit into another novel, *Love's Hour*, published in 1932. Clara Bow came to London that year, told Elinor she regretted not following her finishing-school advice, and made amends by giving her a photo signed: "To Elinor Glyn, whom I respect and admire more than any woman in the world." (Clara, in bright green lounging pyjamas, would surface three years later at a party hosted by Marlene Dietrich, where the perennial flapper posed on the piano, drank too many champagne-cocktails, and finished the evening throwing up in the powder room, while her Great Dane, Duke, guarded the door.) Gloria Swanson also visited Elinor in 1932, to find her, as did everyone, amazingly unchanged. When she asked sixty-eight-year-old Elinor her secret, the latter showed her how to exercise her facial muscles. Elinor's appearance (with surgical and cosmetic help) seemed to sail serenely on past all vicissitudes, beyond time, beyond fashion.

By 1934 Elinor had earned enough money to move to a larger London flat in Connaught Place, Bayswater, which she decorated in her usual sumptuous style with French period furniture, antique damasks, lacquer screens, great jars of lilies, and five tiger skins, each named for the lover who'd given it to her. She flirted through the mails with a Polish prince in America, an Austrian prince in Vienna, and a field-marshal in Finland. Cecil

Beaton, clever young photographer, artist and future costume designer for the stage, summoned Elinor to his mother's flat to be photographed, amid arum lilies and lengths of silver tissue. Elinor wore a long gown of black velvet with tasseled train and flowing sleeves. Cecil couldn't detect even "a spider's web line" around her eyes. But several years later, like Chaplin, he would use Elinor for parody, a fate awaiting every highly individualized person who swims against the tide of popular taste. Cecil turned up at a costume ball dressed, to hilarious effect, as Elinor Glyn.

Elinor's sister Lucy died in obscurity and comparative poverty in 1935, and their mother died two years later, still straight-backed and elegant, at the age of ninety-six.

Elinor's autobiography, *Romantic Adventure*, appeared in June 1936. In it she never drops her rosy veils, assuring readers that the "fundamental impulse behind every action" of her life has been "the desire for romance." Even her two biographers, grandson Sir Anthony Glyn, who wrote *Elinor Glyn: A Biography* (1955) and Joan Hardwick, author of *Addicted to Romance* (1994), were fooled by Elinor's designing ways, and viewed her mainly as she wished to be seen. However, if we peer closely at her memoir, and read between the lines, the other, more authentic Elinor emerges: a fiercely ambitious, hard-working novelist, essayist, journalist, lecturer and film producer, a woman who was huckster, opportunist and media hustler, and who held the public by its tail.

One canny English journalist, Beverly Nichols, penetrated Elinor's disguise. Interviewing her for an article for the *Sunday Chronicle*, he first took her to lunch on smoked salmon at London's Ritz Hotel, where Elinor put on her usual act. She drew herself up, fixed him with "a glistening eye" and said: "Tell your readers that sex has never touched the hem of my garment." "It was the most wonderful sentence," writes Nichols, for "there was something agonizingly nostalgic about it; it made me think of rich interiors in the 1900s, and sofas and tiger skins and joss-sticks burning in brass pots, and a gentleman with a moustache – from a Guards regiment, of course – fumbling about in the hopes of reaching the hem, but never quite succeeding." We can add that Elinor's remark was more revealing than she knew, in that it shows her thinking of sex in terms of clothing.

When, after a further meeting at Elinor's flat, Nichols sat down to write his article, he saw her whole. She didn't "spend most of her time on a tiger skin, smoking scented cigarettes, writing passionate passages with a purple pen." No indeed. She sat habitually "bolt upright in a straight chair." (One friend complained that there were no chairs for relaxing anywhere in her flat.) "Discipline – discipline – discipline," continues Nichols, "that is the rhythm of Elinor Glyn's life." Elinor had learned discipline and decorum long ago from Grandmother Saunders during harsh Canadian winters, and Elinor dutifully passed the lessons on. When her own thirteen-year-old granddaughter came to see her without wearing gloves, Elinor asked icily: "Are you especially proud of your hands?"

She could still come up with a good public relations stunt when necessary. At a literary luncheon at the Dorchester Hotel in March 1939, where seventy-four-year-old Elinor was guest speaker, she wore her cat Candide, who had an orange coat and plenty of "It," draped around her neck as fur-piece. The speech Elinor gave put Candide instantly to sleep, but Elinor's appearance and delivery kept the audience spellbound. "Great success!" she wrote in her diary.

Our final glimpse of her comes near the end of her life, during World War II, when London was suffering through nightly bombing attacks. The Honorable David Herbert, with another young man, came to visit. Elinor suddenly materialized in a darkened room in "a flowing green peignoir," holding a candle, and made the two young men sit on either side of her in an alcove lined with leopard skin. She had let her hair go white, and it hung in a silver curtain down her back. She was almost blind, but she stood up, stretched out her arms, and placed them on the heads of her visitors. She then prophesied her own imminent death, but told them that they and their country would survive, would "win through to complete and final victory." Cecil Beaton, hearing this story, pronounced Elinor "a figure of great bravura and courage." Beverly Nichols also commented on her courage and regretted that he didn't get to see her "in her post-henna days," when her hair had turned frost white. "I am told," concludes Nichols, "that she never looked more beautiful."

Elinor died in a London nursing home on September 23, 1943, a few weeks before her seventy-ninth birthday. When Clara Bow heard the news, she wept, declaring that "the world has lost a truly great person." But the friend who perhaps drew the best sketch of Elinor's character was fellow-snob Chips Channon, a rich American who lived in England and chronicled society. On the day Elinor died, Chips wrote in his diary: "She was an extraordinary woman; feline, theatrical, a 'poseuse' and a vulgarian, but a personality" and "a brave old girl, tough, upright." The London *Times* obituary correctly noted that Elinor "was by nature intense and lived every moment of a long and adventurous life," while the press in the United States, where hucksters were recognized and appreciated, applauded Elinor's supreme salesmanship. The *New York Times* noted that she described herself habitually as "the high priestess of the God of Love" to market her "bestsellers of slightly seamy, romantic love" and *Time* magazine dubbed her "the sex novel's impeccable grandmother."

Elinor Sutherland Glyn swept proudly through her life in robes with trains, while her hair flamed like a high-placed beacon. As child and bride, her mantles were made of dreams and edged in silver. As novelist, her gowns swished over tiger skins and fierce ambition. As film producer, waves of purple velvet pooled at her feet, and spread across Hollywood screens into America's consciousness. Elinor Glyn walked always straight ahead, in dignity, splendid vitality and conscious design, leaving in her wake the strange, contrary scent of musk and roses.

CHAPTER 3

Marlene Dietrich

The very first thing Dietrich did upon arrival at the Manhattan photo studio was to ask for a full-length mirror. Without it, she could do nothing, *was* nothing. For all her feature films, a huge mirror on rolling platform, framed in six high-wattage light bulbs, was positioned on the set so that, out of the corner of her eye, she could see what the camera saw. The mirror measured her progress towards perfection; it was tyrant, taskmaster and sternest critic. When one of the studio crew had rushed to Dietrich's side with a mirror, she shook out the glistening mink coat, and began slowly, meticulously, stroking and schooling to perfect alignment every hair of its many minks. One of America's greatest fashion photographers, Richard Avedon, stood respectfully, silently, off to the side, waiting to capture her image.

When young Peter Rogers, assistant to ad agency owner Jane Trahey, who'd conceived the "Blackglama" name and ad campaign for the Great Lakes Mink Association, had first asked Dietrich to pose in 1969, she'd refused. She was sixty-eight years old; both camera and mirror had turned from friend to foe, demanding ever more strenuous effort to maintain the Dietrich image. Besides, she wasn't the first star asked to lend her likeness, draped in mink, to appear above the words "What Becomes a Legend Most?" Seven "legends" had preceded her, including on-screen rivals Lauren Bacall, Bette Davis and Joan Crawford. Dietrich had seen their smug faces gazing up at her from full-page spreads not just in the fall issues of *Vogue*, *L'Officiel* and other fashion magazines, but also in the *New Yorker*, *Architectural Digest* and the *New York Times* magazine. Peter Rogers had told her that for doing the ad, she would receive a Blackglama mink coat custom-made to her own design by New York's best furrier, Maximilian. (Bette Davis had just taken the coat she'd posed in, but then Bette Davis had no style.) After Peter's pitch, Avedon phoned to tell Dietrich that it wasn't the mink coat that would shine in the ad, but rather her own fabulous, inimitable, justly famous self. Three days before, Dietrich had turned down $150,000 to pose for a hosiery ad; hosiery wasn't a main component of her carefully constructed image; fur was, so, at long last, she said yes, she'd drape herself in mink, and pose. Then Peter Rogers had eagerly sent round box after box of mink coats and capes to Dietrich's Manhattan apartment, twenty-eight in all, delivering the final three in person, before she'd settled on this one. It was floor-length and hooded, and contained far more than the sixty-odd skins which made up most coats. She who understood so well exactly how glamour worked, both its imagery and its effects, knew that the first rule of fur was it had to be as lavish and prodigal as possible. So here she was, shaking and flicking, bringing a hundred prostrate little mink vassals up to form.

She'd scorned Peter Rogers' offer of both limousine and make-up man Way Bandy. She had preferred to arrive at the studio in her own limo, and, as always, she'd done her own make-up at home, complete with artificial eyelashes as lush as the mink. "Dahlink, bwing me a stool," she instructed Peter Rogers in her throaty voice. When she felt comfortable on the stool, she licked her index finger and held it high towards the studio lights. She was such an accomplished technician that Hollywood's lighting and cameramen's union, years before, had made her an honorary member, and she'd been doing her smoke-and-mirrors act so long that she could tell from the heat on her finger whether or not the lights were positioned at exactly the right distance. For illusions, distance was important. She never worked without a key light placed exactly eight feet above her head and a little to the right. She even had a key light in her living room, above the fireplace, so that when visiting photographers and journalists came, she could glide into the room, seem to move on whim towards the fireplace, lean nonchalantly against the mantel, and raise her head to just the right angle for maximum loveliness.

It took some time to get the key light in exactly the right spot, while Avedon sighed and waited. Let him wait; it had to be exactly where Jo von Sternberg had placed it forty years before when, together, they'd first created the legend. She glanced at the mirror; yes, the overhead light hollowed the cheeks and placed a sharp shadow under the nose of the woman-in-the-mirror. Slowly, taking her time, the real woman draped the mink coat this way and that, checking every movement in the mirror, draped and redraped, pulled the hood up and down. Yes, up was better, but not so stiff, glamour had to look easy, languid; one must never let the effort show. She was oblivious to everyone in the room, totally focused on the woman-in-the-mirror. Chin a little higher; eyelids lower; head more to one side. When the face looked right, and fur slid over the body in the most becoming, reverential folds, Dietrich hitched her skirt higher and crossed the million-dollar legs, clad in sheer pantyhose and the spectator pumps which she'd invented for one of her films thirty-eight years before, and which Coco Chanel had copied. Dietrich gazed critically at her legs in the mirror, the famous legs which made Emil Jannings go stark raving mad on screen in *The Blue Angel*; Gary Cooper drink himself into a stupor in *Morocco* and César Romero shoot his best friend in *The Devil is a Woman.*

When coat and body were perfectly placed, Marlene Dietrich gave her first smile of the day and the woman-in-the-mirror smiled back, knowing full well that now she was the most glamorous woman in the world, and that the answer to the question "What Becomes a Legend Most?" was style: conscious, calculated, consistent.

The Goddess sat on high, beyond motion, beyond time, beyond criticism. Against a black matte backdrop flowed a wide river of gleaming black mink all the way to the floor. Standing out from this mysterious surround, in full radiance, were The Face, as white and subtly shadowed as the moon, and The Legs, impossibly long and pale, sublimely shaped and most skilfully angled. The only other visible object was the left forearm, gloved in rippling black leather, pointing straight as an arrow to the incomparable knees. Here was Glamour to the nth degree, the very soul of it. There was a sharp, unanimous intake of breath from every male in the room as they felt the impact of this astonishing icon in black and white. The object of their gaze finally tore her eyes from the fascination of the mirror, and it was quickly taken away. Ready for her close-up, Dietrich looked straight into Avedon's lens and said in commanding tone: "Now!"

At the end of the photo shoot, Peter Rogers, an ambitious young man who in another ten years would become head of his own ad agency, Peter Rogers Associates, thanked Dietrich and voiced the general approval. "Dahlink," she told him, "the legs aren't so beautiful. I just know what to do with them." And she was right. Like every great artist, she had moulded her chosen material (herself) into art by a combination of talent, taste and an infinite capacity for taking pains. It was one of the most disciplined and sustained creative acts of the twentieth century.

She was born Maria Magdalene Dietrich, on December 27, 1901, at 9:15 in the evening, in Schöneberg, a suburb southwest of Berlin. Her handsome father, Louis Otto Dietrich, a Lieutenant of Police, had served heroically as cavalry major in the Franco-Prussian war which had driven Empress Eugénie from Paris. Otto Dietrich had married seventeen-year-old Wilhelmina Elisabeth Josephine Felsing in 1898; her family owned the Felsing Watchmaker and Watch Shop, situated on Berlin's most fashionable shopping street, Unter den Linden. Maria Magdalene and her older sister Elisabeth, always called Liesl, were raised in an upper middle-class household where discipline and duty, as they had for Empress Eugénie and Elinor Glyn, filled all the neat, right-angled spaces, leaving little room for fun and frivolity. Maria Magdalene's Prussian father expected her clothes to be as crisp and spotless as his uniform, her shoes polished to mirror-sheen, her posture arrow-straight. Maria's mother was equally strict and conventional. No lady, she told her daughters, ever appeared in public without hat, gloves and male escort. On her two little girls, Frau Dietrich imposed a regimen of cold baths, exercise in freezing playgrounds, and lessons, lessons, lessons that swallowed up their after-school leisure. Instructors came and went from the house on Sedanstrasse teaching Maria and Liesl French, English, piano, violin, deportment. When she did get a moment free for dreaming, Maria smoothed and admired the pretty satin ribbons in different colors that she was collecting to tie to her mandolin.

In 1911, when she was ten, her father died; for the next six years, Maria developed her tastes in an all-female household, excelling at school, for she was highly intelligent, and honing her keen aesthetic sense. She seemed to know instinctively even then that her pursuit of beauty would find its main focus in the aesthetic presentation of self. She began her life-long creative act where, logically, one had to begin: with a new Christian name. She needed something truly distinctive and only hers. Maria Magdalene was too long and too ordinary. She scribbled various elisions across the pages of a blue notebook until she came up with one to fit the image already shaping in her mind. She announced to family, friends and teachers that henceforth she was Marlene, and on that day, at age thirteen, she began her climb to stardom and supreme style.

She would have three women to guide and inspire her. The first was Grandmother Felsing, whom Marlene remembers as "the most beautiful of all women" with dark red hair and violet-blue eyes. "She wore expensive clothes and even her gloves were made to measure," recalls Marlene. "She was naturally elegant and didn't concern herself with what was fashionable. She awakened in me the longing for beautiful things." Grandmother would hand Marlene one of her shoes, custom-made by a French shoemaker, saying, "Shoes are a serious business. This is how light they must be," while Marlene balanced the delicate shoe on her little finger. For Marlene, her grandmother was both "very real and very mysterious, a dream image, perfect, desirable, distant and fascinating." In time, Marlene herself would become exactly that, but for millions of females, not just one.

Marlene's second ideal of style was her mother's sister, Tante Valli. On February 4, 1916, when she was fifteen, Marlene wrote in her diary: "Tante Valli is so heavenly sweet! Yesterday she wore a black dress with white collar and cuffs. She looked completely divine. Chic. She also had black patent shoes." Six days later, Marlene scribbled happily: "She gave me a silver bracelet which I am not allowed to wear at school."

Marlene found her third and most important role model some years later in Tante Jolie, a young Polish woman only one year her senior who had once lived in Hollywood and who had married Uncle Willi Felsing who ran the Unter den Linden shop. Aunt Jolie's real name was Marthe Hélène but because she was so very "*jolie*" (pretty), that's what everyone called her. Her daughter-in-law, years later, would claim that Jolie was definitely Marlene's main prototype: "The long fingernails, the way she wore her jewels, the way she moved, the aura, the glamour, were all the same. They could have been sisters." Jolie wore jeweled turbans and casual flings of sable or fox which she lent to Marlene when the latter needed to impress. Jolie was a spendthrift where clothes were concerned, as Marlene would be, but she did have a trick for economizing. She ordered diamond necklaces and bracelets from her husband's firm to be made with every third stone fake.

It was during those early years that Marlene learned to be an accomplished seamstress. Much later in her life, she once returned home from a late-night party, ripped out the sleeve of her golden gown with cuticle scissors because she'd found a pucker in the seam, and expertly reset it, using especially thin needles begged from a French couturier, before she went to bed.

In 1917, Marlene's widowed mother married another straight-backed, strict, military man, Eduard von Losch, and moved with her two daughters to central Berlin. "Here one only goes out to see what other people are wearing," wrote Marlene in her diary on April 2, "and always worries if one is dressed well enough – and modern!" By now dark-blond, doe-eyed Marlene had plenty of sex appeal and boy friends, and fell in love at least once a week. "It's so much nicer if one has someone – it makes you feel so pretty," she confided to her diary on June 18, expressing the sentiment which would always fuel her love affairs. "Now I wear my hair up, and when something special is happening, I let a curl fall."

By the time she'd taken some dramatic training and become an actress, securing small parts in Max Rheinhardt's Berlin theaters and in a few films, Marlene had already found a distinctive, dramatic self-presentation through apparel. Long before she got to Hollywood, she was already a woman of style, enjoying and exploiting it as essence and tool of both her public persona and private self. On October 27, 1917, during an acting stint, she scrawled in her diary: "Sunday we have the first dress rehearsal. I have stage fright. I am playing the part of a man and am wearing my black sports trousers, Mutti's [Mother's] riding coat and white lace shirt. When I play Franzika, I hope she'll lend me her pink evening dress, because it's so well cut and suits me and I must have a long dress." In the beginning, like Elinor Glyn, Marlene sometimes had to settle for second-hand style. When she couldn't get small acting roles, she sold gloves on commission, performed in cheap cabarets and played violin in a pit orchestra which provided background music for silent films. She had little money but ordered her first custom-made suit. "I have always had to have clothes made for me," she would later tell a journalist, "because of my unusual shape – broad shoulders, narrow hips." A friend recalls that while most of the young actresses wore socks and flat shoes, Marlene, perhaps thinking of her grandmother, "wore the most exquisite hose and the finest high-heeled shoes" and that "she could knock your eye out at seven o'clock in the morning." Another colleague recalls her as "quite a glamour girl" in bright red costume and cloche hat who managed to give style to clothes that were not of the finest quality. "Her taste, her selection of colors, made up for, and to some extent concealed, the cheap materials she wore." She owned a black velvet coat and a matching chic little hat. For one casting call, she turned up in a pirate's hat, with pheasant's tail feather as exclamation mark, a panne velvet coat, a dangling four-legged red fox pelt, and her father's monocle. She got the part. Sometimes she wore five fox skins all at once, or a wolf robe, the kind you spread on beds. People followed her through the streets of Berlin, fascinated with the original way she'd put herself together.

In 1922, she played a bit part in a film called *Tragedy of Love*, directed by Joe May. His assistant was a twenty-six-year-old Slovakian-German called Rudolf Sieber, handsome, blond, and athletic. He remembers that it was a pair of long absinthe green gloves and matching shoes which first drew, and kept, his eyes on Marlene. Absinthe green is the color of an intoxicating drink and of the feathers of jungle parrots.

Marlene and Rudolf married on May 17, 1923, at Kaiser Wilhelm Memorial Church. Marlene wore a modern white wedding dress which showed her white-stockinged ankles, with a wreath of myrtle holding her veil. She had wanted to make a spectacular progress to church in open horse-drawn carriage so that her veil would billow and wave behind her, but her mother hired a closed Packard instead. Marlene had found a husband who would give her life-long dependability; he would always be her mentor, adviser, friend – but only briefly her lover.

Shortly after they were married, Marlene had Rudi's tailor make her a man's evening suit. At age twenty-one, she had indeed come of age where her style was concerned, for she had already found, in furs and trouser suits, its two main components, both hinting at the exotic and the erotic. Later, she would join her two main motifs together by buying a man-tailored polo coat in white ermine. With the love and security of Rudi to wrap her round, Marlene's lust for life burst into joyous expression in her raiment. Perhaps no woman of style ever got more positive enjoyment from her attire. Her relationship to her wardrobe was one of passionate engagement and relish which would last to the very end of her life.

At one important Christmas party attended by the Crown Prince of Germany and the country's top actors, Marlene arrived late, carrying a parcel, and shot straight into the ladies' room to change. She emerged in a stunning dress which she'd designed and which local dressmaker Mrs. Becker had finished only minutes before. The gown featured seven silver foxes cascading down the back, and stole the show. Long before she chose her 1969 Maximilian mink, Marlene knew that furs had to be as prodigal and generous as her own large-hearted spirit. To wear a few mean little pieces was worse than wearing none. In love and in fur, one had to go all the way. Her animal furs, as they had for Elinor Glyn, suggested unleashed sexual appetite and exploration of the exotic. Leopard and ocelot implied a steamy jungle where monkeys hung pendulous from trees and parrots screamed into civet-scented air; sable evoked the snowy steppes of Russia; mink, wolf and fox were redolent of secret, earthy dens.

Furs and feathers would both become almost a part of Dietrich's nature; she didn't feel whole without them. "You wrap yourself in feathers and furs which seem to belong to your body like fur to a wolf or feathers to an ostrich," friend Jean Cocteau would comment years later. Marlene never let conservation laws stand in her way. She frequently smuggled bird of paradise feathers from one country to another, later storing them carefully in old trunks, between acid-free tissue paper. Animal skins, no matter how old, moth-eaten or dried out, received the same loving care. Gone from her back but not forgotten, they would all go on resting in peace inside her trunks, waiting for their resurrection. (It would come after her own death.)

On December 13, 1924, Rudi and Marlene's only child, Maria Elisabeth, was born, two weeks before Marlene turned twenty-three. After that, she and Rudi stopped sharing a bed and sexually went their separate ways. Marlene lavished affection on her daughter when she was with her, and the rest of the time kept on with her acting and swash-buckling style parade.

In September 1929, when she was appearing in a Berlin revue aptly titled *Two Bow Ties*, Marlene met the man who, more than any other individual in her life, would help her market her glamour. For her first meeting with director Josef von Sternberg, then looking for a female lead for his UFA (*Universum Film Aktiengesellschaft*) film *The Blue Angel*, Marlene, at Rudi's urging, dressed like a lady in heliotrope suit and hat, with white kid gloves. But she couldn't resist adding, as her own racy signature, two dangling silver foxes. Von Sternberg was a small man with brooding brown eyes who looked like a decadent poet. He affected parrot-green coats, oriental dressing-gowns, riding boots, knobbed canes and, from time to time, a turban. (He had, after all, a nodding acquaintance with those of Elinor Glyn, having directed some segments of *It*.) Fleeing Vienna's anti-Semitism, von Sternberg had landed in America at age fourteen, found work as apprentice to a milliner, and then to a Fifth Avenue lace house in New York which sold the same sorts of veilings and nettings with which he would later adorn Marlene. He got into films by cleaning and patching their celluloid before moving on to the fun of directing them.

When parrot green met silver fox, Glamour began its slow, sure rise to highest billing and greatest beauty. After *The Blue Angel*, which would get them both invited to Hollywood, Marlene and Jo would make six more feature films together in which Glamour was both package and product, and in which its glorious material and its two master craftsmen worked in perfect harmony and understanding of its power and presentation.

"Glamour is what I sell," Marlene would later tell a reporter. "It's my stock in trade." But what exactly does glamour imply? Webster's Dictionary defines the word as "an elusive, mysteriously exciting and often illusory attractiveness that stirs the imagination and appeals to a taste for the unconventional, the unexpected, the colorful or the exotic." Marlene herself defines it more succinctly in her autobiography as "something indefinite, something inaccessible to normal women – an unreal paradise, desirable but basically out of reach." Glamour catches up the viewer's imagination, and makes it fly. On that September day in 1929 when Marlene met von Sternberg, she found the first, and more important, of two catalysts and critics for her chosen art. In the following year, she would find the other.

Shortly after their first meeting, von Sternberg arranged for Marlene to have a screen test. She worried about her nose which stuck up, as she wailed to Rudi "like a duck's behind," and which she'd already seen on screen in the few "terrible films" in which she'd briefly appeared. After the screen test, she returned in high excitement to Rudi. "That man is brilliant!" she exclaimed. "You know what he did today? He pinned that awful dress they put on me in Wardrobe for the test. He did it, himself. A BIG director! Then he told them what to do with my terrible hair. I told him that it always looks like a cat had just licked it, but he wouldn't listen."

In her autobiography, Marlene describes von Sternberg, with her usual generosity, as "the greatest cameraman the world has ever seen" and goes on to say that "one of his greatest talents lay in making everything appear opulent and radiant when in fact he worked on a very thin shoestring." It exactly suited Marlene's own keen aesthetic eye that "von Sternberg always began with the image, not the story." Playing the waterfront tart Lola-Lola in *The Blue Angel* would be an exhilarating learning experience for Marlene, who would later tell a film critic that she began to see how "the image of a screen character is built not alone from her acting and appearance but out of everything that is cumulatively visible in a film." Shortly after shooting started, Rudi asked von Sternberg: "Jo, have you thought of giving Marlene the chance to create her own costumes? She has an uncanny knack, an instinct. I have never seen it fail, once she knows the character." Von Sternberg agreed to give her free rein, and Marlene was thrilled to be creating what she called Lola-Lola's "imagery." She ransacked closets, chests of drawers, hat-boxes and old trunks and crowed with delight when she found such items as a cheap belt with big rhinestone buckle, or a threadbare kimono. She even made "costume sketches which I relished doing" and when finally she stood before von Sternberg in "everything that in my opinion was within the means of a B-girl in a sleazy, waterfront saloon", Jo cried "Wonderful! Simply wonderful!" and beamed his approval.

Marlene was happily cavorting on the set in her sleazy fringes and spangles from November 4, 1929 to January 30, 1930. It was while viewing the rushes that she took the next important step on her road to consummate style. Metaphorically speaking, it was a step back, aimed at distancing herself. She watched, fascinated, while on the screen Lola-Lola moved like a cat, sat astride a barrel, spread her silk-stockinged legs wide enough to show her frilly panties and sang "Falling in Love Again." The face on the screen, as it always would, looked world-weary, as wise and secret as the Sphinx, fully adult, with no hint of Clara Bow's insouciant young flapper. Those deep-set, hooded eyes had seen it all, and that beautiful mouth hinted at both humor and cynicism. "Mister von Sternberg is a god! A Master!" Marlene told Rudi excitedly after she'd seen the rushes. "He paints like Rembrandt, with his light. That face up there on the screen, a real sea-front harbor tart – she is *right*!" This was the first time, comments her daughter Maria, that she heard her mother "refer to herself in the third person. It was the beginning of her thinking of Dietrich as a product, quite removed from her own reality." Distance from the artifact she was creating would be the key to Dietrich's style, and its power. Distance allowed control, criticism and the saving grace of irony and self-mockery; it also kept her from sinking into narcissism and total self-engrossment. This distinction between self and glamour product would prove crucial to her well-being – and, in the beginning, would be firmly in place.

For the Berlin première of *The Blue Angel*, at the Gloria Palace on March 31, 1930, Marlene turned up in a big-collared white ermine coat, carrying the usual conventional spray of red roses. But when she tossed coat and roses aside, the audience snickered and pointed, for she had deliberately pinned a most unconventional lesbian symbol, a bunch of violets, to her white chiffon dress, "just where the legs part." After the showing, the audience went wild, shouting "Marlene! Marlene!" as the lights went up. She felt both euphoric and surprised as she stood, in angelic white and naughty violets, taking her bows. Only later would she look back and realize that on that last day of March, 1930, when she was twenty-eight, a star was born.

As soon as she'd taken her curtain calls, Marlene left that very night for Hollywood, having just been hired by Adolph Zukor and Jesse Lasky at Paramount. She headed for the luxury steamer *Bremen*, set to sail next morning, in the back of a large UFA truck, drinking champagne, dancing the Charleston and dizzy with excitement. Her metaphors of style lay around her, carefully folded into thirty-six pieces of luggage lashed down with ropes. Rudi stayed behind in Germany; he and Marlene would live more and more apart, but she stayed married to give herself a useful cloak of respectability while she conducted her endless amours. She would support Rudi and his long-time mistress Tamara Matul financially until they died. Tamara became a Dietrich clone with the same plucked eyebrows and general make-up, dressed in Dietrich's cast-off designer clothes. Marlene's daughter Maria would join her mother in Hollywood in the following year, and be conscripted at a young age as unpaid dresser and helper on the set.

The *Bremen* reached New York one day late, on April 9. Marlene prepared to disembark, as she tells us, "wearing a gray dress, my favorite travel outfit in Europe," but Mr. Blumenthal, Paramount's envoy sent to meet her, explained that she couldn't leave the ship looking like an ordinary woman, but only as Hollywood's newest star. Marlene obediently grabbed her keys, trotted down to the hold, found the place where her trunks were still stored, extracted a black dress and mink coat, and in the warm sunshine of New York's April weather, posed in full glamour sitting on top of twelve pieces of her luggage, while photographers' cameras clicked. Then she was hustled to a breakfast press conference at the Ritz, where Jesse Lasky introduced her to the press, just as, ten years before, he had introduced a flamboyant, tiger-frisky Elinor Glyn. Marlene was feeling, as she tells us, "both fearful and enthusiastic," and let Lasky do the talking.

When Marlene reached Hollywood, which she described as a place where one had to "concentrate on keeping every eyelash right," she found a town with only three important streets, Sunset, Wilshire and Hollywood Boulevards, and air smelling of gardenias and orange blossoms. After Paramount had given a reception for her at their studios on Marathon Street, the star-making machine revved up. On studio orders, Marlene had to lose thirty pounds, have her wisdom teeth extracted to hollow her cheeks, her ankles massaged free of fat and her natural eyebrows plucked almost to extinction. When her figure was properly gaunt, Paramount's make-up chief, Dotty Ponedel, went to work on the Dietrich face. Dotty penciled in new eyebrows in their first, but not last, placement, darkened and lengthened Marlene's upper lashes, drew a white line along the lower eyelid to "open" and enlarge her eyes. Along Marlene's "duck" nose, her only imperfect feature, Dotty drew a fine silver line which straightened the bridge and, by catching the light, narrowed the nose's width. Von

Sternberg's camera and lighting magic would do the sculpting which make-up couldn't, and a gilding powder which Marlene bought at a specialty store, having refused to bleach her hair, would make it look blonder and shinier on screen.

Paramount launched a $500,000 publicity campaign, beginning with a fact sheet which informed the press that their new star "has fair hair with a reddish tinge, blue-green eyes and a supple figure. She looks very unlike the popular conception of a continental. Height: 5'5". Waist: 24". Weight: 120 pounds." Paramount gave Marlene a dark green Rolls Royce and uniformed chauffeur, and installed her in a one-bedroom apartment on Horn Avenue, decorated for the delectation of future movie-magazine fans with over-stuffed sofas, mirrors galore, crystal decanters and real leopard-skin rug, not a fake like the one Elinor Glyn had brought to Hollywood. Marlene settled in, unpacked her thirty-six trunks, stacked around her the books she bought by the yard, for she was a voracious reader, and invited von Sternberg, who had fallen madly in love, to share her bed. He was there almost every day for breakfast on the patio, with Marlene in cream silk lounging pyjamas and wide organza hat.

In the evenings, Marlene dressed for Hollywood parties in the current fashion, inspired by Paris couturière Madame Vionnet, of slinky, bias-cut, backless evening gown. Because it had no back and was cut low under the arms, Marlene couldn't wear a bra to uplift her sagging breasts, always a problem for her. So she taped them with wide surgical tape, a practice she would continue for years. No pain or inconvenience was ever too great if it achieved the Dietrich look and line. One party guest recalls that "Marlene always arranged to make a tremendous entrance, escorted by a famous and handsome movie star," wearing "a backless dress or gold lamé lounging pyjamas while every man in the room ogled her."

But it was after breakfast and before the evening parties that Marlene, that May and June, felt happiest and most alive, totally engrossed in an exciting new activity. She was closeted all day, every day, until she began shooting *Morocco* in July, with Paramount's head costume designer, Travis Banton, who, like von Sternberg, would play a crucial role in the evolution of the Dietrich image. Travis had studied at Columbia University, the New York School of Fine and Applied Arts and the Art Students League. He worked briefly in New York for the couture houses of Madame Francis and Elinor Glyn's sister Lucile before opening his own salon in the East Fifties. There he shot to fame in 1920 by designing Mary Pickford's wedding gown for her marriage to Douglas Fairbanks. Producer Walter Wanger had enticed Travis to Hollywood in 1925, as assistant to Paramount's head designer, Howard Greer, at a salary of $150 a week. Promoted to head in 1927, Travis would design brilliantly for more than 160 movies, one of his final memorable efforts being Rosalind Russell's wardrobe in *Auntie Mame* (1958).

Early each morning, Travis would greet Marlene looking as elegant as his designs, in paisley ascot tucked into cream silk French-cuffed shirt, cashmere blazer, white flannels and custom-made English shoes. His favorite pair had black scrolls on white leather. His domain at Paramount, where he and Marlene worked so hard and so happily, was painted and carpeted in greige, a neutral tone hovering indecisively between gray and beige that didn't compete with the colors of the clothes. The rooms were filled with satin-covered banquettes, multi-view mirrors and padded, carpeted platforms on one of which Marlene would stand for her fittings. There were other rooms with miles of shelves stocked with bolts of lamés; silk chiffons, satins, crêpes and velvets; lightweight woolens; veilings and trims, all of which Travis bought on his yearly trips to Paris. Since talkies had replaced silent films, fabrics such as taffetas and stiff moirés, which made far too much noise on the soundtrack, had been outlawed in favor of crêpes and satins which had a sinuous, silent flow.

Dreaming up attire for the nascent Dietrich myth was a creative act for both Travis and Marlene. They were a formidable team. Alfred Hitchcock once called Marlene "a professional dress designer" and Travis' assistant Edith Head, who would succeed him as head designer, asserts: "You don't design clothes for Dietrich. You design them with her."

Travis began by sketching ideas for outfits on large sheets of drawing paper. Marlene liked to arrange the sketches on the greige carpet, viewing them from every angle while she walked about, stabbing at them with her cigarette to point to some detail which she thought should be changed. If she and Travis couldn't agree, there would be pitched battles, which Marlene called "discussing." When both of them considered a sketch perfect, Travis would turn it over to drapers to create a muslin pattern on Marlene's personal dress form, while the two of them chose fabric and accessories, including shoes and handbags from the store of Hermès – ones which Travis had bought on his annual trip to Paris. Marlene worked long hours, completely absorbed, fulfilled, without stopping to eat or even visit the bathroom. Often she and Travis worked till late at night. "The costume work is good and I enjoy it," Marlene wrote enthusiastically to Rudi. "Travis Banton is talented. Jo tells us what he wants and Travis and I discuss what the clothes should be. He is willing to do the sketches over and over until they are right. We have the same kind of endurance, we never tire."

Together they designed some of the loveliest clothes ever seen on screen. When, in 1976, Diana Vreeland, head of the Costume Institute at New York's Metropolitan Museum, wanted to mount a show called "Romantic and Glamorous Hollywood

Design," which included some Banton-Dietrich gowns, the Met's Director, Tom Hoving, asked Diana: "Why in the name of God Hollywood?" She replied: "Tom, I've been looking at French couture for the last forty years, and I can only tell you that I have *never* seen clothes made like these."

The creative collaboration of Dietrich and Banton would influence every woman in America, for Hollywood was just then beginning to take over from Paris as the western world's fashion capital, an influence which would peak in the thirties and forties, then decline in the fifties when television began to compete with movies. The major studios hyped their designers as "the most creative fashion minds in the world" and sent American newspapers and magazines photos of their stars wearing not just gowns they'd worn in films but also ones designed specifically for these publicity shots. In the same year Marlene arrived in Hollywood and teamed up with Travis, the female public first looked to movies for fashion guidance, and to movie magazines, which for the next twenty years would supplant *Vogue* and *Harper's Bazaar* as major source of new trends.

It was in 1930 that women stopped looking like girls, influenced by Clara Bow's short skirts and Mary Pickford's Peter Pan collars, and suddenly turned into women. The Wall Street crash of October 1929 had ushered in an economic depression so severe that America's females had to grow up overnight. Dietrich, as well as Garbo, Crawford, Harlow and other stars of the thirties, were fully mature, gowned on screen in bias-cut crêpes or satins which clung to breasts and hips and accentuated feminine curves. Suits acquired a wide, padded look at the top of the sleeve to show that women could shoulder their burdens and were equal to the task. Skirts grew longer; knees dimpled like Clara Bow's seemed suddenly frivolous and irrelevant. The mature woman as fashion ideal would reign until the end of the 1950s, to be superseded, right up until the present day, by girls again, skinny and waif-like in mini-skirts, baby-dolls, school jumpers, T-shirts so tight they look outgrown, ankle socks and hand-me-down grunge from a child's dress-up box.

When Marlene's clothes for *Morocco* were ready for fittings, she often spent as much as six hours at a stretch standing patiently on a padded platform while she and Travis pointed and

pinched, and the fitters pinned and repinned. In those days, when every film showed their heroines in at least twenty different outfits, stars would be condemned to standing stock still for fittings for as many as 120 hours per film. Greta Garbo, for one, came to hate her fittings; not so Marlene. However long it took to get it right, she was ready to stand and endure. "In films," she would later explain to a friend, "with the screen getting bigger and bigger every year, the close-ups twenty, fifty times life-size, every ruckle looks like the Rocky Mountains."

During July and August 1930, when *Morocco* was being shot, Marlene's chauffeur drove her at dawn each morning to the Paramount lot, where she had her own bungalow in the eclectic row of Tudor, Georgian or Wild-West façades built to serve as film backdrops. Marlene's 60 x 30 foot space contained living room, dressing room, make-up room and bathroom. Nearby were the bungalows of Clara Bow, Jeannette MacDonald, Carole Lombard and Mae West, whose talent for self-parody made Marlene warm to her instantly.

Each day Marlene marveled at von Sternberg's art and became his eager pupil. Sam Jaffe, Paramount's production manager, recalls that whereas other directors would have tried to teach Marlene to act, von Sternberg "simply arranged for her to move exquisitely." He would tell her: "Look up, look down, look aside, look this way," controlling her – but only in the beginning – like a puppet on a taut string. He taught her exactly how to present herself for maximum beauty of still pose or movement, something Marlene would always remember and profit by. Elinor Glyn would have approved of the ways in which von Sternberg shot Dietrich for maximum mystery, using filtered lenses, shadows, gauze over the lights, veils over the face, even cigarette smoke. "I am his product, all of his making," Marlene wrote to Rudi. "He hollows my cheeks with shadows, widens the look of my eyes, and I am fascinated by that face up there on the screen and look forward to the rushes each day to see what I, his creature, will look like." Von Sternberg also back-lit and thus lightened her hair, "causing a glow like a halo," as Marlene told Rudi. She considered Jo "a poet who writes with images rather than words, and instead of a pencil, he uses light and a camera." In *Morocco*, von Sternberg followed the convention of thirties Hollywood, and used a lot of close-ups of what he called the "face that lives – really lives." "They don't need an actress here," moaned Luise Rainer, who collected two Academy Awards before she left Hollywood in the late 1930s. "What they need and want is a face and the camera to go around it."

With the "It" girl and other flappers, the erotic emphasis focused on legs. In the 1930s, it moved to the eyes: Garbo, Crawford and especially Dietrich had amazingly eloquent eyes. In the 1950s, eros would shift to the mouth – best exemplified in Marilyn Monroe's iconic lips, always open and inviting – and in the 1960s and 1970s, eros would go wild, spreading gradually to the complete female body, bared in the 1990s to the camera's prurient gaze.

Marlene's face on screen had a luminous whiteness and a rare, perfect symmetry, unlike most faces, which have a good side and a bad side. As the filming of *Morocco* continued, both von Sternberg and Marlene were falling in love with The Face; his affair would be finite; hers would last a lifetime. Marlene reported to Rudi that one close-up was "the sexiest come-hither look that's ever been filmed." But she still had the necessary detachment from her screen image firmly in place. "If while you are seeing it," her letter continued, "you know that I'm counting one, two, three – it can be very funny."

As well as self-presentation, Marlene was learning the art of make-up. Very soon she pushed other skilled hands away in those dawn hours when she stood – she never sat – before her lighted dressing-room mirror and put on her make-up herself, dipping the rounded end of a thin hairpin into white greasepaint to line the inside of her lower eyelid. "God, she was good at that!" recalls her daughter who, after her arrival in Hollywood, used to sit entranced as her mother painted her face. "One marveled at her skill and lightning speed."

By the time *Morocco* finished shooting in August, the Paramount executives had seen Dietrich as Amy Jolly in the rushes, and they knew that they had a spectacular new star. By then, they had also seen the amazing box-office figures out in Europe for *The Blue Angel*, and began negotiations for its American release the following December. Paramount began to sell Dietrich in earnest, ordering Eugene Robert Richee to take plenty of still photographs to be distributed to the press. One of them was blown up to billboard size and plastered across America with the heading "Paramount's New Star – Marlene Dietrich." In her gossip column, Louella Parsons headlined the "Famous Actress" whom nobody had seen expect on billboards, and movie magazines encouraged fan clubs to form based on nothing but Richee's still photos. Dietrich was a star firmly fixed in American consciousness even before they'd ever seen her on the screen.

Morocco premiered on November 14, 1930 to great acclaim. The public flocked to see it, and loved it, as did the film industry. Both von Sternberg and Marlene, to her delight, were nominated for Academy Awards. (She lost out to someone with no glamour at all: Marie Dressler, for her role in *Min and Bill.*)

Marlene had insisted on wearing black for *Morocco*'s opening scene "so as to appear slimmer." Black is hard to photograph, but finally von Sternberg had capitulated. He was aiming for an image more mysterious and alluring than Garbo's at MGM; in fact Marlene had been brought to Hollywood for the express purpose of giving Garbo some stiff competition. So *Morocco* opens with Marlene posed à la Garbo, swathed in black, veiled in night-time fog aboard ship, slowly moving towards the camera. In the next scene, Marlene dons top hat, white tie and tails; leans nonchalantly against the balustrade of a seedy Moroccan nightclub and croons "*Quand l'Amour Meurt.*" Marlene would conspire with von Sternberg to present her briefly in male attire in all but their final film together. She appears in top hat and tails in *The Blue Angel*, *Morocco* and *Blonde Venus*; dons a military coat and peaked cap in *Shanghai Express*; a white Cossack uniform in *The Scarlet Empress* and a helmeted aviator's suit in *Dishonored.* Marlene's masculine garb made her body look even more erotic than her slinky, bias-cut crêpe gowns did. "Sexuality itself gets a sharp specific emphasis if someone uses the clothes of the other sex," writes Anne Hollander in *Sex and Suits* (1994). Sartorial borrowings from the opposite sex show a sophistication beyond mere procreation; sex isn't just for perpetuating the human race; sex is for private titillation; sex is *fun.* Sexuality, says Marlene's male attire on screen, is something fluid, whimsical, shifting, even dangerous. There she is on film, marveled America's women, looking at Dietrich in top hat and tails, seemingly immune to housework, male domination and sexual demands, even menstrual pains and childbirth. American women, who had secured the vote only ten years before, watched Dietrich's elegant trousered legs striding into areas of male power, social supremacy and unpredictable sexual inclination. Clothes make the man; by wearing his pants, Marlene started women dreaming of further emancipation. In another two years, her message would be broadcast with far more emphasis and effect.

On screen, as off, it was Dietrich's erotic energy which counted, not her gender. Pure eros would always be the motive force behind her style. Marlene's powerful, and active, female libido gave her more "It" than Elinor Glyn could have imagined in her wildest dreams – far more than screen rivals Greta Garbo, who was merely tender and vulnerable, or Mae West, who came too close to parody. Marlene was all-Female, especially in a trouser suit. "It's very nice to be a woman," she declared. She celebrated that fact every time she got dressed.

In addition to concentrated eros, Amy Jolly in *Morocco* and all Dietrich heroines keep their cool. They have none of the Theda Bara-type vamp's frantic, obvious desires. Dietrich was woman fulfilled, almost sated, shaded with the slight melancholy which always follows sexual union. Dietrich was partaker and onlooker all at once; on screen, as off, detachment showed, and male attire helped to convey this casual, carefree stance to an audience.

In her next film, *Dishonored*, shot in October and November 1930, Marlene played a Mata Hari-type spy with a far wider range of clothing than emotion, running the gamut from a prostitute's sleaze to a fur-trimmed long dress, lamé mini skirt, Russian peasant costume, aviator's leather pants and jacket and, for the final scene, a fur-trimmed suit. Preparing to face the firing squad who will execute her, she asks a young officer for a looking glass; instead he offers her the blade of his sword. Dietrich looks into that make-shift mirror, adjusts her stockings and, for the very last time, puts on her lipstick. This symbolic act conveys the real Dietrich's creed. By paying attention to her appearance at the moment of death, the heroine demonstrates that clothes are the stuff of life, that beauty is synonymous with courage, and style with content.

By the time *Dishonored* premiered in March 1931, less than a year after she had arrived in the United States, Marlene Dietrich had become one of the most famous women in the world, admired, applauded, envied and talked about. As von Sternberg recalls in his memoir, "enthusiastic reviews poured in, fan mail kept an entire department busy, photographs were requested, men wished to lay their fortunes at her feet. Actors wanted to be her partner on screen, producers and directors longed to work with her." For Marlene, it was an exhilarating time, and all very gratifying, but she kept her head and stayed focused on her art, perfecting the Dietrich habit.

For *Shanghai Express*, made in November and December 1931, in which Marlene again plays a prostitute, she and Travis devised costumes of no particular period full of mystery and teasing, using mainly black in egret feathers, chiffon, maribou and veiling. In one scene, Shanghai Lily is memorable in narrow black crêpe; coq-feather skull cap with veil; coq feathers spilling and cresting wantonly around neck and shoulders; one long strand of crystal beads drawing the eye downward to woman's ultimate mystery; beige pumps with black toe-caps, in the style Chanel would copy and Marlene would wear for her Blackglama ad thirty-eight years later, perhaps consciously returning then to this earlier symbol. To find exactly the right veil for Shanghai Lily's saucy little hat, Marlene and Travis had labored for hours, unrolling bolt after bolt of veiling, trying each one across her face, and rejecting forty different ones before they unrolled a veil with faint Venetian-blind stripes. When Marlene put it across her face, as her daughter recalls, "something amazing happened" and "Travis let out a wild whoop" while Marlene merely smiled.

She was a thorough professional, working always with incredible energy and discipline. Early each morning during a shoot, after Marlene had put on make-up and costume in her Paramount dressing room, she was taken by limousine to the sound stage. Her daughter recalls such rides: "Never a blink, swallow, shift, pull, twitch, cough, sneeze or word" as Dietrich sat "weight balanced on one buttock, shoulder and thigh, fingertips braced against the car seat to decrease body pressure" and thereby prevent her costume from crushing, "eyes open, locked into nonmovement, painted lips ajar, frozen."

After all the hard work of designing costumes, having them fitted, shooting the movie, watching rushes for ways to improve herself, Marlene had to pose for still studio portraits. During her Paramount years, she sat for 870, and spent long hours rejecting some, choosing others, then retouching them herself, with a wax pencil, until they conformed to her ideal. This was cosmetic surgery of a sort, performed on paper rather than on a person. When she'd finished the photos, Marlene ordered dozens of copies for herself in 8 x 10 or 16 x 20 sizes. She got into the habit of taking a pile of these with her to dinner parties, to display to guests while wives fumed and food cooled. With that gesture, her long, slow descent into solipsism had begun.

In July 1932, Marlene met a woman who would not only influence her own style profoundly, but, through her, that of thousands of women in the western world. At a Hollywood dance recital, Marlene saw a striking figure sitting near her: a dark-haired young woman dressed in white slacks, white turtleneck sweater and white tailored top coat. Even though Marlene had worn trousers on screen and years before in Berlin, no woman in North America at that time wore them in private life, unless one counts the cocktail pyjamas popular for evening since the late twenties with a few trend-setters. The woman-in-white, Marlene learned, was Mercedes de Acosta. She had married portrait painter Abram Poole in 1920, taken a girlfriend on their honeymoon, and boasted thereafter: "I can get any woman from any man." She had come to Hollywood in 1931 as scriptwriter, and soon became Greta Garbo's lover. Mercedes dressed with singular style in black, white, or both, favoring stark lines, cloaks and tricorne hats.

On the morning after the dance recital, Marlene appeared at Mercedes' front door with a large bouquet of roses. "White roses," said Marlene as she handed them to her, "because you looked like a prince last night." Next evening, Marlene came to dinner. As they sipped champagne, Mercedes stared at Marlene's face. "You have exceptional skin texture that makes me think of moonlight," she told her new friend. "You should not ruin your face by putting color on it." Marlene marched into the bathroom, scrubbed her cheeks and vowed: "I will never put rouge on my cheeks again," and she never did. It was during this same evening that Mercedes suggested that Marlene wear "slacks," as they were then called, for ordinary day wear, since she'd looked so smashing in them in *Morocco*. Next day, Mercedes took Marlene to her tailor where, with her usual prodigality, Dietrich ordered twelve pairs of trousers and matching jackets.

One day soon after, when a photographer called while Marlene was loafing at home in a pair of her new slacks, she told him: "If you want to shoot me this way, all right." Several days later, newspapers around the world carried a photo of Marlene in trousers and a new world fashion was off and running. Marlene began wearing creamy white flannel slacks for tennis, often with cream shirt and matching beret. One night, she created a sensation at a Hollywood party by arriving in navy blazer, white bell-bottomed trousers and peaked yachting cap. Paramount printed more fan photos of Dietrich in pants, with the daring slogan "The Woman Even Women Can Adore." Every new photo of a trousered Dietrich emptied the few racks of women's slacks in stores, while manufacturers rushed to supply more.

Women in pants signaled a radical shift in both female silhouettes and consciousness. Women down the ages had always worn skirts, which by hiding them from the waist down, left full play for female modesty and masculine fantasy and myth. Trousers first appeared as underwear just as Worth and Empress Eugénie got women into crinolines. If the crinoline should suffer some trauma, legs might very well come into view and so they had to be sheathed, hence the invention of white cotton pantaloons, whose crotch was left unstitched. Pants moved from underwear to exterior garb in the 1890s, when women first rode bicycles and needed them for safety's sake. After all those years of skirts, to emphasize women's legs and the shadowed place between seemed like sexual heresy, a slur on the purity of the "Angel in the House," still on the pedestal where Victorian men had placed her.

Feminist advances have always been in direct ratio to the number of trousers appearing on women's bodies or in their closets. Since the 1930s, it has been socially acceptable for women to assume male dress because they raise themselves by so doing in the social hierarchy. But no man, unless he's wearing a Highland kilt, dare put on a skirt, for he is then debasing himself to the lower status of women. When in the 1930s, women copied Dietrich's trousers, they signaled their desire for the kind of successful career and financial freedoms she had. She was then earning a quarter of a million dollars a year (four million in today's currency) and – although her fans didn't know this – supporting husband, husband's mistress, daughter and assorted relatives. She also commanded the attentions, either paid for or voluntary, of plenty of men. Women looked at her wearing men's clothes, sighed, dreamed, identified, if only subconsciously, with her emancipated image, and sartorially followed her lead. Converts to feminism grew in the 1940s when women worked in factories for the war effort and literally wore the pants in the family while husbands served at the front. Trousers and feminism both lost ground in the 1950s when women put on housedresses and aprons and stayed in the suburbs, baking apple pies and raising their children. In the late 1960s and 1970s, trousers became a political statement as women stormed all-male boardrooms in the protective coloring of suits tailored exactly like a man's. In the 1980s and 1990s, women got all the main designers on their side, particularly Yves St. Laurent, Giorgio Armani, Ralph Lauren and Donna Karan. Today, every woman who steps into trousers carries Dietrich's spirit in one of her pockets.

Marlene's love affair with her trouser-model Mercedes was hot and heavy from September 1932 until May 1933, when it cooled only because Marlene then departed for Europe to spend the summer with Rudi. She arrived at Paris' Gare St. Lazare on May 19, to be greeted by Rudi, photographers and a large pop-eyed crowd, for Marlene was wearing a man's polo coat, pearl-gray suit, tie and her signature beret. Transvestism was illegal in Paris, and the Chief of Police warned her that such a costume made her liable to arrest. Marlene paid not the slightest attention to this intimidation.

She spent her days in Paris ordering new couture from the designers which best accommodated the glamour image still firming in her mind: Patou, Lanvin, Molineux and Madame Grès. (Chanel was already popular, but Marlene wouldn't patronize her until the 1950s.) Dietrich's chosen couturiers soon learned to design clothes with her in mind. Dietrich could afford to buy lavishly, since couture dresses then cost no more than $200 each. She loved the whole, delicious process. First she made an appointment with her particular *vendeuse*; then chose quickly, without advice or indecision. Sometimes Marlene altered color or fabric; she liked neutral colors rather than bright ones. (Later, in *Marlene Dietrich's ABCs*, she would advise women on a budget never to buy a dress in "green, red or any other flamboyant color," but to assemble a basic wardrobe of one gray suit; two black dresses; a black wool skirt; several black or gray sweaters.) After choosing came the fittings; most women had three; Marlene had at least six and sometimes as many as eighteen. Ginette Spanier, costume manager of Pierre Balmain, a house which Marlene would patronize in the 1950s, recalls what these fittings were like:

> Marlene is intelligent, ruthless, and quite extraordinary over clothes. She knows exactly what she wants. She knows a great deal about fitting. She also knows how a dress is made. She never smiles. She never says, "Good morning." She stands there in the fitting room, hour after hour, incredibly beautiful, without a smile, pinching a tenth of an inch of material here or there to show how it puckers. As the hours go by she pinches a bit lower down the dress. That is all. I have known her to have a garment fitted six times because of a seam in the *lining* of which she didn't quite like the angle.

"I dress for the image," Marlene would tell a fashion journalist. "Not for myself, not for the public, not for fashion, not for men. The image? A conglomeration of all the parts I've ever played on the screen." Consistency was the secret of her power; past and present image merged, as did public and private. Like Elinor Glyn's, Dietrich's clothes were classic, never strictly geared to current fashion. Her screen rival at MGM, Greta Garbo, was a protean creature on screen born anew with each film; Dietrich, as she progressed from role to role, kept on wearing her past, using the same language of furs, feathers, men's suits and hats with veils, on screen and off. Often she had two identical outfits made: one for the screen and one for private use. In everyday life, Garbo wore baggy pants and old raincoats and had no glamour at all. Dietrich was always Dietrich; she never took off her style. That was why her image burned like an eternal flame. "She never changed," attests her daughter. "She was a law unto herself, knew it, lived it" – or, as someone else put it – "Age cannot wither nor custom stale her infinite sameness."

Ginette Spanier notes in her memoir that Dietrich "thinks out a whole wardrobe in terms of her various appearances. She goes straight for her needs, bearing in mind what background she will appear against, what other performers she will top." To be instantly visible and to photograph well when traveling, Dietrich usually dressed in white or beige, and always wore high heels, because, "I'm too short. Heels preserve the *line*." Like Elinor Glyn, she needed no publicist, no advance notice handed out of where she would be; the press gathered like moths to a light.

After Marlene had reinforced her image through her new couture wardrobe, she summoned her glovemaker to her Paris hotel, who arrived with suitcases full of tissue-thin leathers. Marlene ordered fifty pairs at a time, demanding an ever tighter fit as he smoothed the leathers over her fingers, pinned and repinned, while the world's thinnest pins showered onto the carpet. Daughter Maria recalls the hilarious time when, her glove order having arrived, her mother put on a pair, taking twenty minutes to do so, and found that she couldn't move her fingers at all. She laughed so hard she had to run for the bathroom before exclaiming: "They will be just right for stills. I won't have to retouch my hands – finally!" The skin-tight gloves were packed in tissue, black for the black gloves, white for the white, beige, pearl gray and tan ones, and each packet clearly labeled: "Studio

Stills. Gloves, black kid, 3/4 length" and so on. Later, Marlene got the glovemaker to make a plaster cast of her hands to be used for fitting, just as her shoemaker used one of her feet when making her shoes.

After Paris, Marlene, Rudi and Maria moved on to Vienna, and went straight to the House of Knize, the justly famous tailors. On the first day, both Marlene and Rudi, who was fond of fine clothes, but not fanatic like his wife, ordered tails, double- and single-breasted suits, dressing gowns and shirts. On the second day they chose the fabric. Marlene considered Knize "the very best in the world" and when its heads escaped to the United States before World War II and opened a Manhattan shop next to the St. Regis Hotel, Marlene was their first eager customer.

While still in Vienna, Marlene had a sudden desire for new nightgowns. She phoned a Paris house, and ordered a selection to be made to measure and brought to her. Two days later, a little brown sparrow of a saleswoman arrived by train, bearing confections in shell-toned pinks and pearls, in satin, crêpe de Chine and gossamer silks. Marlene chose the nightgowns she wanted, picked out a few modest ones for Rudi's mistress Tamara, and sent the saleswoman on her way. Apart from her nightgowns and bras, which were always a fitting problem, Marlene had no need of lingerie. She seldom wore panties and never wore slips. "Slips are for women who buy cheap clothes and have to try them on in stores," she maintained. Since all her own garments had linings, no slips were necessary.

By 1934, the power of Dietrich's image was earning her a yearly income of $350,000, making her the third highest paid person in the United States, number one being William Randolph Hearst, and number two, Mae West, who also knew a thing or two about image. That same year, Marlene earned the title "The Most Imitated Woman in the World," as women copied her trousers;

slinky, bias-cut dresses; head-hugging hats with little veils; high heels; berets and trench coats. They plucked and redrew their eyebrows in Dietrich's latest shape, and bleached their hair blond. But they probably didn't realize, as they rushed to copy, that, in fact, they were acquiring a whole new way of perceiving their clothes. This new way of seeing began when Gloria Swanson and Clara Bow lit up the screen in Elinor Glyn's silent films, and reached full flower in the thirties and forties when the clothes of ordinary women became invested with new drama, significance and glamour because they looked like Dietrich's, or Jean Harlow's, Joan Crawford's or some other star's. When some woman in Kansas City looked in the mirror and put on a tiny hat with Venetian-blind veil like the one Marlene wore in *Shanghai Express*, the woman thought: "That's Dietrich's hat," and suddenly the one on her head, exactly like a hundred others selling for $2.98, became iconic, special, transcendent. Today's movie stars don't possess this artful power of creating icons because they are focused primarily on their acting rather than appearance, change character with every role, and don't much care what they wear on screen or off. Their glamour is sporadic and particular, not part of a grand design.

The clothes which Marlene and the other thirties' stars wore in black-and-white films got America's women not only into similar grown-up, glamorous garb but also out of brightly colored clothes. In those pre-technicolor days, the garments women saw on screen were never colored, so in real life black, white and gray became favorite hues for fabrics, and silver or platinum jewelry replaced gold. Silver lamé or gunmetal satin, which fell in rivers of light over Dietrich's or Lombard's slim hips, became fashionable for evening. A new sensuality flowed from those screen images onto real-life women suddenly grown seductive in sequins, black lace or slithering satins.

To the creation of Dietrich the Glamour Goddess, Marlene brought to bear the remarkable intelligence, self-confidence, energy and willpower which impressed all those who knew her. Douglas Fairbanks Jr. called her "a glamour girl with brains." Arthur Kennedy considered her "the most self-assured woman I ever met in my life" and Danny Thomas thought her "one of the most powerful people I ever met." Cecil Beaton commented on her "genius for believing in her self-fabricated beauty." Marlene needed only five hours sleep a night, and was never idle. To maintain "the line" she was always on a diet. On the set, to keep her stomach from bloating, she never ate; when the rest of the crew broke for lunch, she redid her face and hair. Sometimes she fasted for days; other times she ate gargantuan meals, for she was a natural gourmand, then stuck her fingers down her throat and vomited.

She liked to be always in control, but she was learning that glamour also depended on an audience. As Richard Avedon once put it, "Glamour gets rid of you, it doesn't invite you in. You have to kneel before it." The public worshipped Dietrich's glamour and used religious terms to describe her, such as "goddess," "divine" and "immortal." Whenever fans pushed and shoved around her, Dietrich would tell her companion: "Don't worry! They won't touch me," and they never did. If glamour demands obeisance from afar, it also creates in the viewer feelings of inadequacy and inferiority, of a hunger never satisfied and an imaginative reach beyond reality and beyond grasp. Like Elinor Glyn, Marlene understood the importance of mystery as an element of glamour. "It is a woman's job to sense the hungers in men and to satisfy them," she told a journalist, "without, at the same time, giving so much of herself that men become bored with her." Glamour thrives on elusiveness – and veils. One must hold back so that imagination has something to work on. "You can't live without illusions," Marlene decided, "even if you must fight for them."

Dietrich spent every cent she had left after routine living expenses on maintaining her glamour image; she never saved or invested a penny. None of the thirties' glamour queens could "wrap it up" the way Dietrich could. (Gracie Fields once complained of the next-generation, younger actresses: "They can act. But can they wrap it up?") For traveling, Dietrich had six steamer trunks the size of small closets, two-toned gray, brass-cornered, emblazoned with large black "MDs," lined and padded in gray silk-damask. Her personal maid carried a huge leather folder of keys, each tagged as to bag and contents. Dietrich's Hermès make-up case, custom-made of pigskin so tender it had to have its own canvas slipcover, had cream suede interior fitted with crystal bottles and jars whose Art Deco lids were enameled in pink and lapis blue. Her "extras" supply cupboard was always stocked with dozens of large bottles of French perfume. She replaced her dark-green Rolls with a custom-designed black Cadillac with gray flannel interior to muffle traffic sounds, recessed triple mirrors on either side of the back seat which unfolded with the flick of a finger, and white Tibetan goat carpet which looked so glamorous that she kept it, even though its long hairs tangled in her high heels and caused her to trip sometimes when she was getting in or out. She bought spectacular jewels, including an emerald-and-diamond ensemble consisting of three bracelets, two clips, one large brooch and a ring. None of the diamonds was less than four carats; one bracelet, with 128.45 carats, wide as a shirt cuff, had a cabochon emerald the size of a small avocado. Like all her glamour props, Marlene's emeralds gave her immense pleasure. "Jo, aren't these wonderful?" she asked as she shot one bracelet-laden wrist under von Sternberg's nose. "The big bracelet is too Mae West, but it will be good for photographs – very – important-looking, what Dietrich should wear!" She wore her emeralds casually about town, and in two of her films.

However, one couldn't *always* be a glamour goddess. Because she was a mere human, Marlene felt the need of an antidote, and alter ego. She found one in her habitual scrubbing of floors, walls, sinks, toilets, playing charwoman with a bandana tied over her hair, smudges of dirt on her beautiful face. She routinely scrubbed every hotel suite, especially its bathroom, before she settled in. Scrubbing kept her sane, but ruined her fingernails. She always traveled with twelve dozen sets of false ones bought at Woolworth's.

In the early months of 1934, Marlene and Travis were busy in the greige workrooms planning her costumes for *The Scarlet Empress*, in which Marlene plays Catherine the Great. By this time, four years into their collaboration, Marlene was feeling superior to her style partner. "He is getting a reputation dressing Dietrich, and I do all the work. He knows nothing about 'line,'" she complained to Maria. "In this, we will use lots of Russian sable," she continued, warming to her work. "That will cost a fortune! Let them scream, Jo will handle the Studio bosses. We could maybe let them sew on the skins – like they used to!" Marlene laughed with her usual abandon.

Once filming of *The Scarlet Empress* was finished, Marlene was off to Paris, where she booked into the Plaza Athénée and immediately went shopping for furs, those used in the movie – such as the world's largest mink muff – having whetted her appetite. At the furriers', she stood at the hub of a giant wheel of pelts laid at her feet, pointing with her cigarette at various bundles of skins, decisively announcing what should be made: a floor-length cape from mink skins; a 3/4 length cape from red fox; a baby seal trench coat; a nutria polo coat; silver foxes for flinging over black suits; blue foxes for gray flannel ones. (She had once owned leopard but now had decided its pattern was too "fussy" and chinchilla was fit only for blue-haired dowagers.)

From October 1934 to mid-January 1935, Marlene was shooting her final von Sternberg film *The Devil Is a Woman.* In various fringes, laces, shawls, and veils with chenille dots as big as golf balls, Marlene and Travis conspired to wrap, drape and festoon her almost to the point of parody of the Dietrich style. Travis designed an elaborate Spanish comb, and hairdresser Nellie Manley braided Dietrich's hair, then wired the braids so tightly to the comb that when at the end of each day's shooting Nellie removed them, with wire-cutters, Marlene fell forward, arms and head on her dressing table, tears streaming down her face from the pain of this device. Like *The Scarlet Empress, The Devil Is a Woman* got disastrous reviews and didn't do well at the box office. Von Sternberg fled Hollywood and went into a professional decline. His career never recovered from the loss of his greatest inspiration. As for Marlene, she spent days in a dark room rerunning all seven von Sternberg films until she felt she'd mastered his lighting techniques and camera angles. Then she got on with her career.

Ernst Lubitsch, whose sophisticated, champagne-dry, very European outlook suited her own, produced Marlene's next film, with direction delegated to Frank Borzage. In the late summer of 1935, Marlene and Travis were concentrating on costumes for *Desire*'s heroine, a jewel thief who steals a pearl necklace. "Travis, she can't wear trousers, but – a man's blazer? Double-breasted, maybe in blue linen, not too dark, with a straight white skirt. For that I have shoes! You won't believe this, but I wore them in Berlin in a play – and they are still modern today! Like the ones you liked so, but in white, with lizard..." Travis was drinking heavily by this time. When his hands trembled too much, assistant Edith Head had to do the sketches, and soon got skilful at forging Travis' signature across the bottom. In one unforgettable session, Marlene kept Edith working for thirty-five hours, with only three of them for sleep, while they concocted the right hat for a scene in *Desire*. "We sat up for hours trying on dozens of different hats," remembers Edith, "changing them, tilting them, taking the feathers off this one and trying them on that one, snipping off a veil or a brim, switching ribbons and bows. Finally we got what she wanted. I was amazed at her stamina and determination."

Before Marlene began shooting David O. Selznick's *The Garden of Allah*, which took from April to the first week in July 1936, he called her into his office and gave her a real dressing-down, so to speak. He told her that he knew that her pictures ran over budget because of her fanatical attention to costumes and make-up and hair. Marlene expostulated, then just ignored his lecture. (She always claimed that David O. Selznick was the man on earth she least wanted to bed.) On June 17, after viewing rushes, Selznick wrote frantically to the film's director, Richard Boleslawski: "Would you *please* speak to Marlene about the fact that her hair is getting so much attention, and is coiffed to such a degree [it never moved] that all reality is lost?"

As soon as she'd finished this truly trashy picture, in early July, Marlene, Maria and Nellie Manley, kidnapped from Hairdressing, set sail on the luxury French liner *Normandie* for the usual summer in Europe, accompanied by twenty-one steamer trunks, thirty-five large suitcases, eighteen medium ones, nine small, fifteen hat boxes, plus the Dietrich black Cadillac and matching black-liveried chauffeur. *Vogue* reported to its readers that Dietrich was ensconced in a four-room suite called "Deauville," with blue satin upholstery and baby grand piano. She had been sent so many bottles of champagne that their coolers on silver tripods stretched like some giant's necklace along one rose wall of the dining room. In the mornings, Marlene sat on her private terrace in lounging pyjamas, and let lesser mortals gape. In the evenings, according to *Vogue*, she "swathed herself in green chiffon, and painted her toes and fingernails green to match her emeralds." She watched the shipboard screenings of *Desire*, and was photographed smiling adoringly at her own image. By 1936, Marlene's life story was looking very much like the Greek legend of Narcissus, the youth who pined for his own reflection in a limpid silver pool, and finally died. Like Narcissus, Marlene was being claimed and manipulated by her image, by the tyranny of the mirror which was slowly spoiling her career and her life.

When she got to Paris, Marlene ordered more couture clothes, left Maria there with Rudi and Tamara, and crossed the English channel on the *Maid of Kent* for her first visit to London in five years. She was mobbed on arrival at Victoria Station, looking, in red velvet and mink, as one reporter noted, "more like her glamorous screen self than any star I ever met." She took a suite at Claridge's, began a love affair with Douglas Fairbanks Jr., obviously not agreeing with Elinor Glyn's assessment of his lack of "It," and in July began filming *Knight Without Armour*, directed by Alexander Korda, taking time off to return to Paris for fittings on her clothes. Whenever Marlene began a new love affair, her clothes grew more womanly. Her trousers stayed in her closet, while she put on superbly cut dresses which showed her curves, and flung furs in all directions.

Her lovers were extensions of her clothes, to be controlled and combined in the same way. All her life she tried on men, for the same reasons she dressed as she did: to feel warm, admired, sexually powerful and utterly feminine. She kept all her old lovers, turning them into loyal friends, just as she kept all her old clothes. Over the years, she tried on, after Jo von Sternberg, Maurice Chevalier, John Gilbert, Brian Aherne, French actor Jean Gabin, U.S. General James Gavin, Edward R. Murrow, Adlai Stevenson, Frank Sinatra, Michael Wilding, Mike Todd, Kirk Douglas, Yul Brynner... the list goes on, for her lovers were as multiple as her garments. For variety, when she was in her pin-stripe mood, she tried on Edith Piaf, Ginette Spanier, Mercedes de Acosta and many other women. "In Europe it doesn't matter if you're a man or a woman," Marlene informed Budd Schulberg. "We make love with anyone we find attractive."

Like her clothes, Marlene's lovers only made contact with her surface. In spite of her incredibly active sex life, fueled by her powerful eros, she never let them touch the inner person. "Close as we became," Michael Wilding remembers, "there was an unfathomable quality about Marlene, a part of her that remained aloof." She told her daughter that the sex act itself was something she tolerated for the sake of warm caresses, soft romantic words and wrap-around adulation. With each new lover, the distance between the glamour goddess and one particularly passionate male worshipper seemed to grow. Spontaneity and naturalness were, at the same time, decreasing. Lovers became costumes of a special kind in a carefully created scenario which she controlled. And like her clothes, ultimately they didn't enrich or satisfy her deepest needs, or her soul.

Marlene began shooting Ernst Lubitsch's *Angel* in April 1937, but as her narcissism increased, her aesthetic judgement wavered, and some of the costumes she devised with Travis, who let her lead, were vulgar and downright ugly, such as a $4000 gown so encrusted with fake emeralds and rubies that it weighed in at fifty pounds. Another beaded gown, only thirty pounds, was in better taste; Diana Vreeland described it as "a million grains of golden caviar" and featured it in her 1976 Hollywood costume exhibit at the Metropolitan Museum of Art. One day on the set Marlene and Lubitsch locked horns over a hat. Lubitsch ordered her to wear it; Marlene vowed she wouldn't. The dispute finally led to reshooting at a cost of $95,000. (Marlene won; she appears in stills of *Angel* in a hat which she doesn't wear in the film, but Lubitsch never worked with her again.)

"I am spending what I have in order to appear very glamorous when really I am lonely and bored and – to you I can admit it – frightened" wrote Marlene to Rudi in 1938. From June that year until September 1939 she received not a single offer of work. Fans no longer listed her among their favorites; she was "box office poison." As her self-confidence shrank, she made further mistakes in clothes. She became friends with Parisian designer Schiaparelli and loaded up on outrageous garments which didn't fit the Dietrich style, such as astrological symbols in silver sequins splaying all over dark-blue velvet, and brocade ropes writhing like snakes on pink-figured damask. She wore each outfit once but kept on buying.

The summer of 1938 Marlene spent at Cap d'Antibes, wearing not her usual whites and beiges but flowing beach robes in Schiaparelli's invention, "shocking pink." Marlene had found a clever French seamstress who, by means of bras bias-cut and darted underneath, managed to give the Dietrich breasts an uplift they'd never had before. For the first time, Marlene appeared in public in bathing suits, and acquired a tan by slathering on a special mixture of olive oil, iodine and red wine vinegar.

Marlene warmed to young Jimmy Stewart, with whom she was acting in *Destry Rides Again* in the fall of 1939. She dressed for one date with him in black silk jersey that trumpeted into absinthe green satin as it neared the hem. With it she wore a black turban with crown made of closely laid, absinthe green feathers. She had snared Rudi sixteen years before with absinthe green; perhaps its magic would work again.

Marlene got another acting job in August 1940, in *Seven Sinners*, in which she performed a most appropriate song, "I've Been in Love Before," in the very first of her many "nude" dresses, made by Universal's designer Irene, of sheer fabric with sequins cunningly placed on the bodice. In terms of Dietrich's art, the nude gown formed a whole new genre destined to take her a long way.

In August 1941, she was making *The Lady is Willing* for Columbia, directed by Mitchell Leisen, who had once been a costume designer for Cecil B. DeMille before he became a director, and who still owned a Hollywood tailoring shop. Even such a clothes aficionado as he was felt "maddened by her endless fiddling around with the lights and with her hats and costumes. It slowed up production terribly." The many hats were designed by John Frederics, with costumes by Irene. Marlene was almost forty, and to maintain the illusion of youth had to wear a constricting, uncomfortable foundation garment under her costumes. On the outside, thick silk and elastic held her in a vise; inside, emptiness spread.

Marlene's depression surfaced in private crying jags. To cheer herself, she went on a buying spree at couturière Lily Daché's in Manhattan, where she bought ninety-eight items in one go, including a Persian lamb jacket, a white turban costing $150, and a silver possum muff. But the clothes meant to cure her loneliness only increased it, luring her farther into the dangerous depths of the mirror.

From October to December 1943, Marlene was shooting *Kismet*, pulling her facial skin into a temporary face-lift by means of tape, braided hair and hooks, and painting her face with make-up which had grown less natural and more formalized with every picture, and which now looked like a face painted on wood. In one *Kismet* scene the famous legs are painted gold. The paint turned Marlene's skin green and its fumes made her nauseous.

Marlene courageously flew to Europe in 1944 to entertain American troops fighting in World War II. As part of a USO group, she was only allowed fifty-five pounds of luggage, a far cry from her usual amount. According to *Vogue*, she packed two

Irene evening gowns with all-over beading so creases wouldn't show; a strapless brocade dress; transparent Vinylite slippers; gray flannel men's trousers; silk-lined cashmere cardigan; tropical uniforms she herself had designed; lingerie; three months' supply of cosmetics labeled in huge nail-polish letters (for making-up by flashlight) and a supply of special soap which would lather in very little water. Danny Thomas was a member of that USO troupe and recalls that Dietrich would appear on stage in her uniform, open a small case, pull out a sequinned "nude" gown and start to change right there before four hundred sex-starved males. Danny would pull her behind a screen, and a minute later an incredibly alluring Dietrich would emerge and sing "See What the Boys in the Back Room Will Have," although the answer was patently obvious as GIs stamped and cheered and tried to mob the stage. Marlene lapped up all this adulation and approval. "I remember how absolutely terrific it is to step out before our boys – the largest audience was 20,000 – and hear them cheer and whistle. That joy you give and get," she told a journalist, "I can't put it in words."

The hardships of those USO tours, like her scrubbing, gave Marlene respite from the Glamour Goddess existence. Her sequinned dresses, rolled up in her knapsack, served as pillow for sleeping in huts where rats ran over The Face all night. She washed her hair in an up-turned hard hat; used crude latrines; she even got crabs. She had never felt happier and conceived along the way an exciting idea for a whole new facet of her career which would come to fruition in 1953.

When daughter Maria Riva had her second child in 1948, Marlene gave the mature woman a boost by appearing on *Life*'s cover as "Grandmother Dietrich." Nobody had ever seen a grandmother who looked like *that*! She was thrilled when she was not only offered a part in Alfred Hitchcock's *Stage Fright* but told she could pick her designer. She chose the newest star on the fashion scene, Christian Dior.

When Dior had launched his so-called New Look in the fall of 1947, Marlene was one of his most enthusiastic customers, for Dior's look was all-woman with full skirts, tightly-cinched waists, high heels and tiny hats with veils. It was a silhouette which appealed to a female world newly liberated from khaki uniforms and factory overalls, but it wasn't really a New Look at all, but rather the last gasp of a vanishing female who had held sway in the western world for four hundred years, with France leading the way, and Worth and Empress Eugénie conspiring to give woman one of her most feminine modes. Dior's New Look was the Last Look at really ladylike clothes before mods, minis, almost-naked full-frontal fashions and other aberrations took over.

When Marlene appeared on the set of *Stage Fright* in June 1949, in white fox and diamonds, actress Kay Walsh soon realized that Dietrich "knew more than the wardrobe people," telling them how to iron her Dior dresses and how to rub the hems with Sunlight soap to make them stand out. That done, Walsh recalls, Marlene "took care of all her dresses herself." Co-star Jane Wyman thought her "the most fascinating person I've ever met. On days when she had no studio call she would come on the set just the same. She'd fix my dress, make suggestions about my hair and make-up, and help me in many ways."

Marlene was always generous with her expertise. Musical producer Moss Hart's wife Kitty remembers asking Marlene if she could copy two of her gowns, one pink satin and the other beige chiffon. Marlene insisted on going with Kitty to the fabric store, and holding bolt after bolt of beige chiffon to her face to get the most becoming hue. Then she took Kitty to her dressmaker and supervised the placement of every pin. The dresses were a "huge success," writes Kitty, "I wish I had that beige chiffon right now."

When American women shrugged on mink stoles in the late 1940s, which covered shoulders and upper arms, Marlene scoffed that such stoles were for "fat old ladies who want to show that they are rich enough to own furs but can't afford the whole coat." Dietrich promptly ordered ten running feet of silver-tipped sable so that she could wrap her whole body in a bandage of pelts. For her appearance in mink in *No Highway*, Marlene went to Balmain, where Ginette Spanier found her one morning standing "blonde, pale, beautiful beyond words" draped in their most luxurious $8000 mink cape. "I find it rather poor," said Dietrich, unsmiling. Ginette added their longest mink stole and Dietrich, still unsmiling, agreed that looked better. She ordered the cape lined with artificial violets, a flower which brought back happy memories of youthful lesbian hi-jinks in Berlin.

Marlene was invited to present the best foreign film award at the 1951 Academy Awards ceremony. She learned that the other female presenters would be dressed in the current fashion of pastel, fluffy ballgowns, all very *jeune fille*. "Mama had better be slinky," decided Marlene, "nice, slinky, black." Would she be walking on stage from the right or left side? she asked the organizers. She ordered her skirt slit to the knee on the side which would show, and upstaged all the other movie queens dressed as hollyhocks all-in-a-row.

Current lover Eddie Fisher reported that by 1953 Dietrich even had mirrors on her bedroom ceiling. Eddie was a critical boyfriend, but Marlene, that fall, was about to discover the perfect lover: one completely under her control, who didn't expect emotional intimacy or anything at all in return for loving, who would be faithful and utterly adoring for as long as they were together.

She would find this many-headed lover seated in respectful rows on the other side of the footlights, for she was about to mount her first one-woman stage show, selling her glamour straight up, presenting her *chef-d'oeuvre*, her self-portrait in cloth, all by herself, without having to rely on directors, film crews or writers. She herself would create and control costumes, lighting, make-up, content. And no one could cut or edit or dub her afterwards. She would skip the emoting – she'd never been very good at that anyway – and go straight to what she did best: she would be Dietrich, plugged into everyone's sexual fantasies. For the next twenty-two years, Marlene's one-woman shows in nightclubs and theaters aimed her image at the whole world. Those stage appearances were Dietrich's epitome and epitaph, the crux and climax of her style. She had progressed to this final point of light: all Dietrich, only Dietrich, the ultimate, amazing, resplendent narcissist.

"Dietrich must be a sensation," she told Yul Brynner, who was then sharing her bed, "and that we can only do with what I wear!" She hired Jean Louis, Columbia Picture's top designer who had once worked for Hattie Carnegie in New York. Marlene decided to market her sex-without-gender in two parts. "The woman's part is for men and the man's part is for women," she explained to Art Buchwald. In the first half she would appear in the most feminine and sexually provocative apparel she and Jean Louis could dream up. In the second half, accompanied by a major drumroll, she would prance on stage in tuxedo tailored-to-a-T by Knize, complete with bow tie and top hat.

She rang up the curtain on December 15, 1953, in the Congo Room of the Sahara Hotel in Las Vegas. Her gown was skin-tight black net lined with flesh-colored silk, with leaf-shaped motifs of sequins and rhinestones *very* strategically placed. The dress cost $6000 and weighed about fourteen pounds. Floating around her as she glided on stage was a black chiffon cape lavishly bordered in black fox. She used it as a tease, finally letting it drop away completely to reveal the world's first topless-but-tasteful show-biz grandmother. The dress was a further refinement of the "nude" gowns Dietrich had designed with Irene for her USO tours, where they had more than proved their effectiveness.

Her costumes were the essential part of her performance, not her songs. Over the years fabrics were gold, black or white, decorated with sequins or bugle beads, rhinestones, crystal tassels or – most fitting of all – tiny mirrors. The enveloping clouds of chiffon or velvet over them when she first appeared on stage were lush with feathers or furs, climaxing in a swans-down coat with an eight-foot circular train for which two thousand swans had given their all.

Like any work of art, a costume progressed slowly through painstaking changes. First, Marlene and Jean Louis would go together to imported-fabric houses to choose the fabric. Then he would construct her foundation garment using Biancini silk imported from Italy, a miraculous fabric with the stretch of silk and strength of canvas, so lightweight it was called "soufflé." Jean Louis dyed the foundation to match Dietrich's skin tone and make it invisible to the audience. It was, as daughter Maria notes, "the best-kept secret of the Dietrich legend," providing the necessary illusion of eternal youth. Marlene flew from her New York apartment to Jean Louis in Hollywood six or more times for fittings on each gown. She would come directly from the plane, and stand motionless for eight to ten hours in front of mirrors while Jean Louis and his assistant Elizabeth made the dress on her. "I don't like symmetry. Move that sequin," Dietrich would command. They would move a pin-head-sized sequin one eighth of an inch to the right or left. But this would make it symmetrical with another sequin, so they would have to move that; on and on it went, while Jean Louis feared that the spiderweb fabrics would go up in flames from Dietrich's cigarettes. "I don't remember how many costumes we made," writes Marlene in her autobiography. "I have preserved them all, and I take those I still wear out of the trunk as carefully as I would take a baby out of a cradle." The dresses were, in a sense, her children, and her bid for posterity.

Critics ignored her singing and praised her gowns. Each one delivered eros with maximum tease by being transparent enough to make you think you were seeing everything and covered enough, given those coy sequins, to make you realize that you were seeing nothing. One reviewer describing a gown concluded: "Houdini must have designed it." When, during a show at New York's Mark Hellinger Theater, a young man near the front raised binoculars, Dietrich stopped right in the middle of a song and said sharply, "You don't have to do that. Don't kill the illusion."

Illusion was crucial, to achieve a beauty beyond time, beyond decay, beyond criticism, beyond reality. And this swan-song for the old glamour appeared at a time when television and Hollywood were beginning to focus on the real, warts and all. As Richard Avedon says, "It would be absurd to photograph Meryl Streep or Anjelica Huston with 'her light.' They'd be embarrassed, because the new artifice is 'I'm real. You photograph me *real*.'"

Dietrich on stage fostered nostalgia by means of both her apparel and choice of songs. The ghosts of 1930s Banton-Dietrich costumes flitted through her wisps of chiffon and pale fox borders, and many of the songs came from her old movies. As one successful stage show followed another, Marlene got back some of her self-confidence. When someone asked her if she got stage fright, she said she never did, because the audience had paid "to see the most glamorous woman in the world, and I am she!"

Her performance was all style. Every lift of an eyebrow or an arm was pre-programmed and precisely on cue. "Technique and control," affirmed Dietrich, "they are all that matter. In every single bar of my music, every single light that hits me – I know it and I control it." She became the world's most glamorous puppet while the legend pulled the strings.

She got parts in a few more movies, including *Witness for the Prosecution*, made during the summer of 1957, in which her acting was much better than usual, and her figure as svelte as always in Edith Head's severe *tailleurs*. Dietrich distilled her life-in-clothes philosophy for Cynthia Kee, who interviewed her for an article entitled "My Clothes and I," appearing in *The Observer* in March 1960. The two women met in a hotel bar, and Kee describes the Dietrich impact:

> She really is quite something. She was wearing a wild mink coat; a black Balenciaga dress embroidered, at the left breast, with the scarlet bar of the Legion d'Honneur; a stiffened black tulle hat; white kid gloves; black patent leather pumps and a black crocodile handbag. That's all. But the quality of her body gave the mink a luxury no advertiser could buy, the black dress was littler and subtler than volumes of *Vogue* could imply, and her single decoration was somehow more worldly and wicked than all the jewelry in Paris, London and New York put together.

"I have good taste," Marlene told Kee. "It must have been the influence of my mother because it has always come quite naturally. No one else has ever had any effect at all on my clothes." She went on to say that at Dior, Chanel and her new love, Balenciaga, "they know me now and they show me only the clothes that are mine. I never consider money when I order clothes." She waxed enthusiastic about Balenciaga, a Spaniard who had had his own couture house in Paris for twenty years and would close it in another eight. Marlene declared that he knew more about actual cutting and sewing of clothes than any other designer, and that the first fitting at Balenciaga was like the third one at any other house. Reading this interview, one gets the impression that Marlene is winding up the Dietrich doll and letting it talk and gesture. Did her green eyes light up when she talked of Balenciaga, or were they as glassy as her cabochon emeralds?

As her one-woman shows continued, and Marlene jetted around the world, something pathetic, almost tragic, began to happen. Marlene was becoming victim and prisoner of her own wondrous creation, well and truly caught in crystal talons and coils of chiffon. As she aged, the accent on youth which North American culture demanded was ever harder for Marlene to maintain, for the world's sexiest grandmother began to look less sexy and more grandmother. By 1962, she had undergone two surgical face-lifts, and on stage had to wear an extremely constricting foundation from neck to ankle. Foundation and gown fit so tightly that once she'd put them on, she couldn't sit down, and had to lie propped against a slant-board as she waited for her cue. When she walked, she could only take tiny, precarious steps and two assistants had to support her as she moved from dressing room to stage. Her clothes, always her solace, her best and most beloved means of expression, mainstay and means of all her art, had turned on her and were wreaking their revenge.

Marlene learned, slowly, painfully, the full meaning and ugly underside of glamour: its sacrifice of actual being for mere seeming, of spontaneity, intimacy, honest maturity, and any possibility of growth or change for an illusion of perfect fulfillment beyond ordinary mortals. For Dietrich, the cost of her glamour was far too high. The woman-in-the-mirror had turned out to be a devouring Frankenstein monster which she herself had created.

Dietrich also found herself becoming an anachronism with a firm place in the past, and in the public's fond memory, but with none in the 1960s present of pink-haired rock stars and tattered jeans. On and off stage the symbols of her style remained – berets,

1. Empress Eugénie (wearing flowers in hair) with her ladies-in-waiting.

2. Eugénie in romantic mood. Engraving of Winterhalter's 1859 portrait.

3. Eugénie dressed for a Tuileries ball.

4. Napoléon III and his Empress, in walking dress.

5. Eugénie in outdoor dress and jacket.

6. (top, right) Couture's first master, Charles Frederick Worth, c. 1864.

7. (middle, right) Eugénie in 1871, exiled to England.

8. (bottom, right) Eugénie in the simple garb of old age. Drawing by M. Ferdinand Bac.

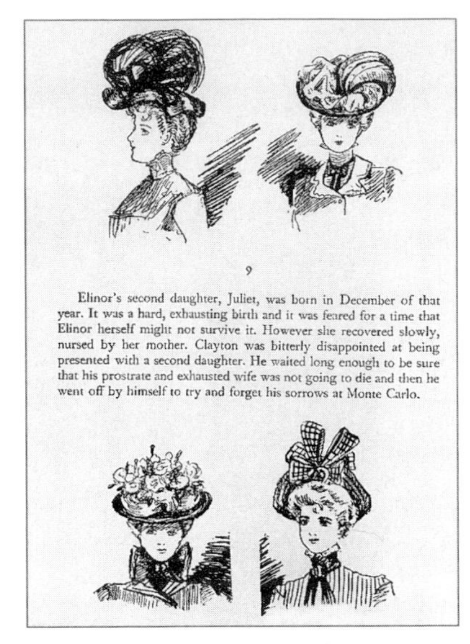

9

Elinor's second daughter, Juliet, was born in December of that year. It was a hard, exhausting birth and it was feared for a time that Elinor herself might not survive it. However she recovered slowly, nursed by her mother. Clayton was bitterly disappointed at being presented with a second daughter. He waited long enough to be sure that his prostrate and exhausted wife was not going to die and then he went off by himself to try and forget his sorrows at Monte Carlo.

9. Elinor's hat sketches for *Scottish Life*, 1898.

10. Wasp-waisted Elinor in 1900, in romantic Lucile gown.

11. Elinor costumed for the 1908 U.K. stage production of *Three Weeks.*

14. (opposite) Love scene from film *Three Weeks* (1924), with Aileen Pringle, Conrad Nagel and tiger skin.

12. Elinor in her veils. Portrait by Philip de Laszlo.

13. Elinor in Paris, 1919.

15. Madame Glyn in Hollywood, c. 1923.

16. Elinor in typical headgear, posing with her cats, 1931.

17. Elinor at age 72, in the midst of her tigers, in her Connaught Place drawing room.

18. Marlene costumed for *Shanghai Express*, in Venetian-blind veil and coq feathers, 1931.

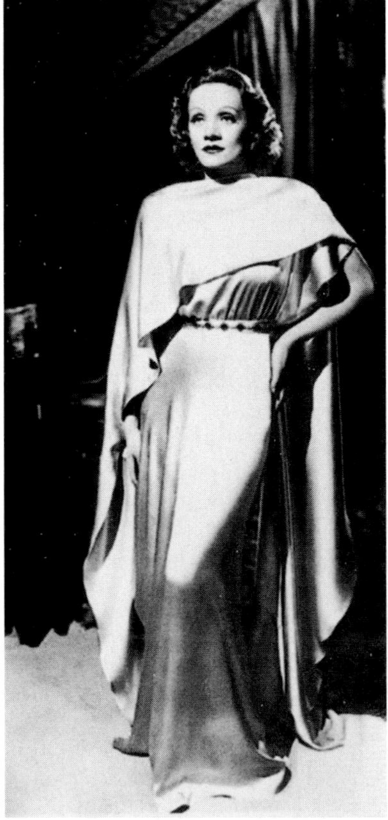

19. (left, top) Marlene in masculine garb, with von Sternberg.

20. (right, top) Marlene costumed for *Desire*, wearing her own emeralds, signing autographs on the set, 1935.

21. (right, bottom) Marlene in slinky satin, costumed for *The Garden of Allah*, 1936.

22. (left, top) Travis Banton's costume sketch for Marlene in *Angel*, 1937.

23. (right, top) Marlene in swansdown coat and nude gown at Las Vegas, 1959.

24. (left, bottom) Marlene and Travis Banton at work, 1937.

25. Marlene in 1969, posing for Avedon in Blackglama mink.

26. Wallis Spencer, young naval wife, in homemade skirt and sweater.

27. The Duke and Duchess on their wedding day, June 1937.

28. Seamstresses at work on Wallis' trousseau, 1937.

29. Wallis in her Paris drawing room, in Mainbocher dress.

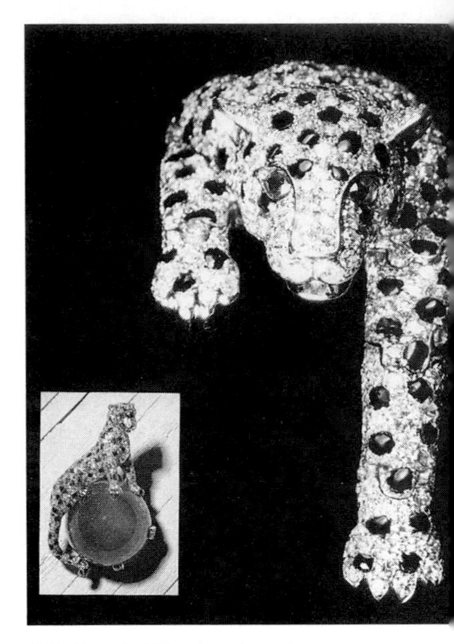

30. Inset: Diamond and sapphire panther rampant on a 152-carat sapphire, bought in 1949. Panther bracelet, bought in 1952, with emerald eyes and diamond and onyx body.

31. Wallis in Balenciaga's 1950s black broadtail suit and white ermine hat. She wears the diamond plume brooch later auctioned off to Elizabeth Taylor.

32. (opposite) Wallis in Balenciaga dress designed to show off her diamond clips.

33. (right) Wallis at a Paris party, wearing a white crêpe Dior sheath as simple background to her ruby and diamond necklace, bracelet and brooch (worn in her hair).

34. Jackie in Jack's idea of a wedding gown. September 1953.

35. (left) Jackie leaves for 1961 pre-inaugural concert in Cassini's white satin gown.

36. (middle) Inauguration Day, 1961. America's new queen in pillbox crown, Cassini coat and touch of sable.

37. (right) Jackie clones: fashion models in Jackie hairdos, pillboxes and suits.

38. Jackie bares her arms to Indira Gandhi and the Indian sun, 1962.

39. Jackie arrives in Washington after Jack's assassination, still in her pink, bloody suit.

40. America's young widow, in deflated pillbox and mourning veil. November 25, 1963.

41. Still svelte at sixty-something, Jackie leaves a meeting at the John F. Kennedy Library with son John Jr.

trouser suits, dotted veils, furs – but the soul of style, the light and life of it, had fled.

She kept on circling the globe, mainlining on applause, while her drinking and her loneliness increased. Her hair thinned, necessitating a false fall made by skilled London wig-maker Stanley Hall, which Dietrich attached to a velvet hairband, usually beige to blend with her hair. Her erotic energy was still amazing. One day in 1963, Marlene burst into her New York apartment, just back from Washington, opened her large black crocodile handbag, extracted a pair of pink panties, waved them under the nose of her astonished son-in-law and exclaimed, "Smell! It is him! The President of the United States! He – was – wonderful!" One wonders if Kennedy's wife Jackie, that other woman of style, knew of this particular coupling.

The Dietrich-doll needed more and more stroking. Australian journalist Hugh Carnow remembers how he and Marlene routinely spent their evenings: "We'd look at her scrapbooks. The scrapbooks were jammed tight under the bed and she'd drag them out and show them to me. She had marked statements she liked in red ink." One evening in the mid 1960s, Marlene and Hugh attended a dinner party hosted at their Paris house by the Duke and Duchess of Windsor. Marlene had brought two records which she insisted on playing. They contained minute after long, boring minute of nothing but applause, briefly interspersed with Dietrich's singing. "Zat was London," Marlene would beam, or "Zat was Rio." The Windsors looked horrified and fellow guest Judy Garland amused, but by now Marlene could see very little beyond the woman-in-the-mirror.

She stepped up the pre-programming of her one-woman show when she opened on Broadway in 1968, adding a few more puppets in the form of handsome young men hired to race down the aisles after each song bearing floral tributes in just the right shades of pink. In its review of the Broadway show, *Time* called Dietrich "Old Gal in Town," mentioned the illusion of youth and the illusion of sex, but admitted that the illusions still worked. *Newsweek* called her "a kind of Mother Courage of the gone glamour world." Survival itself was cause for pride. In the course of her life Marlene had abundantly proved the point first made in the final scene of *Dishonored*: beauty is courage, and style can be content.

She was paid $250,000 in 1973 to do a television special called "I Wish You Love," with a set all in shades of pink. "No one else is 'doing' glamour anymore," she complained to reporters from her hotel suite in London, where the show was being produced. Dietrich's faith in herself, like her external style, was still there, for she told a friend: "I look at my face on the television screen and I remember how every tooth was capped, how every hair in that head was dyed and shaped, how every inch of skin on that neck and face had been pulled and shaped, and, in spite of knowing all that, I sit back and say to myself, 'That is *still* the most beautiful thing I've ever seen in my life.'"

When, during the summer of 1973, French *Vogue* asked Dietrich to edit the December issue, which would have a black cover bearing in gold the words "VOGUE *par* Marlene Dietrich," she turned in eighty-three pages of Dietrich photographs and tributes, divided into sections: "Myself, viewed by the great photographers"; "Myself, viewed by the great poets"; "Myself, viewed by myself."

In November of that year, Marlene, in an alcoholic haze, fell off the stage in Washington, D.C., and deeply gashed her left leg, in which the circulation had been very poor for some time. She had to have vascular surgery and skin-grafting on her leg in January 1974. By April 1, however, Dietrich, age seventy-three, was back on tour. The catheter briefly inserted in her bladder after surgery had left her incontinent; she had to suffer the indignity of wearing absorbent pads under her stage dresses, a terrible affliction for one always so meticulous and elegantly groomed.

In August 1974, while in Paris, Marlene fell again and this time broke a hip. For the stretcher trip across the Atlantic to New York for surgery, Dietrich wore a candy-pink caftan with a Chanel chiffon shawl in the exact same shade of pink draped around her face. Style was her only real comfort now. Twenty-nine days after hip surgery, she opened at the Grosvenor House in London, without a limp, and with Princess Margaret in the audience. (When performing for royals, Marlene's gowns were made less revealing by adding a layer of silk between skin and sequins.) "Don't they have anyone who can tell them how to dress? You should have seen her," Marlene scoffed to her daughter over transatlantic wires, describing the appalling get-up on the queen's sister, and deploring the royal clothes sense in general.

Marlene fell off the stage in Sydney, Australia, in September 1975, and suffered a broken femur of the left leg. By that time, circulation in both legs was so poor that they were always cold as marble and as pure white as they'd appeared on paper in the 1969 Blackglama ad. Marlene recovered slowly, with her leg in traction, in the University of California Medical Center where Rudi lay in a different room, drifting in and out of coma after a severe stroke. Rudi died on June 24, 1976, aged seventy-nine, her husband and steadfast friend for fifty-three years, and a part of Marlene died with him.

In 1978, three years after her final stage show, seventy-seven-year-old Dietrich appeared in her last movie, *Just a Gigolo*, tempted by the $250,000 she was offered for two half-days' work in a Paris studio. She who had always spent so lavishly on herself, family and friends was short of funds. Director David Hemmings recalls: "Dietrich got out of the car very slowly and came up the ramp to the studio very slowly, supported by a cane on one side and Maria on the other. She didn't look remotely like 'Marlene Dietrich.' She looked like my Granny, like your Granny, like everybody's Granny if Granny wore a jeans pantsuit, a Dutch-boy wig and cap, and huge dark glasses." After Marlene had shuffled unsteadily into the immense silence that had fallen on the sound stage, Hemmings was shocked to see that "she had made herself up at home. She had painted on a mask of what Dietrich looked like to her forty or fifty years before, an image and age-fix from which she either didn't know how to retreat or just couldn't *see*." In the film Dietrich wears a black costume in homage to her past: hat with veil, skirt slit up the side. She looks on screen, poor thing, like a grotesque caricature of herself, or like some second-rate male Dietrich impersonator.

By the time she made that final movie appearance, Marlene was drinking herself into a daily stupor. She turned her back – too late – on cameras, press and public, and walked away.

She retreated to a flat in Paris, became a total recluse, and let the Legend swallow her whole. She stayed in bed, and organized her world on its counterpane. It was all very orderly, everything in its place: pads of paper, stamps, Dietrich photos for fans, photo-mailers, diaries, books, on the left; pills, dishes, frying pan, liquor supply decanted into green mineral-water bottles on a nightstand to the right. Nearby stood two small lidded garbage cans, one for urine and one for feces. Style appeared in the pretty Limoges pitcher into which she urinated. She stayed in bed for more than a decade. By 1982 her leg muscles had atrophied and she'd developed what is known medically as "drop foot." She could no longer stand or walk even if she'd wanted to.

Eros stayed almost to the end. When Marlene was eighty-five, she received a Lifetime Award from the Council of Fashion Designers of America, one justly deserved. She called ballet dancer Mikhail Baryshnikov in New York, asking him to accept the award for her (he couldn't) and proceeded to flirt outrageously with him on the phone. (Calvin Klein accepted it instead, and Katharine Hepburn wrote a charming prose poem.) When a California physician wrote Dietrich a series of passionate fan letters, she ordered some panties from Dior, "those little itsy bitsy ones, like chorus girls wear," scented them suitably, and sent them to him in the mail.

When, in the spring of 1987, the Duchess of Windsor's fabulous jewels were put up for auction by Sotheby's in Geneva, Marlene decided to sell some of her own to raise needed cash. In the following November, she allowed Christie's to open her Geneva bank vault and auction off diamond and sapphire cufflinks, gold cigarette cases encrusted with diamonds and a necklace of seventy graduated diamonds from Van Cleef and Arpels. In the same year, she sold the famous swans-down coat and one jewel-studded gown to the German Cinematic Foundation.

When Eros went, Dietrich still had Style. She ordered trunks containing her old clothes brought to her bedside, rummaged around in her essential past, until she found a thirty-year-old Balenciaga raincoat made of heavy rubberized material. "The worms could never get through *this*!" she exclaimed to her daughter, and asked to be buried in this couture-made shroud. Even in her grave, there would be a faint glint of Dietrich glamour.

She lay lost in a mist of drugs and alcohol, her skin like the yellow-white kid of an old glove, her eyes which had feasted lovingly on so much beauty, clouded by cataracts. Around her on the bed, scrapbooks, photos and clippings showed hundreds of best-dressed Dietrichs, the most glamorous woman in the world. She died on May 6, 1992, in her ninety-first year. Like the last ripple on a silver pool after a swan has sailed on by, glamour gleamed until the final calm.

After Dietrich's death, officials of the German Cinematic Foundation, who had already purchased her swans-down coat, paid five million dollars for 680 suitcases and crates full of Dietrich relics. In addition to 350,000 written documents and 15,000 Dietrich photographs, the suitcases contained hundreds of garments, her life story told in fabric, including dozens of hats and handbags, dress patterns, 400 pairs of size 5 shoes, and 2500 stage and screen costumes. These artifacts were laid to rest in a factory warehouse in Berlin's northern Spandau district, until they could be properly catalogued by a fashion specialist. The Dietrich wardrobe goes on permanent display in Berlin in 1997.

Style, as Marlene would have wished, thus forms her epitaph, and has the very last word.

CHAPTER 4

The Duchess of Windsor

She had measured out her life with Cartier gems. Jewels from that famous Paris house, and others, formed the main facets of her stylish existence, giving it most of its color, hope, fantasy and passion, matching its cold glitter and its surface polish. Her gemstones were all genuine: nature's minerals, magical, catching every light; the life which surrounded them was all artificial: painstakingly manufactured, mundane and non-reflective.

The well-dressed audience of one thousand assembled in the auction room on Thursday evening, April 2, 1987, knew that the jewels were significant. That was why they had flown to Geneva from the world's four corners, ready to pay thousands of dollars, even millions, to pry out a piece of the legend and carry it off to spark their own plain lives. Poised in the air around them that evening, unseen but palpable, as they sat hushed and expectant, was the primitive power of the jewels themselves which for their deceased owner, Wallis, Duchess of Windsor, had been reward and religion and revenge. Possessing a clarity and dazzle never achieved in her relationship with the duke, the gems were milestones in her marriage, points of illumination marking its changing sentiment, its gratitude and guilt. The duchess had written her autobiography in 1956, netting herself an advance of $700,000 with which to buy more gems; but her real biography was there in the Geneva auction room, throwing new light on the life. There was no real crown among the jewels, but all of them stood in place of one.

The sale was advertised as the auction of the century. Since Alfred Taubman, millionaire owner of Sotheby Parke-Bernet in New York, was putting on the Biggest Jewelry Show on Earth, it seems appropriate that in the lakeside gardens of the Hotel Beau Rivage where the auction was being held Taubman had erected a red-and-white striped tent, the kind one sees at circuses.

Many of the important pieces, the awesome emeralds and rubies which had empowered the duchess' life, would be sold that evening; the rest, along with such minor indulgences as gem-studded lipstick cases and gold pencil holders, would be dispersed at 4:30 p.m. on Friday afternoon. For both sessions, there would be a live link-up with New York, where a thousand more people in Sotheby Parke-Bernet's auction room would have a chance to bid, as slides of the pieces were projected on a screen. The jewels had been previewed in the New York showrooms at a party on Tuesday evening, March 17, where such celebrities as Barbara Walters, Malcolm Forbes, Donald Trump, designers Carolyne Roehm and Arnold Scassi, best-dressed socialites C. Z. Guest and Brooke Astor had paid $125 each to peer and marvel, while security guards dressed as waiters passed among them with trays of champagne and canapés.

For the following five days, New York's general public was allowed to enter the showrooms to gape and dream. On the first day, a line of eager people a block long was in place more than an hour before Sotheby's 1 p.m. opening. By 2:30, staff were turning newcomers away because they had no hope of getting in before the 5 o'clock closing. In addition to their Geneva and New York engagements, the jewels had also toured Monaco and Palm Beach.

The Thursday evening auction in Geneva was late starting, while excitement mounted, but finally, as the clock moved towards 9:25, handsome Nicholas Rayner, Sotheby's Geneva jewelry expert, sporting a ruby-red pocket handkerchief, walked importantly to the podium with a gold gavel in his hand. Above him was an illuminated screen which showed the opening bid for the first item, a ruby and sapphire gold clip in tassel shape. A pretty girl held it aloft on a black velvet cushion while the bidding progressed. The clip went to Alexander Acevedo, a Madison Avenue art dealer, for $47,667, ten times its actual worth. But then, nobody present was interested in the dollar value of anything offered; what they were buying was a chip off the old blockbuster myth in which the romantic hero makes a mighty sacrifice for the woman he loves. The general public who had come to look, and the not-so-idle rich who had come to buy, were both drawn to the force and flash of Celebrity, which, in American culture, sometime around the middle of the twentieth century, had replaced religion as the Highest Power and Greatest Good. The duchess who had worn the jewels was a media darling and cult figure, a modern-day Cinderella who had come from humble beginnings to snare Prince Charming, setting him a wondrous task by which to prove his love and devotion. The duchess had succeeded – and America loved success before all else – in two ways: first, by making her personality reside memorably in jewels and clothes; and secondly, by elevating both to the level of myth. On that April evening, the jewels, like so many shooting stars, were poised for far trajectories; the clothes were even then finding resting places in the august halls of the Victoria and Albert Museum in London and the Metropolitan Museum in New York.

Slowly, as well-manicured hands on well-massaged arms were raised and lowered, each jewel had its moment center-stage. There were maharajahs' emeralds, trumpeting their memories of elephant processions through red-gold dust; canary-yellow diamonds shining as boldly and brightly as the noonday sun; aquamarines and sapphires coalescing into smallest, calmest oceans. And all these stones, plus a few modest, opaque ones, such as turquoises and corals, that kept their own council and didn't scream to be noticed, were fashioned into charming conceits: single feathers and entire flamingos; butterflies and jungle beasts; royal crowns, sized, alas, for a lapel and not a head; princely plumes and little frogs. In all, there were 230 lots to be sold, including eighty-seven from Cartier and twenty-three from Van Cleef and Arpels.

After only thirty lots had sold, the take stood at three million dollars. As the sale continued, a ruby and diamond bracelet, bearing the cryptic message "Hold tight," fetched $486,000; the duchess' 19-carat emerald engagement ring brought $1.98 million. A pair of stunning yellow-diamond clips sold for $2.27 million and a ruby necklace for $2.6 million.

"All done New York?" Nicholas Rayner would ask at the end of each bidding contest, gold gavel poised mid-air. "*Adjugé!*" he would then declare in a plummy voice, as silence replaced the murmur of voices and gavel tapped on wood. Mr. Acevedo, who had caught the bidding fever on the very first lot, found himself at evening's end 2.7 million dollars poorer, but he resold a $733,326 pearl necklace at a profit before he even left the salesroom. Marvin Mitchelson, a Los Angeles divorce lawyer who'd grown rich on failed love, bought a diamond bib necklace for $373,996 and dedicated his newsworthy achievement to his mother. By the end of the evening, the auction had netted close to ten times what it had expected to, and when Nicholas Rayner banged his gold gavel down at the end of next day's session, jewels valued at seven million had fetched almost $51 million.

The duchess would have been pleased. In death she had achieved even more fame and social prominence than in life – which, after all, had always been her primary ambition. She might have been less pleased, she who never gave to charity, to know that her lawyer, Maître Suzanne Blum, had arranged for the auction proceeds to go to the Institut Pasteur, the research center and hospital in Paris which, in 1987, was channeling most of its funds into AIDS research. The duchess would also not have been pleased to know that Elizabeth Taylor, *not* a woman of style, who usually made it to the top of Mr. Blackwell's Worst-Dressed List, had phoned from poolside at her Los Angeles home to buy a diamond brooch in the Prince of Wales' three-plume motif, and that Kelly Klein, designer Calvin's hip young wife, had bought a large pearl choker with one pendant pearl as big as a goddess' teardrop, which she would routinely wear with her jeans. The duchess had never, ever worn jeans, and *pearls* with jeans was unthinkable. The duke, too, would not have been pleased with the sale, for, unlike the duchess, he was a romantic, and had requested that the jewels be dismantled after her death so that they would never touch any female flesh but his beloved's. In this, as in one other sovereign instance, the duke's wishes had been thwarted.

The duchess had come a long way from her humble beginnings before reaching the pyrotechnics of the Geneva jewelry auction. Born Bessie Wallis Warfield, on June 19, 1895, she was illegitimate, a cruel fact which no jewel in her view, however large, could ever obliterate. Her mother, Alice Montague, from a

Virginia family with more breeding than money, didn't marry her father, Teakle Wallis Warfield, of the hard-working, trading-class Maryland Warfields, until Bessie Wallis was seventeen months old. Nor was she ever baptized, an embarrassment which made two of her three marriages, if one cared to press the point, illegal, including the one to a former king. The marriage of her parents, coming as it did so long after the plump, dimpled fact of Bessie Wallis, couldn't take place in a church, but was a modest affair in the Episcopalian minister's living room, with Alice, who loved clothes, looking pretty in a green silk afternoon dress, with hat and gloves to match. As her daughter would in years to come, Alice derived comfort and confidence from her apparel, and the sable trim of her green silk did much to alleviate the sordid circumstances. Bessie Wallis' father Teakle had tuberculosis, and died on November 15, 1897, when she was only two. Alice had no money, and no skills beyond sewing and cooking. She got a job altering clothes with the Woman's Exchange, and made Bessie Wallis' dresses on its sewing machines during her lunch hours. Montague cousins in England, showing the same largesse as Elinor Glyn's French relatives, dispatched their discarded garments to Alice to be remade for herself and Bessie Wallis. Although this gave mother and daughter free dresses and coats, they often didn't have enough money to buy stockings. A Warfield cousin remembers that Bessie Wallis sometimes had to borrow them, or wear ones that were darned. In little Bessie Wallis' world, everyone she encountered had nicer clothes and bigger houses. The seeds of her life-long ambition were planted very early. She would somehow, someday, restore herself to the social and material level which her cousins enjoyed and which she felt she deserved.

If she was short on apparel, she was long on love and approval. Alice adored her only child and had her photographed weekly as she grew; by age five, as Bessie Wallis played with her dolls, three hundred more Bessie Wallises encircled her. It seems logical, in light of this, that her first words weren't "Mama" but "Me-Me." She was, it seems, born a snob, for she named her first dolls Mrs. Astor and Mrs. Vanderbilt after the reigning queens of New York society. Her favorite picture books were fashion magazines which showed these and other matrons in diamond chains and stately trains.

Like Elinor Glyn and Marlene Dietrich, Bessie Wallis was influenced by a formidable grandmother who cared mightily for appearances. Grandmama Warfield, in perpetual mourning, wore black dresses with tight, white-edged collars to her chin, small white linen caps with three black-ribbon bows, and jewelry suitably pared to one pearl brooch and one black-enamel bracelet. "Bessie Wallis, how will you ever grow up to be a lady," Grandmama would ask sternly, "unless you learn to keep your back straight?" She also told her granddaughter never to drink coffee: "It will turn your skin yellow."

Bessie Wallis was trained from childhood to be a genteel wife and well-turned-out accessory to some man of wealth and breeding. But in addition to little money, Bessie Wallis had another handicap in the matrimonial stakes. She wasn't a beauty. Her face was too square, with a large mole on her chin; her nose was too large and her hair too straight, facts which were brought home to her every time she looked at those three hundred photos, or at her pretty mother, who had a cute little nose, golden curls and feet so dainty she took a size 2 1/2 shoe. "Nobody ever called me beautiful or even pretty," sighs Bessie Wallis pathetically in her autobiography. If God had denied her beauty, she could still impress through original style and neatness. For her very first party, Alice wanted her daughter to wear a blue sash with her white dress. Bessie Wallis stamped her feet and insisted on a bright red one, so that the boys would notice her. When she was naughty, her mother spanked her with a hairbrush, fit symbol for one whose life would be disciplined by grooming.

Bessie Wallis' schooling began in Baltimore at Miss O'Donnell's, where a classmate recalls: "She made up her mind to go to the head of the class and she did. She was poor, mind you. The Warfields had nothing. She had no pocket money, not a penny." At ten, Bessie Wallis was enrolled at the Arundell School for Girls, and when classmates laughed at her because her mother took in boarders, she hit them with her heavy walking shoes. One classmate thought her a "fly-up-the-creek" girl who screamed a lot at parties. "She had smartness and style without real beauty."

When, on June 20, 1908, her mother Alice married a penniless alcoholic named John Freeman Rasin, Bessie Wallis looked charming in a dainty gown of embroidered batiste laced with blue ribbons. But in the middle of the ceremony she left the parlor where it was taking place, repaired to the next room and began tearing the wedding cake to pieces, intent on finding the ring, thimble and dime hidden inside. Just one day after her thirteenth birthday, Bessie Wallis thus gave evidence of her rampant materialism and its focus: jewelry, clothes and money.

Just before graduating from Arundell in June 1912, at age seventeen, she wrote to her Aunt Bessie Merryman, a lighthearted widow to whom Bessie Wallis was always very attached, "I am wearing corsets now and am crazy about them." After Arundell, Bessie Wallis moved closer to her goals by changing schools, friends and name. Millionaire Uncle Sol Warfield, who could often be persuaded, if Alice and her daughter pleaded hard enough, to foot their bills, paid for Bessie Wallis' "finishing" at Oldfields, Maryland's most expensive and élite girls' school. Bessie Wallis made sure her three closest friends, Renée duPont, Ellen Yuille and Mary Kirk, came from rich families. She also, like Marlene Dietrich, and for similar motives of soft-sell and image, gave herself a new Christian name. Henceforth, Bessie Wallis told everyone at school she was to be called Wallis. There were other Bessies at Oldfields, not to mention those four-legged, milk-giving ones in nearby fields, but there was only one Wallis.

During her two years at Oldfields, Wallis was totally focused on rich young men and on clothes as a means of attracting them. One beau was Lloyd Tabbs, whose family owned an estate called Glen Ora, just outside Middleburg, Virginia. (Glen Ora would later become the weekend home of President Kennedy and his wife.) Due to her quick wit, liveliness and facility for stroking male egos, Wallis had plenty of beaux. Along with all the other young ladies of her day, she also swooned over the golden-haired Prince of Wales, the world's most eligible bachelor, carefully pasting his picture clipped from a magazine onto a blank page of her diary.

In 1913, when she was eighteen, Wallis found her second clothes mentor, the first being her mother. Her pretty, stylish cousin Corinne Mustin (née Montague) invited Wallis to spend the summer with her and husband Henry at their lovely home on Boston's North Shore. From Corinne, Wallis learned the difference between style, which was what one wanted to achieve, and mere fashion. Style, according to Corinne, made the *woman* stand out; fashion, the *clothes*. At that stage in her life, Wallis was still choosing flashy garments which drew attention to themselves rather than to her. A friend recalls one evening gown which had a bodice of cloth-of-gold patterned in little flowers, and a full crêpe de Chine skirt in a blazing hue called "sunset."

That same year, Wallis attended the Princeton Ball with a young man whom, in her usually forceful way, she'd persuaded to take her. She debated long and hard with her mother on the subject of her gown. Alice favored pink; Wallis wanted blue to match her best feature: her extraordinary, violet-blue eyes. When she learned that no other girl at the ball would be wearing blue,

Wallis opted for blue organdy. By this time, she was well into the first stage of her life in style, which we can neatly divide into three distinct chapters. In this first one, she used style as springboard for her social ambition, and to satisfy the need to be special and superior, her life's driving force. It would be "Me-Me" all the way, herself alone against the world. Her strengths were internal; her greatest resource was the rock of her determination to direct, control and better her life. In her blue organdy, Wallis may have looked like the usual languid, passive Southern belle content to float prettily down the stream of life, but in fact she was more steel than magnolia, a daring and adventuresome prospector. She kept that part of her well hidden under her corset, playing the traditional female role to the hilt, using her charm, essential frivolity and support of the male to achieve her goals through marriage, which was the only possible career for a woman of her time and upbringing.

In December 1914 came the challenge of Baltimore's Bachelor Cotillion. Only forty-eight young women out of a possible five hundred could be chosen; those that were had an assured place in society and hopes of a brilliant marriage. When Wallis found herself one of the lucky forty-eight, she longed for a ballgown in which she could really shine. She couldn't afford to order one from Baltimore's most fashionable shop, Fuechsl's, so instead copied a model made for dancer Irene Castle by the man who'd dressed an empress, Monsieur Charles Worth, and got a black seamstress named Ellen to make it for her. The gown was white satin under a knee-length white chiffon tunic with embroidered band. Wallis went by streetcar many times to Ellen's house, and stood happily for hours while the gown was fitted to her slim, boyish figure.

Two years later, Wallis met the first of her three husbands, a handsome Navy lieutenant called Earl Winfield Spencer Jr. As

Wallis tells us in her autobiography, it was "the gold stripes on his shoulder-boards, glimpsed out of the corner of my eye" which "acted like a magnet" and drew her to him. They were married in November 1916, with Uncle Sol digging into his pockets to pay for a trousseau. Wallis chose a wedding gown designed by Elinor Glyn's sister Lucile of white panne velvet with long court train, its bodice embroidered in pearls, quite the smallest ones to figure in Wallis' life, whose pearls would grow ever larger as her fortunes rose. Wallis herself designed the six bridesmaids' dresses. Rather than the usual bland pastels, they were striking and unusual: bouffant gowns of orchid faille with French-blue velvet girdles. Matching hats had blue velvet brims and orchid faille crowns. For going away, Wallis changed into a prophetic ensemble in the exact shade of amethysts. (Later she would own a huge latticed bib of these stones.)

Win was stationed in San Diego, a social backwater where Wallis was bored and restless. At twenty-eight, Win already drank too much, while Wallis consoled herself by running up smart little numbers on her Singer sewing machine. By 1921, at a time when Wallis' mother Alice was working as housekeeper and Aunt Bessie as paid companion, Wallis was living with Win in a small apartment hotel in Washington. Win would go off for an evening's drinking, having first tied Wallis to the bed or locked her in the bathroom. He routinely fell down drunk at parties and had affairs with other women. Wallis grew up quickly. She soon realized that she would have to leave him. She spent little time with him after 1922, and would finally divorce him in June 1926, although no one in her family had ever been divorced and all her relatives were against such flouting of convention.

In January 1924, Wallis had her first and giddiest trip to Europe, traveling with cousin Corinne and carting around an ironing board so that her dresses would never have a wrinkle. It was in July, still living apart from Win, that Wallis began what she called her "lotus-eater's dream": a year in China, staying with rich friends Kitty and Herman Rogers, who lived in great luxury – the kind of people Wallis was always drawn to – in Peking. At this point in her life, she looked, according to Cecil Beaton, who would later see an amateur film of Wallis with the Rogers, "much less individual, her hair thicker, her head bigger, her body fatter." Wallis was still tentatively experimenting with style, but had not yet found her own distinctive look. She earned money for clothes by gambling and – according to some biographers – by drug dealing. She designed the clothes herself with some help from British and American fashion magazines, and had them expertly and cheaply made by local tailors. She was happy in China because she was, for the first time ever, able to live the superficial, social, luxurious life which suited her best. In the mornings, she would swim or play a game of tennis. In the afternoons, she went to polo matches or satisfied her hunger for pretty things by shopping in the bazaars and markets for porcelains, pieces of brocade, or another little elephant for her growing collection, carved from ivory, jade, turquoise or rose quartz. In the evenings, she donned a slinky evening dress and went off to flirt outrageously at parties at the American or British Legation. This taste of the sybaritic, self-indulgent life was enough to get Wallis hooked on it permanently.

In 1925, her mother married Charles Gordon Allen, a man who, like her previous two husbands, was neither rich nor strong-minded. Wallis would repeat her mother's three-husband pattern, but with more financial rewards. While awaiting her divorce from Win, Wallis cast about for a source of income to support her clothes habit. She entered a contest run by a fashion magazine in which applicants had to write an essay on spring hats, with the winner to be appointed to the magazine's editorial staff. Wallis was then staying in New York with friend Mary Kirk, who had married Jacques Raffray and taken an apartment in Washington Square. Wallis stayed up all night, laboring over her entry, and was very disappointed when she didn't win. This was her one abortive bid for financial independence.

She then reverted to more conventional methods, and used her Southern charm on the Raffrays' friend, Ernest Simpson, well-heeled partner in a family company which bought and sold ships, with offices in London and New York. They met at Christmas time, 1925, when Ernest still had a wife, Dorothea, who later declared: "Wallis was very smart. She stole my husband while I was ill."

"I've decided definitely that the best and wisest thing for me to do is to marry Ernest," wrote Wallis to her mother in the following July, even though she knew full well that she wasn't in love with him. "I can't go wandering on the rest of my life and I really feel so tired of fighting the world all alone and with no money," she continued. Wallis married Ernest in London's Chelsea Registry office on July 21, 1928, in a sunshine-yellow dress and sky-blue coat custom-made in Paris, and set up housekeeping in a rented London flat. Ernest had an American mother and British father. After Harvard, he'd become a British citizen, served in the Coldstream Guards and got as far as the fringes of London society. He was well-read, dull, dependable, loyal and utterly conventional. His character is neatly contained in an incident which would take place two years later when he was traveling in Europe with Wallis and Aunt Bessie. A fire broke out in their hotel in The Hague. Wallis and Aunt Bessie rushed downstairs with coats thrown hastily over nightgowns. Ernest appeared shortly thereafter, immaculate in bowler hat, suit, clean shirt, Guards' tie, handkerchief neatly folded in breast pocket, suitcase in right hand, inevitable rolled umbrella in left. "Good Lord!" laughed Aunt Bessie. "The best-dressed man at the fire!"

Wallis had to dash across the Atlantic to Washington in late October 1929, because her mother lay terminally ill. "Isn't that a brown dress you have on?" Alice asked in a weak voice, squinting at her daughter from her sick bed. "Yes, Mother," Wallis replied meekly, glancing at the brown checked dress she'd bought in London. "Thought so," sniffed her mother in the same exasperated tone which had greeted Wallis' childhood misdemeanors and preceded the hairbrush's whack. "Whatever made you choose such an unbecoming color?" moaned Alice, style devotée to the death. Wallis felt extremely sad and bereft when her mother died on November 2, for she was one of the few people Wallis really loved. Fortunately, she still had Aunt Bessie, who would live to be one hundred.

After trying several flats, Wallis and Ernest moved into a smart new apartment building, Bryanston Court, in George Street, near Marble Arch, and Wallis began her climb up the social ladder. She asked American Syrie Maugham, English writer Somerset Maugham's ex-wife, who always dressed in white, to help her decorate the flat. Wallis would invariably look to professionals to assist her own taste, which, she knew, wavered from good to bad. She bought a dining table with mirror top hoping to reflect society's chic, and chose the color of aquamarines for walls and curtains in her bedroom.

Wallis had inherited some money from Uncle Sol in his will, and when in 1930 she found herself in Paris, she decided to spend it all on three or four couture-made outfits. Both Ernest and Aunt Bessie tried to dissuade her from anything so reckless, telling her to invest the money instead, keeping the principal, and spending only earned interest. "But the prospect of at last having a few chic clothes from the great couturiers," as Wallis tells us in her autobiography, "was more than I could resist." What she didn't know was that her clothes investment would, in another four years, start paying truly princely dividends.

It was in January 1931 that Wallis' life took an exciting new turn. Her American friend Thelma Furness, the Prince of Wales' current lady love, invited Wallis and Ernest to come to her sister Consuelo Thaw's country house, Burrough Court near Melton Mowbray, for the weekend, to meet the Golden Prince himself. Thelma was one of the famous Morgan twins, both willowy, raven-haired and clothes-mad, both adventurers like Wallis. The twins liked to wear the same dress design made up in contrasting colors. Thelma might wear an outfit in white with black gloves, and Gloria in black with white gloves. Gloria married rich Reggie Vanderbilt, while Thelma, after eloping at age sixteen with a roué twice her age and divorcing him, married older but also richer Lord Furness, an uncouth character ironically known as "Duke." Thelma had met the Prince of Wales one day when he was awarding rosettes to prize-winning cows at the Leicester Fair. He stopped long enough to cast an appraising eye on her. The prince preferred to romance women already safely tethered to husbands and had settled – for the moment, anyway – on Thelma.

After three years of fruitless efforts to penetrate English society, Wallis was thrilled at the prospect of reaching, or at least brushing up against, its very pinnacle. (It was Prince Edward who led society; his parents, King George V and Queen Mary, preferred quiet evenings at home, he pouring over his collection of stamps, most of which bore his likeness, she embroidering.)

When the invitation to Burrough Court came, Wallis was in bed with a fever and severe cold. "Friday I got up," she told Aunt Bessie in a letter, "and spent the entire day on hair and nails." But in spite of this, she was still red-nosed, bleary-eyed and terrified. "Ernest, I'm really scared," Wallis wailed to her husband, between sneezes. "I haven't the faintest idea of what's expected of me." There was something, however, to give her courage: those Paris couture models hanging in all their glory in her closet. "Among my acquisitions," she writes, "was an attractive blue-grey tweed dress with a cape of the same material edged with nutria, which I had bought on my shopping spree. This, I felt confident, would meet the most exacting requirements of both a horsey and princely setting and would give me the added assurance that came from the knowledge that in the dress was a little white satin label bearing the word Molyneux." Handsome Irishman Captain Edward Molyneux, who had apprenticed himself to Elinor Glyn's sister Lucile before opening his own Paris salon in 1919, let the clothes shine by putting his entire staff, some six hundred people, into pale gray uniforms to match the pale gray décor. His clothes were understated and subtle, and Wallis was probably drawn to him after seeing his elegant designs – which every woman in the audience wanted – in Noel Coward's *Private Lives*, produced in 1930.

With her blue-gray tweed and little white label to bolster her, Wallis on that historic Friday, round about five p.m., made her curtsey to the prince. As usual, she noticed clothes first – "very loud-checked tweeds" – and that he was smaller than expected (only 5'7"). His face was tanned, and wrinkled like last year's apple from days in strong sun on his Empire tours. His hair shone like gold, and his manner was surprisingly natural and off-hand, if a little shy. He laughed easily, but when he stopped, his expression was that of a sad little boy, his blue eyes lost and wistful. They never seemed to quite focus, and one was slightly lower than the other. He was full of nervous mannerisms, tugging at his necktie, holding his head to one side when spoken to, constantly clutching his right wrist with his left hand. (This was probably because, when he was growing up, his mother had made sure he never put his hands in trouser pockets by having them sewn shut.)

Christened Edward Albert Christian George Andrew Patrick David, called David by his intimates and Edward by the rest of the world, the Prince of Wales was born on June 23, 1894, eldest son of George and Mary, the Duke and Duchess of York. David grew up inside a constricting, stiff Eton collar and environment to match, in which his parents paid far more attention to his clothes than to the boy inside them. His father, who would be crowned king in 1910, when David was not quite sixteen, was so hide-bound and conservative that he had used the same collar-stud and hairbrushes, as he proudly told a friend, for more than fifty years. He also dressed exactly as *his* father, portly playboy King Edward VII, had, in frock coats and side-pressed trousers. "I hope your kilts fit well. Take care and don't spoil them at once as they are new," wrote David's father to his son and heir. "Wear the Balmoral kilt and grey jacket on weekdays and green kilt and black jacket on Sundays."

David's mother was equally conservative and, as he puts it, "never once changed her style during the whole of her lifetime." She dressed for daytime head to toe in one pastel; toque hat, fox fur, severe tailleur and buttoned kid boots would all be pale blue or lavender, cream or pale rose. Once, in the 1920s, when skirts were rising at an astonishing rate, Queen Mary got her lady-in-waiting, the Countess of Airlie, to shorten hers first, as a sort of trial run, and when King George roared his disapproval, Queen Mary meekly kept her skirts forever after at an unfashionable ankle length. She also kept David in ruffled dresses and long ringlets until age four, so that he looked like an early version of Shirley Temple, and developed some odd sexual kinks. Queen Mary's four sons were paraded before her daily as if for military inspection while she looked them up and down with eagle eye. Stockings had to be pulled tight over knees; Eton collars had to be well starched and spotlessly clean; neckties had to be straight;

sleeves had to hide, tucked into their cuffs, not one but *two* clean handkerchiefs. Neither parent gave David any physical affection at all, although his mother did teach him to knit and crochet. "I am a most bum specimen of humanity," David wrote to brother Bertie when he was twenty, and indeed he seems never to have developed to full puberty; he remained small and puny, never grew body hair and, according to three accounts, including that of his future wife, had the world's smallest penis. He also had some queer infantile regressions. At parties, he sometimes rode in a baby carriage, wearing nothing but a diaper. Beside his bed he kept a stuffed donkey with white ears, a scruffy teddy bear and the chimney-sweep doll made for him by his domineering and unloving mother. After dinner, the prince liked to suck single-mindedly on a wet cigar which he never bothered to light. His only revolt against his parents, once he attained majority, was to dress extremely casually in loud checks, turn-up trousers, plus-fours and ascots instead of ties. From 1919 to 1925, the Prince toured the Empire, traveling 150,000 miles and visiting forty-five different countries and colonies, picking up en route the spectacular loose gemstones from cowed maharajahs and other colonials which would eventually find their way to Sotheby's 1987 Geneva auction. Elinor Glyn's beloved Lord Curzon was at Portsmouth in 1920 to see the Prince off on one of his tours. "In a little tight naval uniform which clung close to his figure he did not look above fifteen, quite a pathetic little person," wrote Curzon about the twenty-six-year-old prince. It was during those years of constant media exposure, nevertheless, that he became every maiden's Prince Charming. The young women of Ballarat, Australia, had presented him with yellow silk pyjamas to which each of them contributed a stitch, just about the time Wallis Warfield was pasting him into her diary. The young men of the world, on the other hand, rushed to copy his Fair Isle sweaters, plus-fours and other fashion innovations, to the delight of the British clothing trade.

As Wallis, in her Molyneux blue-gray tweed, began a conversation with the prince, he noted that she spoke in staccato sentences, with little explosions of laughter which surprised her dark eyebrows and made her large, loose mouth turn down at the corners. She had the Southern woman's gift of focusing totally on him as they chatted, drawing him out, listening attentively, making him feel witty and wanted. In repose, her face had a deep horizontal crease across the forehead. An artist would have sketched her in angles rather than curves. Later, the prince would come to admire her slim-hipped boyish figure, her clear skin, as smooth and polished as the inside of a shell, and her large blue eyes which sparkled like sapphires when she told a funny story in dry, deadpan fashion with a comedian's timing.

There is no doubt that visually Wallis and Edward matched. The prince's body was as sinewy and hairless as hers; their blue eyes had the same prominence; he was barely taller than she; in their dress they were both superbly groomed and fanatically style-conscious. Wallis and Edward: "WE" was the term they would later inscribe on jewelry and little notes to each other. And to any eye craving symmetry, they did make a most consonant pair. Reproduced on a smaller scale in porcelain, they could have stood pleasingly at either end of a mantelpiece.

"It was quite an experience and as I've had my mind made up to meet him ever since I've been here I feel relieved," Wallis wrote to Aunt Bessie on the following Tuesday. Had she made a lasting impression? She needed to see the prince again to consolidate. "I have bought a black satin evening dress – the first thing to wear I've bought since our orgy in Paris," she told Aunt Bessie on February 5. "I do hope Thelma Furness will ask us again with the prince." Wallis was still waiting in vain for an invitation a month later. "I would go to Paris for clothes if I had the cash. Don't know what I'll do for spring clothes as have put everything into the flat," she complained to Aunt Bessie on March 6. "The Thaws are giving a party May 24th and I'm hoping HRH [His Royal Highness] will be there," wrote Wallis to Aunt Bessie on April 6. "I would like to be given the once-over without the cold." She didn't have to wait quite that long, for Thelma Furness gave a cocktail party on May 15, where Wallis, to her great delight, encountered the prince for the second time and tried to ingratiate herself further.

The next excitement in her life, on June 10, was her presentation at Court, a necessary step for anyone with social aspirations. She borrowed friend Tamara Thaw's simple white satin, floor-length slip dress, "which fits perfectly," and added Thelma Furness' ostrich feather headdress, large fan and white satin embroidered train, which fell loosely from shoulders to floor and trailed fulsomely behind. (In 1936, when Wallis' name was emblazoned across every American newspaper, a man came into the New York dress shop Thelma then owned and asked to buy this white satin train for a proposed Baltimore museum and "shrine" of Wallis artifacts. Thelma refused to sell it.) Since all the ladies to be presented would be wearing the same requisite costume of white gown, train and three-plume headdress, Wallis felt the need to make hers stand out. "I am buying an aquamarine and crystal ornament and large aquamarine cross," she told Aunt Bessie, "imitations but effective." No one could miss the cross; it was four inches long, suspended around her neck on a cord. Wallis didn't know as she curtseyed to King George and Queen Mary, the latter blazing with jewels, and smiled at the Prince of Wales, that she was soon to part company forever from imitation gems – but not from crosses. "My aquamarine jewelry really looked divine with the white and Thelma's train is very handsome and longer than regulations. Also her feathers were higher which helps a lot," wrote Wallis smugly to Aunt Bessie on June 13. "I hope I can have HRH here for a KT [cocktail] some afternoon."

Her friendship with the prince was advancing far too slowly to suit Wallis. Then in mid-January 1932, His Royal Highness dined with the Simpsons at Bryanston Court, and stayed till four a.m. At the end of January, Wallis was thrilled to be invited, with husband Ernest in tow, to the prince's weekend retreat, Fort Belvedere, situated on the edge of Windsor Great Park. The house looked like a child's idea of a fort, and as Wallis drove toward its battlements and turrets on that Friday evening, she felt that the inert page of one of the books of fairy tales which little Bessie Wallis had eagerly perused was about to spring to full, wondrous, amazing, unbelievable life.

The prince's weekend parties were casual and relaxed affairs. Everyone gathered in the drawing-room, which had yellow velvet curtains, Canalettos and pine-paneled walls, for the cocktail hour, which went on and on until dinner was finally served around ten p.m. After dinner, Wallis was amazed to see the prince bend his blond head over a large flat screen, and begin poking a needle in and out as he did needlepoint, a skill taught him, unbeknownst to Wallis, by an obliging Thelma Furness.

For Wallis, the prince was "the open sesame to a new and glittering world that excited me as nothing in my life had ever done before." Soon they were calling each other "Wallis" and "David" in private – she still called him "Sir" in public – and he was turning up often at Bryanston Court for cocktails, staying on to take "pot luck" at dinner. By the following December, he was utterly, obsessively, irrationally in love. He would telephone at three or four a.m. – the matched pair both had lifelong insomnia – to talk and talk, needing Wallis more and more as substitute mother and nanny to resolve his private complexes. Wallis' greatest concern during this period wasn't the growing rift in her marriage, but having enough smart clothes for the social set into which the Prince had drawn her. She talked Ernest into a trip to New York in May 1933, to buy new outfits, and wrote exultantly to Aunt Bessie, after her return. "My clothes are really a huge success. PW [the Prince of Wales] calls the piqué one my white tie dress." "I have ordered two evening dresses as the U.S. ones are falling apart," she informed Aunt Bessie on October 14, as she and the Prince whirled from one nightclub to another. "I have put blue moiré where the white piqué was," she added, trying to make her older dress appear new.

"We have inherited the 'young man' from Thelma," wrote Wallis to Aunt Bessie on February 12, 1934, after Thelma had sailed innocently away to New York, asking Wallis to look after the prince in her absence. "He misses her so that he is always calling us up and the result is one late night after another," scribbled Wallis. "I think you better send me the dress as soon as possible as I'm really naked. I want something sophisticated either red, blue, black or combination of colours." In her next letter, on February 18, Wallis mentions that the prince is telephoning two or three times a day, and that the "sophisticated" new dress should be given to her good friend Thelma to bring to England. "It's all gossip about the Prince," Wallis reassured her aunt, who had heard disturbing rumors of her niece's affair with him. "I'm not in the habit of taking my girl friends' beaux."

On her return, Thelma spent a weekend at Fort Belvedere (her last one) with Wallis, the prince and some other guests. When, at table, Britain's future king, Lord and Master of all he surveyed, picked up a lettuce leaf in his fingers, Wallis slapped his hand and told him sharply to use his knife and fork. Thelma stared across the table dumbfounded at this intimate Nanny-child exchange, and knew, at that moment, that the Prince was permanently lost to her and that even if Wallis had once dutifully returned the white satin court train and fine feathers she'd borrowed, she had no intention whatsoever of returning the prince.

Wallis had by this time also adopted a motherly attitude to the prince's clothes. She would reach out to straighten his necktie, or adjust a collar tab. Once she made him take a cigar out of his breast pocket. "It doesn't look very pretty," she told him curtly. "The royalty stuff [is] very demanding on clothes," she sighed to Aunt Bessie on April 21, 1934. "Any cheap pale blue summer dress for country wear you see for about $20 get for me," she demanded. "It naturally takes more money to play around with him," she wrote on April 25, requesting two more dresses, one linen and one wool; "he demands one to look chic." At this point, Wallis tripped the light fantastic of her novel storybook life without a worry in her head except filling her wardrobe with enough beads and spangles.

In August of that year, the prince invited Wallis to accompany him on an eleven-day cruise on the borrowed yacht *Rosaura* from Biarritz to Cannes. One member of the party reported that Britain's future sovereign "has lost all confidence in himself and follows W. around like a dog." When the cruise ended, the prince and Wallis boldly moved into the Hotel Miramar at Cannes together. One moonlit night at one a.m. the prince summoned the night manager to his suite and told him to wake up the staff of the local branch of Cartier. The prince then went to the store and returned with an armload of little velvet boxes which he stashed away for later occasions, presenting Wallis with only one. Thus far in their relationship he'd given her nothing except an orchid plant and a cairn terrier which was most appropriately named for its role in this Cinderella story, for it answered to "Slipper." Wallis excitedly opened the velvet lid, and saw a diamond and emerald charm for her bracelet winking up at her, her first solid artifact from the "new and glittering world" which was sprinkling its riches around her. There was no doubt that the prince was deeply in love with her; she, however, was in love not with him but with his lifestyle, in which "trains were held; yachts materialized; the best suites in the finest hotels were flung open," as she herself put it. She told Ernest on her return that she felt like "Wallis in Wonderland," to which he snapped that in his view, she was playing in never-never land with Peter Pan – his new nickname for the prince.

Wallis marked the newly intimate stage of her relationship to her prince by ordering three enchanting custom-made nightgowns from the lingerie shop near Berkeley Square which future *Vogue* editor Diana Vreeland then owned. Wallis chose one model in white satin cut on the bias à la Madame Vionnet; a second in pale blue with a neckline composed of bias-cut petals; a third one in pale blue crêpe de Chine. The nightgowns, Diana told her, would be ready in three weeks. Wallis called twice in the first two weeks to ask, "How are the nightgowns getting on?" In the third week, she telephoned every day. The new nighties were Wallis' conventional way of arousing the princely libido, but she had others less tried and true. She was discovering that David had a rather peculiar sexuality, not quite the usual manly thing. He was a foot fetishist, for one thing, and he wanted other special attentions which Wallis, who had learned a thing or two in China, felt duty-bound to give him. (Years later, she told one reporter that the prince had "a small penis complex" and another that he wasn't "heir-conditioned.") His Highness' sexual relations with his earlier lady loves had been far from satisfactory. He thought Wallis perfect in bed, utterly wonderful, absolutely amazing. The prince glowed with gratitude and more little velvet boxes changed hands.

His Highness' gratitude also surfaced in gifts of clothes. "The blue-eyed charmer is still the best beau and keeps me pretty busy," wrote Wallis to Aunt Bessie on October 27, 1934. "I bought a coat and dress with the $200 the Prince gave me and some leopard skins which I think will make a lovely sports coat." She assured Aunt Bessie that she intended to stay married to Ernest: "I shall try and be clever enough to keep them both." In November, there was a ball at Buckingham Palace in which the prince resolved to present Wallis to his parents; they in turn resolved to ignore her; and Wallis, for her part, resolved to upstage every woman in the room. Princess Marina, whose forthcoming marriage to the Duke of Kent was the occasion for the ball, looked beautiful and bride-like in white satin. Queen Mary was regal in silver brocade and the other female guests were innocuous and indistinguishable in assorted pastels. Wallis, however, wore violet-colored lamé with an emerald-green sash, designed by Eva Lutyens, daughter-in-law of the famous architect Sir Edwin Lutyens, and had the satisfaction of having Prince Paul, Regent of Yugoslavia, lean close to her ear to tell her: "There is no question about it – you are wearing the most striking gown in the room." It was some small compensation for both king and queen turning a cold shoulder.

"I have two more bracelets and a small diamond that sticks in my hair. Smart," Wallis gloated to Aunt Bessie on December 3, and added to her hoard, "a lovely pin with two large square emeralds," when Christmas came. Society knew that she was now the prince's lady, and suddenly she found herself the object of much attention. It was a heady time for Wallis. She writes in her autobiography of "new doors opening. I was stimulated; I was excited; I felt as if I were borne upon a rising wave." Gossip about her new gems flew about town. Lady Diana Cooper, daughter of the Duke of Rutland, noted at one party that "Mrs. Simpson was glittering and dripped in new jewels and clothes." Another society matron, seeing Wallis at the opera, wrote of "a simple black dress with a green bodice and dripping with emeralds – her collection of jewels is the talk of London." The prince couldn't verbalize his love and devotion – his letters to Wallis are full of silly baby-talk and banality – but he could speak of it in the language of gemstones, could strike their seam of passion. The jewels pinned to Wallis' meager bosom or encircling her neck and thin wrists blazoned his love to her and to the rest of the world as blatantly as if he had announced it in a full-page advertisement in the Sunday *Times*. The cuckolded Ernest remained a loyal monarchist, protested hardly at all, and meekly increased his wife's personal property insurance.

For Wallis, the jewels had a different cost. A 1934 letter to Aunt Bessie reveals that she was distressed by the prince's infantile dependence on her and by his escalating demands. As she did up her safety clasps carefully, Wallis reflected that nothing in life was free; everything had its price. Oblivious to her internal grimace, the prince kept on ransacking the royal coffers for loose gems, most of them empire loot from India, and trotted off with them to Cartier or Van Cleef and Arpels to have them set.

Her new jewelry and social prominence were so marvelous that Wallis felt the rest of her appearance wasn't quite worthy. "At that time," Thelma Furness recalls, "she did not have the chic she has since cultivated." Another friend agrees that "in those days Wallis didn't dress well at all," and remembers her wearing "a big floppy hat" that looked terrible on her. When Cecil Beaton first met Wallis he thought her "somewhat brawny and raw-boned in her sapphire-blue velvet," but when he met her again in 1934, he found her "improved in both looks and chic." It was in 1934 that Wallis, with her usual drive, set about improving her image.

She started with her grooming, which was already good. Now, as inner turmoil over her situation with the prince grew, her neatness became fanatical, a trait which psychologists maintain is a sign of unfocused anxiety, of which Wallis had plenty. It surfaced, in addition to her neatness, in fear of flying and chronic ulcers. Her center-parted hair became so smoothly brushed "that a fly would slip off it," as Cecil Beaton noted. She looked, at London parties, as if she'd just emerged from an airless glass dome.

Having groomed herself to the nth degree, Wallis moved on to general style. She once told a society photographer, in reference to his proofs of her, to "please pick out the ones that make me look least like a horse!" She knew she couldn't become a beauty, but she could become what the French call *une jolie-laide*. Wallis' style would never be instinctive or spontaneous. Unlike Eugénie, Elinor and Marlene, Wallis wasn't born with infallible good taste, although she always worshipped beauty. Taste she had to acquire, laboring as intensively at creating her style as any ballet dancer did over her pointe work or pianist over her scales.

That year in London Wallis found a fine teacher in American Elsie de Wolfe, married to Englishman Sir Charles Mendl. During her New York stage career in the 1890s, Elsie's costumes, bought annually in Paris from Worth or Doucet, were so copied in the United States that her Saturday afternoon performances in a new role were known as "Dressmakers' Matinees." At these, a full house of seamstresses ogled such creations as a teagown called the *Déshabille Troublante*, made in thirty shades of red chiffon, which graduated downward from pink under the chin to intense rose below the waist and deepest carmine ruffling around the hem. Another one of Elsie's memorable outfits in blue crêpe de Chine had chinchilla rippling round every edge and overflowing into muff and hat. In 1902, Elsie wrote a series of articles, "How to Dress by the Best-Dressed Yankee Actress" for the New York *Evening World*. Two years later she ended her acting career and in 1905 launched herself in the vocation she invented, that of interior decorator. Later she would start the fashion for shorts and blue-rinsed hair.

She took Wallis firmly in hand and taught her everything she knew about style. Quality was what counted, said Elsie, not quantity, and the cut of clothes was crucial. Like Wallis, Elsie had a plain face, but, as she says in her autobiography, when she got her "first smart wardrobe, my whole outlook on life changed and I realized that, if one has health, a good figure, and knows how to dress, one need not be ugly." Elsie assured Wallis (whose measurements were 34–25–34) that their similar flat-chested, slim-hipped figures showed clothes to best advantage. Like Marlene Dietrich, Wallis was blessed with broad shoulders, and hips so narrow that she looked marvelous at a London costume party dressed as a tube of toothpaste, in blue and silver oil cloth. Elsie hated her ugly hands so she covered them up by wearing short white gloves always, even at home for her own dinner parties. "A smart little touch," writes Elsie, "and an original one." Wallis, who also considered her own hands ugly, copied the white gloves, and, as Marlene Dietrich's friend Ginette Spanier, then a salesgirl at London's Fortnum and Mason's, recalls, her regular customer Mrs. Simpson "had the whitest white gloves I have ever seen."

Elsie then got down to wardrobe specifics. She advised Wallis to dress very simply and starkly in a way that would make the best background for her jewels and accentuate, rather than attempt to disguise, the angular lines of her body. Elsie introduced Wallis to her own favorite couturier in Paris – Mainbocher, who would do for Wallis what Worth had done for Eugénie: he would make her clothes which suited her perfectly. Born October 24, 1890, in Chicago, Main Rousseau Bocher was the first American to succeed in the Paris world of couture. He had studied singing in Munich and Paris, sketched fashions for American *Vogue* and *Harper's Bazaar* and edited French *Vogue* before opening his Paris couture house in 1929. He designed extremely simple, understated clothes whose only extravagance was their price tag, higher than that of all other couturiers. He would move his business to New York in 1941, acquiring C.Z. Guest, Babe Paley and Gloria Vanderbilt as loyal customers, before closing it in 1971. "Even the simplest dress," according to Mainbocher, "must not look timid" but have "quiet assurance." Elsie Mendl and Mainbocher together helped Wallis step permanently out of mere fashion and into her distinctive style. She and the prince both attended Mainbocher's 1935 spring showing, where Wallis bought carefully and His Highness paid the bills.

Wallis learned her lessons well. It is rare to see someone photographed as often as she would be down the years who never, ever looked ridiculous or dated. This, of course, is the true test of style: clothes must look exactly right for the woman, rather than for the period. "I began with my own personal ideas about style," Wallis told a journalist in 1966, ignoring her two main mentors. "I've never again felt correct in anything but the severe look I developed then." She chose her plain, pared garments in blue-gray, mauvey-blue, raspberry, navy, dark brown and black. In summertime she opted for such shades as powder blue, fondant pink or ivory beige. For day, she favored suits with fitted jackets and slightly flared skirts, or high-necked, long-sleeved dresses. She liked lightweight fabrics for evening, such as chiffon or gazar, and kept necklines high in front to hide her prominent collar bones. Hats were usually small and off the face. Wallis' rigor, restraint and consistency in dress paid off, for in 1935, to her great delight, she was, for the first time, named to the Paris couture's Best-Dressed List. The French, who had been getting out a best-dressed list since 1922, would do so until World War II. After the war, the list was compiled in New York by the New York Couture Group's Eleanor Lambert and a committee, who made their twelve choices from approximately 1200 ballots returned from designers, fashion editors, celebrities and restaurant owners. Wallis would stay on the list for forty years, and in 1959 would, like other perennial winners, be elevated to the Hall of Fame which honored those whose long-term contributions to style had been significant.

Wallis never unbuttoned or relaxed her style. She was "chic but never casual" according to one friend; "chic and worried about it," according to Diana Vreeland. "I never saw her in a blouse and skirt in the country," couturier Hubert de Givenchy would recall. "I remember her in a pearl grey suit with a white blouse and a good brooch on the lapel." Wallis' body matched her style. Schooled to Grandmama Warfield's directives, Wallis never lounged in a chair but, like Elinor Glyn, sat bolt upright at all times. Wallis had a peculiar way of sitting down whereby she crossed her legs, puppet-like, just before she sat.

Like Marlene Dietrich's, Wallis' wardrobe would eventually develop its own magic and mystique. Lady Abdy recalls a 1979 fashion show of dresses couture-made between 1900 and 1945. Among the Doucets and Worths was "a marvelous dress made for Mrs. Simpson by Mainbocher in 1935. When I saw it I really understood her legendary chic; it was so supremely elegant one longed to wear it and to be thin enough to do so." "She elevated sobriety into an art form" would be the women's magazine *Elle*'s epitaph for Wallis after her death. She stands as model and inspiration for all plain women who aspire to elegance and who are prepared to bring to style a lifetime's discipline and dedication.

Nineteen thirty-five was the most thrilling year of Wallis' life, her *annus mirabilis*. She found herself where she had always dreamed of being, at the very apex of society, hotly pursued by all the most prominent hostesses in London and by all the richest Americans who came over for the Season. Thanks to the prince, she had both money to dress divinely, and opportunity – Ascot, Goodwood, Henley – to parade her style and really be noticed. Everyone wanted to dance with the girl who danced with the Prince of Wales. Wallis' letters of 1935 to Aunt Bessie show her whirling across polished floors, clutching her jewels and her Slipper, aware that midnight and the pumpkin loomed, but determined, until that time, to relish and remember every miraculous moment of her new life.

When Wallis stepped into her supremely elegant and appropriate Mainbochers, she put on a brand new self-assurance. Her couture and jewels, like Eugénie's crinoline, proclaimed power and influence to the world. Bessie Wallis Warfield had captured the heart of the Golden Prince whose picture had once adorned her diary. She was no longer the poor relation in secondhand clothes and darned stockings, the little girl on the outside looking in. She felt, for the first time, a great rush of personal pride. One guest at an April 5 luncheon party, who had described Wallis in January as a "quiet, well-bred mouse of a woman with large, startled eyes and a huge mole," now finds she has "the air of a personage who walks into a room as though she almost expected to be curtseyed to."

This new self-confidence translated into her 1935 clothes choices. Wallis bought a black crêpe evening gown, severely plain in front, but with tiers of white-edged ruffles spreading in back with all the aplomb of a peacock's tail. Another black evening gown of classic cut had bands of bead embroidery in startling, neon hues. With her severe Mainbocher suits that summer Wallis sported a satin blouse made with alternating blocks of two vivid colors, as in a jockey's shirt. She also put on royal purple, appearing in a black and purple costume with a coronet of braided purple ribbons anchored to her smooth hair instead of a hat. (Her maid made these bands in various hues to match particular outfits.) With sporty day clothes, Wallis often wore a triangular brooch with sides almost three inches long, encrusted with stones in many colors. With daytime dresses, she aped the royal women by wearing spectacular jewels, including a necklace of baguette diamonds and large emeralds.

"I have some lovely jewelry to show when we meet," Wallis wrote in high excitement to Aunt Bessie on April 29, "with awfully nice stones." When writer Mrs. Belloc Lowndes observed to her female friends one day that she was surprised that a woman as well-dressed as Mrs. Simpson would wear such garish costume jewelry, the women all hooted with laughter, exclaiming that the jewels weren't fake but real, and that the prince had given Mrs. Simpson £50,000 worth of jewels at Christmas, followed by £60,000 worth a week later at New Year's. Across the channel in Paris, Monsieur Jacques Cartier noted that the Prince of Wales was fast becoming an expert gemologist. "He knows more about diamonds than I do!" exclaimed Cartier.

In June 1935, King George and Queen Mary celebrated twenty-five years on the throne, and the prince gave Wallis a Jubilee present – "lovely diamond clips." That month Wallis assured Aunt Bessie that she and Ernest weren't getting a divorce even though "I have got some pretty jewelry and it's clever of the U.S. papers to know who gave it to me." "I have been in a rush getting rags together for Ascot," wrote Wallis breathlessly. "I go on Monday for a whole week." She merely smiled indulgently when the prince, who'd gone off for two days to a naval review, sent her two cables and a letter which said: "A boy is holding a girl so very tight in his arms tonight. A girl knows that not anybody or anything can separate WE – not even the stars – and that WE belong to each other for ever. WE *love* [twice underlined] each other more than life so God bless WE. David." "You also can think how spoiled I am getting with so much luxury," Wallis told Aunt Bessie on August 17, reveling in a Riviera holiday with the prince. "We had a week in Paris," reported Wallis on October 14. "I went with Foxie Gwynne to Mainbocher and she got me everything at half price and the Prince brought them [the clothes] over in his airplane [thus avoiding duty]. . . . What a bump I'll get when a young beauty appears and plucks the prince from me. Anyway I am prepared," sighed Wallis in the same letter. While she was in Paris, Ernest was in New York, and, unbeknownst to her, was romancing her friend Mary Kirk Raffray.

On the first day of 1936, Wallis' *annus mirabilis* ended with a jolt. A note from the prince for the first time mentioned marriage. "Your lovely New Year message helped a boy a lot in his lonely drowsy and he was feeling sad. Oh! My Wallis I know we'll have *Viel Glück* to make us *one* this year. God bless WE." Wallis felt a cold little chill. She didn't want anything to change. She liked being wife to good old Ernest and mistress to the prince.

On January 19, 1936, King George V breathed his last and the Prince of Wales became King Edward VIII. With his succession to the throne, the whole refraction of Wallis' life shifted forever. While the dead king's body was being borne through the streets in procession to lie in state in Westminster Hall, an ominous and prophetic event occurred. The royal crown was resting proudly on the royal coffin. Atop the royal crown sat a Maltese Cross containing two hundred diamonds and one huge sapphire. Suddenly the cross toppled from the crown and clattered along the pavement. The Sergeant-Major of the Grenadier escort quickly retrieved it, but not before a pale, startled King Edward VIII had watched it fall.

"As I always wear so much black for economy I got into mourning with no expense," Wallis blithely informed Aunt Bessie. "I shall wear it until the end of March – that is what we are all doing." Her jewels looked particularly well on black, thought Wallis, smiling into her mirror. In early March, she was off to Paris with friend Foxy Gwynne to buy more Mainbochers. But in her luxury suite at the Hotel Meurice, which the king had commandeered for them at a ridiculously cheap rate, Wallis' anger surfaced. "I need not tell you the state of exhaustion, rage and despair," she wailed to Aunt Bessie as she felt herself paying the price for the king's obsession with her. "The little King insists I return and I might as well with the telephone [ringing] about 4 times daily – not much rest." The king ordered; Wallis had to obey. She was no longer in control of her life, and resentment mounted.

On March 27, her debt to the king increased a hundredfold in the form of a very expensive Van Cleef and Arpels ruby and diamond bracelet inscribed on the clasp with the words: "Hold tight." The accompanying note from David said: "A boy loves a girl more and more and more." There is something ludicrous, almost laughable, in the contrast between the jewels themselves, so fiery and sophisticated, and the donor's lisping, nursery words. There was also something jarring in the spectacle of a king demeaning himself to a commoner subject the way this one did. One day, while Wallis was weekending at Fort Belvedere, she tore her fingernail. The king instantly rushed off, and came back bearing two little emery boards, which he duly presented. When one of the footmen at the fort saw "His Majesty painting Mrs. Simpson's toenails," he gave notice at once. "My Sovereign, painting a woman's toenails! It was a bit much, Madam," he told his next employer.

When he wasn't painting toenails, the king was busy making his kingdom conform exactly to his liking. He sent his private plane to Paris to bring Wallis' friend Elsie de Wolfe Mendl to Fort Belvedere, having ordered her to redecorate it. When he'd first telephoned her, saying, "Elsie, this is David," she'd thought it was some joker and shot back, "And I'm the Virgin Mary!" On May 4, Wallis wrote to Aunt Bessie to say that she and Ernest were separating. "The K. on the other hand has another thing only on his mind. Whether I would allow such a drastic action depends on many things and events," Wallis added, without being more specific. "The financial side has been attended to for my lifetime," Wallis declared happily. The king had settled £300,000 on her, the equivalent of 1.5 million dollars, later scaled back to £100,000. At Buckingham Palace, widowed Queen Mary, who was packing up to move down the Mall to Marlborough House, got wind of her son's attachment to a vulgar American. "He gives Mrs. Simpson the most beautiful jewels," she worried aloud one day to her lady-in-waiting. "I am so afraid that he may ask me to receive her," the queen added, with "bright spots of crimson burning on her cheekbones."

For her forty-first birthday, on June 19th, the king gave Wallis a stunning Van Cleef and Arpels necklace with two ribbons of Burmese rubies and diamonds closely, inextricably, entwined. One guest at a party that summer noted that "Mrs. Simpson was literally smothered in rubies." She felt smothered, too. On the reverse side of the ribbon necklace, next to her skin, lay the words: "My Wallis from her David." The whole tone of their relationship chafed her very core. He was adoring, abject, pleading for approval and protection, forcing her, always, to play mother. "Sometimes I think you haven't grown up where love is concerned," Wallis told him.

She didn't really want to divorce Ernest, of whom she was genuinely fond. Ernest, at least, was a self-sufficient adult. To remain king's mistress, close to power with none of its responsibilities, was what Wallis wanted. Until that day at Burrough Court when, smug in her Molyneux tweed, she'd first met the king, Wallis had almost always got what she'd set her sights on. Now Ernest wanted a divorce so he could marry Mary Kirk Raffray, and the king wanted marriage, and talked of it constantly. "When we marry... when we marry," on and on, like jabs from a pin. The ruby necklace felt more and more like a halter, or a noose. Wallis could feel husband and lover both pushing her where she didn't want to go.

In July, Ernest moved out of Bryanston Court and in with Mary Raffray, and in August Wallis joined the king and a party of friends, including Diana and Duff Cooper, for a Mediterranean cruise on the yacht *Nahlin*. The British press was still ignoring the king's liaison, but the American press pursued them at every port, where the little king was usually clad only in shorts and sandals, with two crosses on a gold chain around his sunburnt neck – crosses which matched the ones on Mrs. Simpson's bracelet. Lady Diana Cooper recalls an evening aboard the yacht when Wallis wore "the most incredible dress" made of some "marvelous filigree material embroidered with dragonflies." At dinner, the king clumsily moved his chair onto Wallis' dress so that the fabric ripped. At once, His Majesty got down on all fours to extricate the dragonflies, and apologized most abjectly and profusely for having ruined her gossamer construct. Wallis glared at him. "Well, that's the most extraordinary performance I've ever seen," she exploded, launching into a long harangue on his inadequacies and former blunders. "Wallis is wearing very, very badly. Her commonness and Becky Sharpishness irritate," wrote Lady Diana to a friend. Her husband Duff decided that Wallis was "a nice woman and a sensible woman – but she is hard as nails and she doesn't love him." "The truth is, she's bored stiff by him," wrote the perceptive Lady Diana some days later. "Her picking on him and her coldness towards him, far from policy, are irritation and boredom." Wallis was beginning to resemble her gemstones, to have the same surface coldness and hardness.

After the cruise, the king flew back to England while Wallis went on to a luxe suite at Paris' Hotel Meurice. Waiting for her were fat letters from Aunt Bessie and other American friends full of clippings from U.S. papers which detailed her affair with the king. The press clippings jolted Wallis suddenly and forever out of her Wallis-in-Wonderland dream. Her shining glass coach, that day in the Hotel Meurice, turned into a pumpkin. She fell ill, took to her gilded bed, and on September 16 scribbled a letter to the king telling him she didn't want to marry. "I am sure you and I would create disaster together," she wrote, her pen scoring the paper deeply. "I want you to be happy. I feel sure that I can't make you so, and I honestly don't think you can me." The king telephoned her the instant he received this missive, and threatened to cut his throat if she went on in that vein. She must come with him for his annual visit to Balmoral. She *must* come. Wallis felt her own throat tighten, beneath its weight of icy diamonds.

On her return from Balmoral, the king installed Wallis at a "more suitable address" than Bryanston Court, in the Regent's Park area of London. No. 16 Cumberland Terrace was a plastered and pedimented yellow mansion built in the days when King George IV in corset, velvet coat and excessive ruffles, dallied with his commoner mistress, Mrs. Fitzherbert. On October 27, at Felixstowe, Ipswich, looking pale and harassed in navy blue felt hat, navy blue double-breasted coat and navy blue kid gloves, Wallis heard the *decree nisi* of her divorce from Ernest Simpson read in court, while in New York, William Randolph Hearst's *New York Journal* ran a banner headline: "KING WILL WED WALLY!" When her lawyer Theodore Goddard spoke of a possible marriage to the king, Wallis replied, with more optimism than truth, "What do you take me for? Do you think I would allow such a thing? I would never think of it. Some day I shall just fade out."

That night, the king gave Wallis an engagement ring bought from Cartier set with a huge 19.77 carat emerald once the property of a Mogul emperor. "WE are ours now. 27.x.36" was irrevocably incised on the platinum band. Wallis looked down at her fourth finger. The emerald's green light meant David was racing ahead full throttle on the road to marriage, refusing to marry some blue-blooded English girl who could produce an heir, while keeping her, his American mistress, in great luxury, on the sidelines. The prince and king had always had his own way; the rock of Wallis' will had met the king's green stone head on, and hers was crumbling.

That month, the Associated Press in America announced that the king had now given Mrs. Simpson a million dollars worth of jewels. (The British press was still mute.) At a November 17 dinner, Wallis was chatting to several guests when someone mentioned tiaras. Princess Olga of Serbia said that hers always gave her a headache. Wallis gave a forced little laugh, her chin held high. "Well, anyway, a tiara is one of the things I shall never have," she announced with bravado. Her jewels, however, continued to spark gossip. "The King is insane about Wallis, insane," wrote American diarist Chips Channon, who lived in London. "Someone at Cartier's foolishly told Bertie Abdy [Lord Abdy] that they are re-setting magnificent, indeed fabulous jewels for Wallis, and for what purpose if she is not to be Queen?" When Chips sat next to Wallis at a Belgrave Square dinner on November 25, he noted that she was "wearing new jewels. The King must give her new ones every day."

On the side which they showed to the world, the jewels spelled power, influence and bountiful riches; on the reverse side, closer to Wallis, were all those inscriptions which spelled obligation and coercion. The whole of London seemed to know of her affair with the king. Strangers began to yell at her and insult her in the streets. Some even stuck pins into her. Pins had always been little silver cohorts of her style, flashing in and out of fabric, pulling it to perfect fit in Mainbocher's salon. Now pins, in this growing nightmare, had turned into weapons. And her beautiful rubies had become a Scarlet Letter, branding her an adulteress.

From mouth to mouth all over England flew the quip: "There's absolutely nothing between the king and Mrs. Simpson – *nothing*, not even a sheet." When news of the king's plan to marry Wallis reached Marlene Dietrich, then in London filming *Knight Without Armour* for Alexander Korda, Marlene sprang into action. She considered Wallis Simpson "frightful, terrifyingly vulgar." "You can't have an American commoner on the throne of England! Impossible!" Marlene exclaimed to husband Rudi. "One of the things that attracted the king to this Simpson is that she is so flat. She looks like his favorite – young boys. But *why* does he want to *marry* her? He must be *very* stupid!" Marlene had never met the King but felt her glamour was powerful enough to convince him of the error of his ways. She put on her most seductive make-up, threw a fetching Aquascutum trenchcoat over a form-fitting dress, summoned her Cadillac and chauffeur, and sped off toward Surrey – only to be turned back firmly by police at the gates of Fort Belvedere. She argued long and eloquently and showed her legs, but they refused to let her pass.

On the morning of December 3, the British press finally broke their silence, and virtually every newspaper in the land carried the story of Mrs. Simpson and the king, with large accompanying photos of Wallis in a tailored suit; in an evening dress; in a teagown, clutching an Aberdeen Scottie; and in a modest dark dress with innocent white collar. Outside her Cumberland Terrace house, an angry mob gathered with signs: "Down with the Whore!" and "Out with the American Garbage!" Bricks and stones were hurled through the windows, but fortunately, Wallis wasn't there. She had already fled to Fort Belvedere to consult with David, shocked to see herself portrayed in the papers as an upstart, aggressive American who was stealing a king and precipitating a terrible constitutional crisis. If only they knew how really passive and helpless she was!

It was a foggy evening at Fort Belvedere, damp and cold, as Wallis and David walked up and down the terrace and he told her where things stood. He and Prime Minister Stanley Baldwin, consulting with his government, had reached a stalemate. The government would never accept Wallis as queen, nor allow their monarch, as king, to marry a twice-divorced commoner. "So now it comes to this," David told her, as the air grew colder and gray fog closed in around her. "Either I must give you up or abdicate. And I don't intend to give you up." Wallis twisted the huge Mogul emerald round and round her bony finger. He was worried for her safety. There had been threats on her life. Wallis had always been a physical coward and agreed with David that she must flee. She could take refuge with friends Kitty and Herman Rogers at their villa near Cannes. Her hands shook as David said that he would send her on the journey with three men to aid and protect her: his lord-in-waiting, Perry, Lord Brownlow, his chauffeur Ladbrook and a Scotland Yard detective.

"This was the last hour of what had been for me the enchanted years," writes Wallis in her autobiography. In the midst of her panic, nevertheless, she took time to increase her jewelry insurance, make a will and pack sixteen trunks and thirty-two suitcases, the contents of which were her shield and comfort against the scary future bearing down on her. (Another dozen suitcases would follow later.) Most of her jewelry, worth about $4 million in today's currency, went with her in the car, a worrisome situation which poor Brownlow only discovered when they were already en route.

In dark brown dress and sable coat, Wallis and her three escorts sped away, crossed the channel and stopped for the first night at a Rouen hotel. Wallis told Perry Brownlow that she was so nervous and frightened she wanted him to sleep in the bed next her own. Years later he confided to a friend that suddenly

Wallis had begun to cry. "Sounds came out of her that were absolutely without top, bottom, that were *primeval.*"

Hounded all the way by the European press, Wallis arrived at the Rogers' Cannes house, Villa Lou Viei, whose name means "the old one," feeling a hundred years old and weighing only 110 pounds. The villa was luxurious, a twelfth-century monastery which the Rogers had modernized, adding six bathrooms and bedrooms, badminton court, tea pavilion and Chinese lanterns in its pink stucco courtyard. Wallis could enjoy none of it. What upset her most was that she who had always valued social esteem before all else had not only lost it, but was now universally reviled. She couldn't bear to be hated as few women in history had been. "The world is against me and me alone," she wrote to the king. Could she ever recoup her losses and make the world envious again?

"A sense of helplessness of unimaginable scope" came over her. "I had the sensation I was sinking in quicksand," she says in her autobiography, as she shouted to David over bad phone connections that she wanted to disappear to South America, and David paid not the slightest attention. On December 10, hands twisting in her lap, Wallis sat in the living room of the Villa Lou Viei while David made his abdication speech on radio, saying he couldn't possibly rule without the woman he loved. King Edward VIII thereby went on record as the world's first drop-out, turning his back on duty and responsibility, embracing self-indulgence and making the first rip in the British monarchy's apparent inviolable respectability – a rent which, given the sexual antics reported in the press of such present-day royals as Prince Charles, may now be beyond hope of mending.

As David's silly speech went on, Wallis moaned and groaned, muttering "the stupid fool," and told herself that "nothing so incredible, so monstrous could possibly have happened." She had lost control of her life forever, and reacted by a further loss of control. She flew into a rage, a real tantrum, shouting and throwing things. She was caged now permanently. She could never, ever leave a man who had sacrificed his throne, his country, everything, for her or she would be called the world's most heartless, cruel woman. And the man she had to marry was stripped of crown and sceptre and orb, stripped of all the social refulgence of a court, stripped of everything which had drawn her to him. But the bitterest pill for Wallis to swallow was that ultimately it was *her* fault. If she hadn't had two divorces, and two living ex-husbands, she, Bessie Wallis Warfield, born out of wedlock to hand-me-down dresses, might have become Queen in all the sunburst glory of her supreme style, with the eyes of the whole world respectfully, admiringly, upon her. Instead of that, she was being shoved into some dark, dusty corner and forced to stay there.

The ex-king decamped to Schloss Enzesfeld, a castle in Vienna loaned to him by owner Eugene de Rothschild, and learned that henceforth he and his future wife would be Duke and Duchess of Windsor. But the bitterest pill for *him* to swallow was that Wallis would never be "Her Royal Highness." Brother Bertie, forced to reign, took this small revenge, urged to do so by wife Elizabeth and mother Mary, and the duke resented it until his dying day. On December 14, Wallis wrote to him from Cannes: "It is plain that York [the new King George VI] guided by her [his mother, Queen Mary], would not give us the extra chic of creating me HRH – the only thing to bring me back in the eyes of the world. It is despair for me to be so badly treated." Wallis' choice here of "chic," usually used in the context of clothing, clearly reveals her belief that social status is tied to dress. "Your Royal Highness" would have bestowed on her ermine robes and high tiara, unseen but not unheeded, exacting a million curtseys and obeisances down the years. Wallis would take her revenge on the female royals who were snubbing her by repeated criticisms of their wardrobes. When the press suggested that Queen Elizabeth, George VI's consort, should, for her public appearances, wear only British-made garments to promote their sale abroad, Wallis snapped that the best thing Queen Elizabeth could do for British fashion was to stay home.

We might pause here to speculate about whether or not Queen Wallis on the throne would have done for fashion what Princess Diana has done in our own day: added real elegance to a royal family long on tradition but short on style. Not since Queen Elizabeth I, who had a dress for every day of the year, has there been a British queen known for her chic rather than for her rubber boots and head scarves. But we might also note, with a glance at history, that no female sovereign who has been obsessed with clothes, whether it was Marie Antoinette, Empress Josephine or Empress Eugénie, has ever stayed on the throne. Perhaps there is something about style and monarchy that just doesn't mix.

For Christmas that year, while the British masses sang "Hark the herald angels sing / Mrs. Simpson pinched our King," the duke gave Wallis a brooch with two large feathers tenderly overlapping: one in passion-red rubies (his) and one in ice-cold diamonds (hers). "You have no idea how hard it is to live out a great romance," Wallis would later say grimly to a friend. From Villa Lou Viei, on January 3, she mailed a letter to David, who had settled down at Schloss Enzesfeld to watch Mickey Mouse movies, prop photos of Wallis all around his teddy bear and wait out his six months until the *decree absolu* of her divorce allowed them to marry. Wallis expressed to the duke her annoyance that their forthcoming marriage got no mention in the court circular, and that they would soon be joining "the countless titles that roam around Europe meaning nothing." It was some small consolation when, in February 1937 (and again in 1938), Wallis found herself still on the Best-Dressed List. At least her status as style icon hadn't been usurped.

On March 2, 1937, Wallis attended her first fashion show in over a year as Captain Molyneux showed his spring collection at Cannes. She chose thirteen costumes for her trousseau, plus a silver fox coat which had none of the generous superfluity of Marlene Dietrich's furs. Wallis' choice was as spare and restrained as the rest of her daytime wardrobe, made from only ten skins sewn lengthwise in ruler-straight lines.

Wallis gave a press conference on March 9, in the library of the Château de Candé, a mansion in the Loire valley near Tours lent to her, with staff, by its American millionaire owner Charles Bedaux for the Windsor wedding in June. Reporters noticed that the Mogul emerald had been replaced as engagement ring by a large sapphire. Was blue her favorite color? they asked. "Yes, and my favorite mood these bleak, rainy days," Wallis replied tartly. As she nervously answered their questions, she kept clasping and unclasping her big hands or raising one of them to smooth her already perfectly sleek hair.

She tried her best to channel her restless energy into the business of assembling her trousseau. She couldn't face the hostile world yet, so representatives of Mainbocher and Schiaparelli bustled up and down the stone steps of the Château de Candé with great armloads of clothes. Including the Molyneux selections already ordered, Wallis chose a total of sixty-six outfits, in accord with her basic rule: sobriety by day; a little fantasy by night. She made sure, once fittings had begun, that long sleeves were shorter than usual so that her spectacular bracelets would show, and that fabric was drawn as tight as a second skin over her narrow hips. Among those sixty-six outfits there was, significantly, only one negligée for intimate moments with the beloved: a Mainbocher design in blue and silver lamé cut very high in front and very low in back. Other Mainbocher choices included a black crêpe day dress patterned with small white turtles and a blue evening dress printed with yellow butterflies. Both turtles and butterflies were evenly spaced, repetitive, and stationary. A black dinner suit and a bias-cut white evening dress had collarless jackets aiming for drama, the former by means of baroque white scrolls and the latter all in sequins with diagonal stripes. The Mainbocher clothes were simple but stunning, guaranteed to turn all eyes when their wearer entered a room, even if she didn't rate a curtsey, yet classic enough to be worn today. American *Vogue* despatched Cecil Beaton to France to photograph Wallis in six Mainbocher costumes for a six-page spread. That issue sold out quickly as American women wove their dreams around their latest cult figure. "Women of the world were little absorbed in the conventional satin gowns of England's new queen," reported *Life* magazine on the eve of the wedding. "What Mrs. Wallis Warfield Simpson would wear, however, roused their avid curiosity."

Wallis chose seventeen Schiaparelli outfits for her trousseau; they formed her requiem to the light fantastic of her lost dreamworld. A blue-wool jacket had jet butterflies caught forever in its tweed; a floor-length coat in open-work navy horsehair lace resembled a large net for trapping the butterflies splayed on the blue crêpe dress beneath. A white evening gown had a huge red lobster frantically clawing its way down the front towards the ground, and freedom.

"Please take care of your precious self for your David, like he is doing for a girl, because it's all he's got left in the world and it's all that he wants," the prospective bridegroom lisped from Vienna, while in London a new quatrain went the rounds:

Gone all the glory, all romance.
"Honi soit" Queen Wally pants.
No golden crown will grace her hair,
Her throne is but a Windsor chair.

On the day before the duke was to arrive at Candé for the wedding, Wallis' dog Slipper was fatally bitten by a poisonous snake hiding in the underbrush. Wallis felt another piece of the Cinderella myth die with him. Next day, all smiles, the besotted duke arrived bearing a multi-colored Austrian peasant costume called a dirndl – not at all Wallis' kind of thing – and a bunch of wilting edelweiss, a mountain flower which he'd picked himself.

On the evening when Cecil Beaton arrived to take the wedding photos, everyone dined by candlelight in a vaulted basement room, with Wallis a literal scarlet woman in a narrow, slinky, ruby-red dress. She picked at the food prepared by Candé's chef, who had formerly worked in Spain for the Duke of Alba, grand-nephew of Empress Eugénie.

On May 11, the duke formally announced to the press his engagement to Wallis, and on May 18 gave her a Van Cleef and Arpels bracelet which she would wear on her wedding day: a wide band of diamonds finished with a buckle of sapphires and baguette diamonds, a bracelet large enough to impress at a hundred feet. "For our Contract. 18.v.37" was the trite message on its clasp.

Wallis' anxiety increased as the big day neared. "From the feminine side, it will be difficult about hair, face, nails, etc." she fussed in a letter, but got around the handicap of being buried deep in the country by summoning a manicurist and Polish-born Antoine from Paris, the latter a hairdresser who coiffed all the best heads, including Elsie Mendl's, and who had been known to dye his own hair lavender. The lingerie Wallis had ordered custom-made duly arrived, in rose pink and almost every shade of blue.

Boxes of pale peach table linens and sheets were delivered, all of them prominently displaying a ducal coat of arms.

On the day before the wedding, Wednesday, June 2, Wallis supervised the preparations, dressed in an optimistic shade of yellow. Cecil Beaton, who had arrived to take the wedding photos, thought she looked far from her best, her face broken out in spots and her general demeanor "especially unlovable, hard, calculating and showing anxiety but no feeling of emotion," while the duke looked positively radiant, "happy as a schoolboy." What on earth, wondered Wallis, could pinch-hit as altar? She decided to use a fake Renaissance chest carved with a row of fat caryatids. "We must have something to cover up that row of extra women!" Wallis drawled with a forced little laugh. From the bottom of one of the many trunks already packed, Wallis got her maid to extricate an embroidered tea cloth to masquerade as altar cloth. The organist arrived that afternoon, borrowed from Notre Dame Cathedral in Paris. When told he had to play "O Perfect Love" he looked blank until someone hummed it for him. A crack-pot clergyman who'd volunteered his services arrived from England, the Rev. Mr. Jardine. (Later, he would head for Los Angeles to exploit his fifteen minutes of fame and get himself a Hollywood agent.)

Cecil sat the duke and duchess-to-be on a pouf and began to click his camera. For the first pictures, Wallis wore a black dress and huge diamond clips. According to Cecil, she "twisted and twirled her rugged hands," while her eyes looked "slightly frog-like, also wistful." Then she changed into her wedding outfit. "Oh, so this is the great dress? Well, it's lovely, very pretty," said the duke. The photo session continued, slowly and stiffly.

Next day, without a single member of the royal family present, and with only Aunt Bessie on the bride's side, Wallis married the duke. Her wedding gown was designed by Mainbocher, who had sent a fitter to Candé on six successive Saturdays and come himself for the final one. The bias-cut silk crêpe dress looked, appropriately enough, like something a nanny might choose: high-necked, plain and neat, its crêpe shirred into an unfortunate heart-shaped seam under the bust which made the bride look more flat-chested than ever. It is a measure of Wallis' general distress and unhappiness that the cut of her wedding dress was one of the few mistakes in clothes she had made since finding her own style in 1934. However, its sapphire-blue color did become wildly popular as "Wallis blue." The wedding gown would end its days in the Costume Institute of New York's Metropolitan Museum, showing its true blue only at the seams while the rest faded to a dull gray. When pictures of the dress appeared in papers around the globe, it became the most copied garment of 1937.

Women hurried into Wallis blue hoping a little romance would rub off on their own mundane lives. Most women of the western world in the late thirties, still homebound by domesticity and child-rearing, still recovering from the Depression, ignored the stains of divorce and adultery adhering to Wallis and saw only the myth, not the reality, of this romance with the plot of a radio soap opera or a Joan Crawford movie. A plain little girl from Baltimore had snared the Golden Prince who, having fox-trotted his way into every female heart, had thrown away a throne and laid a shining pile of gems at his beloved's feet. With her marriage to the duke, Wallis' public image, if not yet in Britain, then certainly in more sentimental America, began to change from wicked witch to heroine-in-halo. Wallis' marriage also gave mature women everywhere new hope. A spate of articles appeared in European and North American women's magazines on the theme of the woman over forty who could still inspire romantic love.

With her blue wedding gown, Wallis wore a matching blue straw halo hat by Réboux, and plenty of jewels, including an Art Deco double clip of sapphires and diamonds at her throat, her immense buckle bracelet on her right wrist, and on her left, a diamond chain with dangling crosses in diverse precious stones – "crosses I've had to bear," Wallis liked to say as the years ground on. Her "something old" was a piece of antique lace stitched to her lingerie; "something new" was a gold coin showing King Edward VIII's profile, minted for the coronation which never took place. Wallis put the coin into one pale blue suede shoe, right under her heel, where she could press down on it, hard, with every step.

Soon after coffee and brandy at the wedding luncheon party, bride and groom, accompanied by 226 pieces of luggage, including 183 steamer trunks, set off on their honeymoon. (When an old beau from Wallis' youth heard about this baggage, he refused to believe it, remembering how, going off for a visit to friends, Wallis "just threw a nightie and a toothbrush into a paper bag, and away we went!")

As she left on her honeymoon with all that luggage, Wallis was entering the second stage of her life, wherein she would take her retribution and revenge. She would never be queen or mistress to a king, but she could live out her life as if she were, robing herself in all possible pomp and privilege. She would try to make, as she told one biographer, "the nearest equivalent of a kingly life that I could produce without a kingdom," suggesting that she did it all for the duke. But in fact she did it for herself. From now on there would be mountains of luggage; ranks of liveried servants; ducal crests on everything that would take one; and, most important of all, jewels fit for a queen. The Duchess of Windsor's plain and sober day clothes aligned her with her plain and sober youth. The jewels displayed on them blazed forth her illustrious present and future. It was a dramatic dichotomy both original and effective, guaranteed to keep all eyes upon her.

From now on, she changed her clothes and her jewelry three times a day. "I have taken you into a void," the ex-king apologized.

She filled that void with style. And, for forcing her to his sovereign will, she made the ex-king pay and pay and pay, in material ways, and other less obvious ones. She felt she deserved high recompense for taking on the lifetime task of replacing a throne and empire for a man who had an attention span of about two and a half minutes. Her method was to recruit the duke as minion for her own life-in-style. He once told a dinner partner that his main activity for that particular day had been to help the duchess choose a hat. On another occasion, the duke staggered into their suite at the Hotel Meurice under a weight of dress boxes which he'd picked up from various couturiers. Wallis leaned close to a visiting friend and muttered: "No one will ever know how hard I work to try to make the little man feel busy!"

Perhaps Wallis' greatest attraction for her husband was that she'd given him the opportunity to weasel out of being king, a job he didn't really want anyway. His greatest attraction for her, however, was simply that he *was* a king. Whenever he started sentences with the clause "When I was King..." she cut him off at once, replying, "Well, you're not King now!" The duchess never relaxed her stranglehold on the duke's psyche. She became his permanent Eton collar. Comments like "Are you out of your mind?...Don't be silly!...I'm not castle-bred like you!" dug into his ego with a sharp, cutting edge.

In the spring of 1938, the Windsors took a ten-year lease on the Château la Cröe on the French riviera at Antibes. It was an oversized villa on twelve acres of gardens, with tennis court, swimming pool, greenhouses, servants' quarters. Wallis turned one room of her suite into a beauty salon; started a collection of *trompe l'oeil* china vegetables displayed on a Chinese escritoire; and had a *trompe l'oeil* design of lacy lingerie, stockings and jewelry painted on a chest of drawers in her bedroom, as if they were spilling out from within. The duchess lived, in fact, a very *trompe l'oeil* life.

The duke, for his part, organized a filing system at La Cröe for the many sets of fine china shelved in the pantry exactly as if he were organizing a government department. He also liked to lurk outside a powder-room door in which the roll of toilet paper, when pulled, played "God Save the King." "Stand to attention!" His Royal Highness would bellow gleefully to whomever was inside.

For their first wedding anniversary on June 3, 1938, Wallis received from the duke a hinged bangle set with a pair of huge Burmese rubies and many diamonds. "For our first anniversary of June third" predictably proclaimed the bangle. That year, the duke, a Nazi sympathizer, took Wallis on a tour of Germany where Hitler raved to Von Ribbentrop about the duchess' "impeccable grooming and couture" and Wallis decreed Goebbels' wife "the prettiest woman I saw, a blonde, with enormous blue eyes and a flair for clothes." She and her gnome-sized husband, decided Wallis, looked like Beauty and the Beast.

The Windsors found a suitably regal mansion in Paris on the Boulevard Souchet in 1939, and Wallis swept into one party at the American Embassy in royal purple, a taffeta *robe de style*, with her hair cleanly rolled upward on either side of her habitual center part. She looked, as one guest recalls, like Mary, Queen of Scots, and was "most formal, stiffened by dignity."

Once World War II began, the British government wisely sent the pro-Nazi duke well away from the action by appointing him governor of the Bahamas. The Windsors arrived in Nassau in August 1940, with Wallis looking nautical in navy-blue silk coat, in spite of the heat, and white hat trimmed in mother-of-pearl. Accompanying the Windsors were three truckloads of baggage, a sewing machine, and two cases each of champagne, gin and port.

Wallis hated her exile on the humdrum island where there was no one to impress and no place to shop. "I hate this place more each day," she told Aunt Bessie, and wailed that she was "a prisoner of war or worse." "It's not an appointment," she quipped to a friend, "it's a disappointment." "Believe me, I would much rather have been the mistress of the King of England," she told a reporter, "than the wife of the Governor of the Bahamas!" The natives composed a new calypso song: "Mrs. Simpson, she no fool / She make her aim the big Crown Jewel." Government House had no air-conditioning, was impossibly shabby and riddled with termites. In the extreme heat, Wallis had to ice her face before applying her make-up, and went down to a gaunt ninety-five pounds, but she set to work to redecorate, at vast expense, her temporary home. The walls of the rooms she would use most were first painted dead white. Then she appeared with a box of her face powder and a puff, and proceeded to pat some powder onto the wall. That, she told the pop-eyed workmen, was to be the color; not Wallis blue but Wallis skintone everywhere. Over the fireplace in the drawing room Wallis hung the 1939 portrait of her painted by Gerald Brocklehurst, in which she wore one spectacular flower brooch on a Mainbocher Wallis-blue silk tussore blouse with pleated chiffon skirt. As Wallis dabbed her high forehead with a lace-edged hankie, she eyed the portrait ruefully. Brocklehurst had chosen to change the shade of blue from bright sapphire to a dull, slate blue.

Once the decorating was done, Wallis turned her attention to her wardrobe. She persuaded Mainbocher to send her a seamstress, Miss Genevieve, while New York's Hattie Carnegie obligingly despatched Miss Rose. Having arrived by plane, the two women set to work in an upper room of Government House making hot-weather dresses in silk shantung and voile; suits in cotton and piqué; evening gowns in organdy and chiffon. Hairdresser Antoine despatched his chief assistant from New York to shampoo Wallis' hair in egg and rum, while Wallis, for her part, despatched her dresses back to New York for dry-cleaning, marking the package clearly but improperly: "Her Royal Highness' Clothes to be Cleaned."

As first installment of payment for her Bahamas exile, Wallis got the duke to commission artist Jeanne Toussaint at Cartier to design a mammoth diamond flamingo clip. The bird stood on one stick-like leg, and, in spite of its lush tail of emeralds, rubies and sapphires, looked precariously posed and quite unnatural.

New gems appeared regularly to fire up Wallis' stalled life. The 1941 New Year's offering from the duke was pleasing in its symmetry, less so in its economy: a matching pair, one for each wrist grown thin, of gilt and silver bangles from Cartier. "For a happier New Year. Nassau. 1.1.41. WE," said the bracelets, with more hope than conviction. There were occasional trips to New York, but not nearly enough of them, so that Wallis could shop frantically for clothes. On a 1944 visit, she ordered fourteen outfits from Mainbocher, twelve from Hattie Carnegie, six from White Russian designer Valentina and five from Saks Fifth Avenue, along with twenty-five hats.

In the fall of 1945, Wallis was vastly relieved to return to France, to vacate the Boulevard Souchet mansion in favor of an even grander one in the Bois de Boulogne which the French government obligingly leased to the Windsors for a peppercorn rent. It may well have been the duchess' chic which made the French, whose economy depended on the couture trade, so eager to keep the Windsors permanently resident in France. "The two poor little old things were most pathetic," decided Lady Diana Cooper when she saw them in September, both "Dachau-thin." Novelist Nancy Mitford thought Wallis resembled "the skeleton of some tiny bird, hopping in her hobble skirt." The Windsors soon got back on the social carousel. In the public's view, Prince Charming still had all the charm in the world, but in Wallis' view, he'd long since turned into a jumpy little frog. He would remain forever loyal and adoring, and in time she would come, if grudgingly, to value his devotion and his habitual good nature.

The Windsors made a visit to England in October 1946, their first appearance on British soil in eight years. Ignored by all the royals, they went to stay with Lord and Lady Dudley at Ednam Lodge, their home near forlorn, abandoned Fort Belvedere. Wallis, as always, was traveling with an enormous case of jewels, including many loose stones and a collection of Fabergé gold boxes. The fact that all this loot accompanied her even on short trips shows how abnormal her attachment to her jewels was becoming. Before going up to London for an overnight stay at Claridge's, having refused to put the jewel case in Lord Dudley's safe, Wallis left it in her bedroom. That night, thieves broke into the house and made off with all the jewels except a few earrings – none matching – scattered, in their haste to flee, across the lawn. Wallis flew into a rage, accused all the Dudley servants, summoned the police. The jewels, insured for $1.6 million, were never recovered. For Wallis, their loss was like a death in the family. The insurance underwriters paid for copies to be made and reinsured the new collection for $3.2 million, with the proviso that half of it had to stay at all times in bank vaults.

After the robbery, Wallis' unfocused anxiety increased; she developed various physical ailments including ongoing gynecological problems. The duke did what he could to soothe. In the fall of 1947, he gave her a bib necklace in lattice design set with large square-cut purple amethysts on a ground of little turquoises. The stones had belonged to David's grandmother Queen Alexandra, so now Wallis could play queen her way, with a bold and modern color combination. It annoyed Wallis mightily that King George

VI and Queen Elizabeth refused to invite the Windsors to their daughter Elizabeth's November 20 wedding to the Duke of Edinburgh. Since the guest list included 2200 people, to exclude the bride's uncle could only be interpreted as a gross snub to his wife. The Windsors wisely decamped to America, where Wallis laughed loudly with a Baltimore friend over magazine photos of the dowdy royals dragging their hems at Ascot.

The duke and duchess were permanently adrift – part of that wealthy, vulgar café society definitely not from the top drawer – moving around the globe with no other incentive than habit and the seasons: Paris in spring, southern France in summer, New York in autumn, Palm Beach, Florida, in January and February... predictable and uniform as little crosses on a chain. As years passed, Wallis' eyes grew as globular as her cabochon sapphires; her thin wrists and ankles took on the translucence of white jade, while the duke, according to Cecil Beaton, looked more and more like a "mad terrier," or like P.G. Wodehouse's vapid Bertie Wooster, nattily if disjointedly dressed in assorted plaids, stripes and paisleys.

For their annual migration to the United States, 118 Louis Vuitton trunks went with them, each one proclaiming loud and clear in gold letters "DUKE OF WINDSOR." During the crossing by luxury liner, never by plane, Wallis stayed put in her cabin, never venturing on deck for fear winds might ruin her hair. Having docked in New York, the Windsors moved into Apartment 28A in the Waldorf Towers, a suite which took up an entire floor. At the end of their first stay there, Wallis assembled the detectives hired to guard the suite and, with *noblesse oblige* bounty, presented each of them with a postcard which advertised the Waldorf on its front and showed on its blank side the autographs of the duke and duchess.

In Palm Beach, the Windsors usually saved money by staying with friends. Planners of winter charity balls soon learned that if they wished the duchess to grace their event with her presence, a piece of jewelry from Van Cleef or Cartier should be sent to her first. The ex-king had abdicated with about three million pounds in his pockets, then worth fifteen million dollars. Nevertheless, the Windsors got very good over the years at selling their pseudo-royal status for whatever it would fetch on the open market, in the form of special rates for clothes, accommodation and travel costs. The duke never, ever picked up the bill in a restaurant, even when he'd invited the guests.

At Palm Beach parties, the Windsors insisted on royal protocol whereby no one could leave before they did. Since they liked to drink and dance until four a.m., Palm Beach social leaders looked more puffy-eyed than usual when the Windsors were in town.

Wallis tried to inject passion into her life in several ways. The first one was to start her collection of great cat jewels. Cartier's Jeanne Toussaint found inspiration for these when she visited the Mayfair mansion of the mad Marchesa Luisa Casati. The extravagantly dressed carrot-haired marchesa, often high on drugs, went to parties with a puma on a leash and drove around London in an ink-blue Rolls Royce naked under her sable coat. In the hall of her house was a stuffed panther with mechanical works inside him which made him spring forward, claws out, eyes menacing and fiery with electricity. "To discourage thieves," explained the marchesa. It seems fitting that the cat jewels, which would be defence mechanisms for Wallis, owed their existence to a larger means of defence for another woman of style.

Wallis bought her first cat in 1948: a panther in gold and enamel, guarding, in fierce crouch, a single cabochon emerald of 116 carats. The next cat followed in 1949: a panther in diamonds with 106 sapphire spots, rampant and triumphant on a cabochon sapphire of 152.35 carats. (At the time of Sotheby's Geneva auction in 1987, Princess Diana, another royal wife who consoled herself through style, pleaded with Prince Charles to buy her a panther; he coldly refused.)

In 1950 Wallis made a grab for passion in a different direction. During her Palm Beach visit, she met Jimmy Donahue, grandson of American billionaire Frank Woolworth. Jimmy was handsome, debonair, and an exhibitionist. At age sixteen, he'd appeared in a Paris night club naked except for a red-and-white checked table napkin tied around his groin. Later in their friendship, Wallis arrived for dinner at his New York apartment to find both butler and footman in the nude. Jimmy also fancied a bit of rough sex. Gossip circulated about how he'd inadvertently sliced the penis from a young lover and forced another to eat an excrement sandwich. His appeal for both Wallis and the duke – for the next few years they formed a tight little threesome – was that he was a real charmer, amusing, original, full of fun and racy stories and cute pranks. He relieved their boredom and made them feel young. How the threesome worked sexually, if in fact it did, is uncertain; was it Jimmy and the duke, Jimmy and Wallis, or three-in-a-bed? Who was jealous of whom? Beginning in June 1950, and continuing until July 1953, which was roughly when Jimmy disappeared from the scene, Cartier's records show that the cat jewels bought in those years were purchased by the duchess and charged to her account with no mention of the duke. Did the duchess resent the duke's love for Jimmy and console herself in jungle cats? Did the duke resent the duchess' love for Jimmy and refuse to pay for them? One wonders.

Lady Diana Cooper recalls an evening when they were all together for dinner out in Paris. Wallis was carrying a large three-plume ostrich feather fan and when some champagne spilled, used her feathers to mop it up. Later they all trooped to a night-club where Jimmy bought her a big bunch of roses. She asked a waiter for a vase; into this Wallis shoved the soggy fan and the roses, exclaiming, "Look, everybody! The Prince of Wales' plumes and Jimmy Donahue's roses!" The duke's face crumpled up and he started to cry. "The whole evening," concludes Lady Diana, "was ghastly."

Wallis had always been a kept woman with no financial independence and consequently no real power of her own. She therefore made her bid for power in the only language she had mastered: that of her personal style. In her clothes and her jewels, she had choice and free will; through them, she could dominate and impress. In 1952 she felt the need for a panther bracelet so highly articulated that every part of its body, composed of diamonds and black-onyx spots, moved when she flicked her wrist. Its fierce head and emerald eyes glared at the world, ready to take on all comers.

Jimmy Donahue disappeared from the Windsors' lives on the night when, dining with them at a German spa, he began an angry, heated quarrel. Jimmy kicked the duchess so hard in the shins that she bled. She screamed in pain; the duke led her tenderly to a sofa; Jimmy made a hasty and permanent exit.

King George VI, who had borne the kingly burdens thrust upon him manfully for fifteen years, in spite of his shyness and stammer and feelings of inadequacy, died of throat cancer in 1952, whereupon novelist Evelyn Waugh wrote to friend Nancy Mitford: "One interesting point stands out. The king died at the moment when Queen Elizabeth first put on a pair of slacks – within a matter of minutes anyway." What Waugh probably didn't know was that Marlene Dietrich was ultimately responsible for those slacks. Waugh was writing tongue-in-cheek, but one feels that Marlene and Wallis, given the importance they attached to apparel, would have agreed that a piece of clothing *could* help do in a parent. After all, Wallis' own mother had succumbed after seeing her in a brown dress.

Queen Elizabeth II was crowned in Westminster Abbey in June 1953, with the Windsors, snubbed again, not there to see it. They ushered in the 1954 New Year at New York's El Morocco, with the duchess in a watermelon pink Dior creation and quite as many jewels as the young Queen Elizabeth could muster. At midnight, as another vacuous year began, the Windsors put on paper crowns and posed for photographers side by side on a zebra striped "throne." "Coronation's over!" quipped Wallis, once the cameras stopped flashing, and crumpled up her crown in one tense, tight fist.

By the mid-fifties, Wallis was entering the third and final chapter of her story, in which style moved from manner to matter, from method to substance. Style as a means of social climbing or of retaliation for a thwarted existence changed to style as main content and *raison d'être*. Style moved into the driver's seat. Elinor Glyn and Marlene Dietrich used clothes to advance their careers; the Duchess of Windsor made a career of clothes, and used style not as aid to a profession but as the very profession itself.

Her appearance consumed many hours of her time. Wallis had her hair done three times a day, three complete hairdressings, not just comb-outs, by hairdresser or maid. Each of them took at least half an hour. She also had a daily manicure, done by a professional, and kept thin on a strict diet, starving herself if she gained 100 grams. As her face began to sag, she had it surgically lifted three times. The horizontal wrinkle in her forehead began to look, as one irreverent acquaintance noted, "as though she'd been hit by an axe." That wrinkle, and all others, according to the duchess' wishes, were always air-brushed from photos so that, in reverse mode to Oscar Wilde's Dorian Gray, the duchess aged but her likeness didn't.

"I adore to shop," she liked to say. "All my friends know I'd rather shop than eat." Twice a year, she ordered a total of 100 couture outfits from whichever Paris house she favored at the moment and, unlike Marlene Dietrich, sold her old models to a used-clothing shop in Paris. Wallis would fill up her working day by booking five or six fittings with couturiers. When she went to Dior, a staff member recalls, she would bring a basket of tiny chicken sandwiches and a coronet-embroidered napkin, and eat sitting straight-backed on a spindly gilded chair. Like any busy executive, she had to grab lunch quickly on the job.

Changing couturiers introduced novelty into Wallis' life. After Mainbocher, she got her clothes from Balenciaga, but complained that he "is such a trying man. He makes one pull everything on over the head. It is ruinous to the hair." To his credit, he invented a brand new shade of blue for her, a purple-blue deeper in tone than Wallis blue. When Balenciaga retired, Wallis moved on to his former apprentice, Hubert de Givenchy. Following Balenciaga's lead, Givenchy made a Wallis-blue linen dress-cover with "S.A.R. [*Son Altesse Royale*] La Duchesse de Windsor" embroidered in white at its top. Under this cover, a dress could make its way discreetly from couture salon to Windsor mansion, without society's inquisitive eyes able to see it. "They all wanted to know what she was ordering," Givenchy explained. "Even women who didn't have her figure or style wanted to dress as she did." When she tired of Givenchy in the late fifties, Wallis switched to Dior. "What she always wanted were little suits, with short jackets cut very close to the body," says Marc Bohan of Christian Dior. "She would pull a tweed tight to her shoulders and say 'make it smaller here.'" Sometimes the duchess grew bold and ordered a button changed, or a color. Dior once complimented her on a linen dress she was wearing: "I don't often admire clothes from other ateliers, but this is something special." Wallis corrected him. "It's not from another atelier. It's from yours – only you made it for me in velvet, and I had it copied in linen."

She spent at least $100,000 a year on clothes, not including furs. Couture houses gave her a discount of at least twenty-five per cent, for she had only to appear in one of their gowns to bring five hundred other women to their door, wanting something similar. One wonders if Wallis kept up her indefatigable social round primarily to make sure her clothes were seen. Were they now directing her life, as well as forming its main business? "When people looked at me and stared, I rather liked it," Wallis admitted to a biographer, "and it pleased the Duke." She was, after all, his vindication and his pride.

She and the duke replaced La Cröe as country dwelling with The Mill, at Orsay in the Chevreuse valley, a stone building with lichened roof and large garden where the duke could dig and potter about and keep out of Wallis' way. At their new Paris abode at 4 Route de Champ d'Entraînment, near Neuilly, which they acquired in 1953 from the city of Paris for an annual rent of fifty dollars, the duchess had a large dressing room where handbags filled six long shelves. Each bore as gold clasp the crest she'd devised, an intertwined WW below a royal crown. Her neatly shelved shoes were all handmade in Paris by Roger Vivier, one pair for each outfit, sometimes in matching fabric. Her 120 pairs of flesh-colored, sheer stockings told their own story of a little girl whose mother couldn't afford even one new pair and so darned her daughter's old ones. In Wallis' extensive closets, dresses were arranged according to color, length and season, with notes attached as to where they had last been worn, and more notes indicating which hats, belts and handbags should be worn with them. In her drawers, gloves and lingerie were also arranged by color. Hats stood in rows, waiting, mute but inviting, on wooden stands. No matter how late the party, or how tired she was, Wallis went through the same ritual of removing her dress, placing it carefully on its padded hanger, then suspending it from a pale bentwood coatrack in her dressing room for one of her two personal maids to file away next morning. At her dressing table, Wallis carefully removed the false eyelashes applied earlier by a professional, and every vestige of make-up. Then Wallis put on the silk nightie which a maid had spread out on her pale blue moiré silk bedspread. On the bodice of all Wallis' nightgowns, woven into the very center of their gossamer lace trim, was the same crest which topped her handbags. In dreams, at least, she could be close to a royal crown.

Her wardrobe, however, took second place in her affections to the jewelry. "Wallis had a love affair with her jewels," recalls Laura, Duchess of Marlborough. "She would play with them like a child with toys, laying them out on a table and touching them." She developed a real crush on canary-yellow diamonds, acquiring huge clips and a 49-carat ring. One of Wallis' most admirable traits was her ability to make, and keep, women friends, to whom she was loyal and sympathetic. But she broke off her friendship with Jayne Wrightsman when Jayne outbid her for an especially fine yellow diamond. Wallis had her jewels constantly redesigned and reset, another way of injecting novelty into her life. In 1958, she had the Mogul emerald of her platinum engagement ring remounted by Cartier in yellow gold and a circle of significant diamonds. Wallis never was sentimental about keepsakes.

She found a new distraction in 1960 when the American dress-pattern firm McCalls persuaded her to lend her name and skills to the "Duchess of Windsor" line of dress patterns. She told Fleur Cowles proudly in 1966, when interviewed for *Harper's Bazaar*, that she'd "designed" three hundred patterns to date, and that she loved doing it. "I usually take my ideas from the clothes I wish I *could* wear – so as not to put every woman in round high necks and the severe lines I insist upon for myself," Wallis explained. She also wrote, beginning in the February 1961 issue of *McCall's* magazine, a column called "All Things Considered," which she continued for the next twelve issues.

In 1964, Prince Charming went to her latest favorite jeweller, New York's David Webb, and bought her yet another bracelet. It was in the highly appropriate form of green enamel frog with little red eyes and a plethora of spots.

By the late 1960s, the Windsors' fake little kingdom had a staff of thirty servants, including two chauffeurs, seven kitchen staff and seven liveried footmen. All of them addressed the duchess as "Your Royal Highness," from whom edicts and orders came thick and fast. The maids were ordered to unroll the toilet paper in the bathrooms, tear it into separate squares, and leave them in a tidy pile ready for royal fingers. The kitchen boy was ordered to cut and trim each lettuce leaf, tomato, chop, piece of fish, whatever, to uniform size and shape before it landed on a plate. He also had to remove all tomato seeds; the duchess had a phobia about them, and would dismiss an entire dish if she saw but one. The laundry maid was ordered to wash by hand the crested tablecloths, each embroidered in a design to match one particular set of porcelain. The duchess demanded that her money be crisp, in bills either fresh from the bank or ironed by a servant. The chef was ordered to bake fresh dog cookies every day for the Windsor pugs, on whom their owners doted. The pugs ate their delicious cuisine from sterling silver dishes, and were taken for walks on short, taut, gold-trimmed leashes. The duchess loathed disorder. A journalist once overheard her berating the duke for littering the dining table with a heap of papers. "I've got twenty guests dining here in two hours! Why didn't you make this mess somewhere else?" she asked angrily. The duke replied: "Darling, are you going to send me to bed in tears again tonight?" If the duchess tried to relax in her drawing room, she found she couldn't stop moving. Perhaps that is how she kept her slim figure. She would jump up to pouf a cushion, remove an invisible speck, or center a vase of flowers on a table.

When in Paris, the duchess subscribed to the Celebrity Service publication and scanned it to see who was in town and could be invited to dine. The duchess' dinner parties were as formal as a minuet. When the last guest had arrived and the Duchess had been so informed, she appeared at the top of her curving staircase and regally descended, past banked lilies and orchids. She kept a tiny gold pencil and pad beside her place at table, so that she could note: "Lettuce leaf not uniform," or "not enough spice in savoury." The dinner table was always so covered with things – little gold boxes, bon-bon dishes, silver-gilt candelabra, flowers sprayed with Diorissimo – that one could hardly see the tablecloth. "After a while I *longed* to escape," remembers Laura, Duchess of Marlborough. "I didn't want any more flowers and perfume and jewels. It was too claustrophobic." But it was Wallis Windsor's world, the one she had so carefully and painstakingly constructed, and it was the only one she had. She was held fast in its platinum claws.

When Cecil Beaton visited the Windsors in September 1970, he noted that the seventy-five-year-old duchess "seems to have suddenly aged, to have become a little old woman. Her figure and legs are as trim as ever, and she is as energetic as she always was, putting servants and things to rights," but she had "the sad, haunted eyes of the ill." It was a measure of her depressed mood that she said to Cecil: "Don't look at me. I haven't even had the *coiffeur* come out to do my hair."

The Windsors hardly ever went out now in the evenings. Instead they sat in their Paris house, usually in the second-floor apricot sitting room between their bedrooms, where leopard-print cushions provided the only wild touch. The duke watched football on television; the duchess leafed through auction-sale catalogues. As the level of whisky in their Baccarat glasses went down, the volume of their bickering went up. "They had nothing and no one. They were just two lonely old people," according to their butler, Sydney Johnson.

The duke died from the same cause as his brother King George, throat cancer, on May 28, 1972, at their Paris home, cradled in Wallis' thin arms. He had always smoked a tin of pipe tobacco a day, a messy habit which Wallis deplored. (Ernest Simpson had also died of throat cancer, in November 1958.) Wallis and David had been married for almost thirty-five years; he had fetched and carried for her; placed a flower, always, on her bed-time pillow; moved dinner-table candles which obscured his view of her. His last word to her before he expired was "Darling."

Wallis at once summoned Givenchy. "It was the only time I ever saw her in bedroom slippers, with no make-up and her hair in a mess," the couturier recalls. (When the duke had begged her to join him and a male friend to watch the televised landing of men on the moon, Wallis had missed that historic event because she simply couldn't appear downstairs without make-up.) "You must make me a black dress and coat for the Duke's funeral," quavered Wallis to Givenchy, her face pale and drawn. "Can you do it?" Givenchy assured her that he could, and worked on it, with his staff, all night.

In elegant black silk dress and coat, the duchess followed the duke's body to England, and, at long last – but too late, too late – Wallis ensconced herself among the royals in Buckingham

Palace. As soon as she'd settled in, she sent word to Queen Elizabeth that hairdresser Alexandre was there to do her hair, and at Her Majesty's disposal, but her offer was spurned. For the duke's funeral in St. George's chapel, Windsor, and his burial in the royal plot at Frogmore, Wallis restricted jewelry to earrings, stark in black and white, and one bracelet. In one ear, she wore a huge black pearl set in diamonds; in the other, a huge white one. Her life story dangled from her wrist: her bracelet of crosses, inscribed with the duke's tender thoughts. "God Save the King for Wallis" said a 1936 aquamarine cross piously. "Our marriage cross" were the ambivalent words on a 1937 one in rubies, sapphires and emeralds. "Get well. Cross Wallis" placated a 1944 yellow sapphire cross.

The duchess seemed dazed and disoriented at the funeral service. "Haven't I seen you somewhere before?" she asked the queen. "Where do I sit? Is this my seat? Is this my prayer book?" wondered Wallis aloud as she took her seat in the chapel, twisting and turning her hands in their black gloves.

The duke's will made no bequests to church, charity, relatives, friends or faithful servants. Everything was left to the duchess. No one knows the estate's exact value, but excluding furniture and art, it was probably around ten million dollars. Sole executor of the duke's estate was French lawyer Maître Suzanne Blum, who had served him since 1947 and achieved fame as divorce lawyer to such Hollywood stars as Rita Hayworth, Douglas Fairbanks and Charlie Chaplin. Maître Blum dressed with the same formality, but far less elegance, than the duchess, whom she would protect for her remaining years from the rapacious world with the fierce loyalty of a Doberman pinscher.

Wallis was certain that she'd been left penniless. When a friend gave her a roll of "divine" tweed from Galway to be made into a suit, the duchess told her that she no longer had enough money to have it made up. Since new clothes were her life-blood,

Wallis gave up on life, and declined quickly, both mentally and physically.

One day in late 1972, walking with a cane in her drawing room, a small rug turned traitor, skidding suddenly beneath her well-shod feet and causing her to fall, breaking a hip. The forced inactivity was hard for one always in motion, who'd never been a reader of anything except fashion magazines, auction-sale catalogues and, occasionally, detective novels. In Biarritz the following summer, Wallis fell again and cracked five ribs. "Her bones are becoming like glass," commented a friend. Put in hospital, Wallis had meals prepared by her own chef, slept on her own Porthault bed linen and surrounded herself with her own magnificent flower arrangements.

From long habit, she tried to keep up the social round. When she arrived at the Waldorf Towers for her final stay in 1974, she leaned heavily on a cane, looked frail and stooped, but still created a stir when she made her slow, dignified progress through the lobby. The panther jewels were locked away now in bank vaults, all passion spent. The duchess settled for sentiment instead and usually wore, just above her heart – *The Heart Has Its Reasons* she'd called her autobiography – the brooch which the duke had given her for their twentieth wedding anniversary: a ruby crown above a diamond heart with WE scrawled on it in emeralds.

By 1975, the duchess was down to eighty-seven pounds, but when she entertained Prudence Glynn, fashion editor of the London *Times*, at luncheon in Paris, she was as beautifully dressed as ever in Wallis blue tweed suit with patch-pocketed jacket and slightly flared skirt; blue silk blouse with pussy-cat bow and cluster earrings of tiny cabochon sapphires. Her outfit, concludes Glynn, was "appropriate." It was Wallis' greatest talent in her chosen art, that perfect propriety of dress. "Whenever you see the Duchess," agreed a friend, "first thing in the morning or at a little bistro dinner, she always looks perfect. She has on just what you'd have liked to have worn if you'd thought of it." Over lunch, Wallis told Glynn that she found current couture prices "dreadful" and sighed over her jewelry: "Most of it's in the bank."

In November 1975, having eased her lonely life with too much neat vodka drunk from iced silver cups, Wallis was taken to the American hospital in Paris suffering from her old complaint, a stomach ulcer. She returned to her Paris home in May 1976, and from then until her death, like Dietrich in her last years, Wallis was a total recluse. The duchess took to her bed two years before Dietrich, in another part of the same city, took to hers. Marlene would lie prostrate for fourteen years; the duchess, for ten. It is a daunting picture: two incredible women of style, moldering away, unseen, unloved, both sinking into complete narcissism.

The duchess would scarcely eat and grew ever more emaciated; did her befuddled mind, like Dietrich's, think always of the *line*? Wallis became obsessed with the fear that burglars might steal her precious possessions, and kept a revolver by her bed. She thought it real; the staff made sure it was a toy. Sometimes she rose in the night and peered out the window with her failing eyes, trying to see if the French paratrooper she'd hired to patrol the grounds was doing so. She scanned the high iron fence topped with sharp golden spears, and the iron gate, locked and guarded around the clock, which protected her property. In addition to the iron fortress surrounding Wallis, Maître Blum maintained an invisible one, allowing hardly anyone, whether friends or press, to visit the Paris house. When Lord Snowdon in 1980 wanted to photograph the duchess for the English *Sunday Times*, Maître Blum refused – which was just as well, for the very last photo of Wallis, taken three years before by Spanish paparazzi by means of long-range lenses, shows her face looking, as one biographer puts it, "a little like a Chinese mandarin but more like a dead monkey."

When her loyal friend the Countess of Romamones came to visit her in 1982, she found the duchess in a wheelchair, wearing a handsome Wallis-blue brocade dressing gown. Her hair was elegantly drawn back behind her ears and she wore her favorite sapphires. In her closets, unworn, were such clothes from the autumn 1975 couture collections as a coral tweed suit from Dior, still in its tissue. The wardrobe Wallis actually used had shrunk to one short row of quilted housecoats which hung on the landing outside her bedroom. At her physician's suggestion, a recording of Cole Porter's "I Get a Kick out of You," a favorite "WE" song, was played over and over in the vain hope of kindling a spark in the duchess' eyes, as blank and unseeing as her gemstones.

When the countess came again to visit two months later, the duchess had not been manicured or made up and her hair was white and lifeless. She looked out the window at the way the sun was lighting the trees and said, "Tell David to come in. He wouldn't want to miss this." On two subsequent visits, she uttered not a word. For the last three years of her life Wallis was completely paralyzed, unable to move even a finger.

She died on April 24, 1986, two months before her ninety-first birthday. The royals who had virtually ignored her in life flocked to her funeral in St. George's chapel, Windsor, prior to burial at Frogmore beside the duke. Queen Elizabeth, supported by her husband, the Duke of Edinburgh, son Prince Charles and daughter-in-law Princess Diana, was seen to shed a tear or two. When Wallis' friend, Laura, Duchess of Marlborough, went to look at the funeral flowers, she thought it "tragic" that they were all from couturiers, jewelers and hairdressers. The duchess herself, however, would have thought it a neat and tidy ending to her tale that these tradespeople, her closest friends in spite of their lowly rank, had sent their pretty tributes to a fellow professional who'd labored just as long and hard in the service of style.

The duchess had made a will, but the details of how she chose to disperse her millions were never published. We do know that she had rejected a proposal to set up a charitable foundation in the duke's name.

Wallis Warfield Spencer Simpson, Duchess of Windsor, climbed from poverty and illegitimacy to riches and a flawed renown, using clothing and gems to claw her way to the top, to express her frustrations once she got there, and finally to fill her days with a singular vocation. One year after the duchess' death, her jewels, reunited from boxes and bank vaults for their final meeting in Sotheby's auction room, spoke in commanding, adamantine tones of wish and will, of dream and disappointment.

CHAPTER 5

Jacqueline Kennedy Onassis

"Jackie, you must show them," said the President, turning to his wife, "the pretty pink suit you're going to wear. You look ravishing in it." "Oh, Jack, it's nothing much," murmured Jackie softly. She and Jack had asked friend and newspaper columnist Joe Alsop and wife Susan Mary to join them at the White House for a private dinner, on a gray day in early November 1963. Over brandy and coffee in the sitting room, they talked about the President's upcoming trip to Texas. He'd barely carried that state in 1960, winning by only 46,000 votes. If he wanted to get re-elected next year he needed solid support in the Lone Star State, and he was going there to get it, taking with him America's Lady Star, his wife Jackie, "to show those rich Texas broads what it's like to be well-dressed." She had protested at first; she hated campaigning, hated having to lower herself to the level of a lot of vulgar, pushy men and their loud, over-dressed wives. (Jackie was a social snob of the first order, but managed, almost always, to hide that personality trait, like so many others, from the public.) But she was feeling really guilty that November, after her magical cruise a few weeks before on the luxury yacht *Christina* with its owner, Aristotle Onassis. He was reviled in the United States because of shady business deals, so the First Lady's cruise had been sharply criticized in Congress and in American newspapers, and Jack had ranted and raved at her for going. Jackie always tried to be a dutiful spouse, true to the Roman Catholic ideals of wifehood, so finally, swayed by guilt and duty, she'd agreed to go to Texas with Jack. Now she trotted upstairs, fetched her pink suit, trotted down again, and stood, holding it against her thin body, while Susan Mary and Joe politely enthused, and the President beamed. Where her clothes were concerned, Jackie knew that Jack only cared about two things: how they affected his political career and how they affected family finances. He was so unreasonable; he wanted her to look like a million dollars but to spend nothing. Fortunately, Jackie had talked father-in-law Joe, who adored her classy image and fully appreciated its political clout, into paying most of her huge clothing bills.

This suit, like others in her closet, such as an off-white one with black braid trim in which she'd shown Empress Farah Diba the White House garden, was by Chanel, whose suits had the understated elegance which Jackie loved. And the color of this one, hot pink, had been Jackie's favorite ever since those days in the 1950s when she'd dashed in to dressmaker Mrs. Rhea's Washington house with a length of pink fabric in one hand and a sketch pad in the other, or sometimes clutching a pile of her latest shopping finds to be altered, always with one hot pink item among them screaming, "me first." Bright pink suited Jackie's coloring, drew all eyes and, as she told Mrs. Rhea, made her feel that "June was busting out all over." Jackie's ten bridesmaids for her 1953 wedding had worn pink silk with hot pink sashes. When Schiaparelli had launched the shade, she called it shocking pink; Marlene Dietrich had worn it on the beach at Cap d'Antibes in 1938. "Think pink," Kay Thompson had advised, playing a fashion magazine editor in the 1957 feature film *Funny Face* in which dowdy bookworm Audrey Hepburn thinks pink, turns into a Paris fashion model and wins Fred Astaire. Pink says "*Yes!*" to life. It is the color of lips, blushes, babies' toes, passion's first flush, sunset clouds, "in the pink" health. Hot pink is pinkissimo, pink at the very peak of ripeness, a sustained siren note demanding attention and appreciation, pink's highest trumpet blast before it modulates to crimson.

Jackie remembered fondly the hot pink peau de soie ballgown in which she'd danced at balls before she married, feeling admiring male glances falling like rose petals on her bare shoulders. Mrs. Rhea had made the gown to Jackie's own design: strapless top, and wide, wide skirt trimmed with many rows of sparkling silver braid.

The pink bouclé wool suit which Jackie was hugging to her as she stood before Jack and the Alsops had a jacket boxy enough to hide her body's shape, with sleeves in the skimpy 3/4 length she liked if she had to have sleeves. The double-breasted jacket showed its navy silk lining in lapels, and had navy-silk slivers, just the merest hint, at the tops of its invisible pockets, two per side. The skirt was straight and didn't show the knees, in keeping with First Lady dignity and decorum. Like all Jackie's clothes, the pink suit gave a contradictory, double message indicative of the personality conflicts beneath. The suit asked to be noticed, but then didn't say much, chary of revelation. It promised, but didn't deliver.

Because it impinged on his own political agenda, Jack had asked to vet Jackie's wardrobe for the Texas trip, which would mark the first time she'd hit the campaign trail with him since the fall of 1960. Jackie had obediently tramped in and out of his room modeling various outfits. Together they'd settled on two day dresses, one beige, one white, three suits in blue, yellow and pink; and a black evening dress. Then Jackie's maid, Providencia Paredes, known as Provi – a pretty brunette from the Dominican Republic who saw to Jackie's clothes, no easy task, given their volume – packed everything carefully between layers of tissue. "Where is the ironing board?" was always Provi's first question when she and Jackie arrived somewhere. But this time Provi wasn't going to Texas, because Jackie's personal secretary, Mary Gallagher, had asked if she could go instead. Provi packed a big cosmetic case and then, on her own initiative, added extra pairs of white kid gloves, in case Texas should have an inordinate amount of filth. Mary typed duplicate lists of everything, including accessories, pasted one copy inside the top of each suitcase, and put the carbons into her handbag.

On November 20, the last night before departure, at a Judicial Reception at the White House, Jackie wore a velvet suit in a color prophetic of events to come: dark red.

Next morning, minutes before they were due to leave, while Jackie was still in her room fussing with her hair and hat and Jack stood waiting beside the helicopter on the White House lawn, he asked aide General Godfrey McHugh what the Texas weather was going to be like. "Jesus," muttered Jack when he heard. He dashed inside again, and phoned Jackie's room, where Provi answered. "Tell her to pack some light clothes." "Too late, Meester President," replied Provi. "They already in the chopper." The earlier weather forecast had been for cool weather, so Jackie's daytime choices were all made of wool fabrics. The clothes were out of joint.

Jackie climbed into the helicopter for the ride to the airport wearing a two-piece white wool bouclé dress. She felt nervous as the president's jet, Air Force One, flew towards Texas, and smoked a whole pack of cigarettes. That evening, November 21, after a full day of appearances, she donned a cut-velvet dress in another prophetic color: black, for a Houston banquet where she made a little speech in Spanish in her usual shy, ladylike manner, while Jack relished the applause. After the banquet, they flew on to Fort Worth, arriving at one a.m. so tired that they could only hold each other up in a brief embrace before going to their separate bedrooms. Jackie's hotel room, decorated in a drab shade of green – she hated green, and never wore it except for a pale pistachio shade – looked out on a deserted parking lot garish with neon, bordered by two loan companies and a bus station. Where on earth had Mary got to? She should have unpacked. Jackie missed Provi already. She was really exhausted, but she knew that the morning would be hectic, so she bent over her bags and laid out the clothes she would wear: pink suit; matching pink pillbox hat; navy silk blouse; navy Chanel chain-handled purse; navy low-heeled shoes. The beautiful clothes, as always, gave Jackie a little rush of pleasure, in spite of her weariness. In that ugly room, the pink suit bloomed like some giant rose in a dusty green thicket. It was the last thing she looked at before she turned out the light; she drifted into sleep warmed by its brightness.

The next morning began with laughter. When the crowd that had gathered in the parking lot outside the hotel to see their president and First Lady asked him where Jackie was, he replied: "Mrs. Kennedy is organizing herself. It takes her a little longer. But of course, she looks better than we do when she does it."

Jackie was always late, perhaps because it gave her a feeling of power to keep America's most powerful man waiting for *her*. He had to wait twenty minutes that morning while she dithered over which length of white glove looked best with her pink suit.

By 12:55 that day, Friday, November 22, 1963, the presidential motorcade was on its way to the Dallas Trade Mart for a luncheon. Jackie and Jack rode in an open black limousine, with a large bunch of long-stemmed roses presented to Jackie earlier lying on the seat between them. Their crimson color clashed with the pink skirt next to them, offending an eye craving congruence and perfect accord. The broiling sun beat down relentlessly as the motorcade wound its way slowly forward. Jackie's face flushed pink; she was feeling far too hot in her bouclé wool. She saw that an underpass lay just ahead, and looked forward to the cool respite of its shade. They were almost there.

Then Jackie heard a loud *crack!*, like a motorcycle backfiring, and inexplicably, as she turned her head to the right and stared, Jack's blood and brains started exploding from his head. (Standing in the crowd, Abraham Zapruder, a local dress manufacturer, started his video camera rolling.) Jackie froze, transfixed, for several seconds, then climbed onto the back of the car, wanting only to flee that terrible sight which no eye should have to look at, but was shoved back into the carnage by Secret Service agent Clint Hill, forced to look, forced to be part of it. Jackie remembered, as she later told journalist Theodore White, looking, in a strange, detached way, at the pink-rose rings on the inside of Jack's skull. "The inside of his head was so beautiful," she said. "I tried to hold the top of his head down, so more brains wouldn't spill out. But I knew he was dead." She crouched in the car, shielding Jack, trying to prevent that secret gray matter which was unspeakable, private, sacrosanct, from being seen by the masses, by the world.

As the car accelerated, Jackie's pink pillbox hat, in a sudden gust of wind, fell forward over her face. She had secured it to her bouffant hairdo with a hatpin so it wouldn't blow off. She'd asked for the extra protection of the bubbletop on the Lincoln today, but Jack had vetoed that. They had to be seen. Jackie yanked the traitorous pillbox off so frantically that a hank of her hair came with it.

It was only when they reached Parkland Memorial Hospital that she noticed in some corner of her mind that splattered on the pink fabric of her suit were gobs of gray, viscous matter and thick, wet blood. This was shocking pink indeed, beauty become sublime, arousing in all onlookers terror and awe. In the language of clothes, the suit screamed a double message, a dichotomy to make all others pale. Bright pink, the dancing color of romance and youth and hope, warring for space with death's crimson flag. Jackie had lost three babies in floods of shocking blood; she'd already had too much crimson in her life, too little pink.

No matter how many people, first at the hospital and then on Air Force One flying back to Washington, suggested to Jackie that she change her clothes, she, who had long ago mastered the art of refusal in her wardrobe, refused to take off her bloodied suit. "Let them see what they've done," she said, "I want them to see." It was the first and last political statement of her life. On board the presidential jet, as Lyndon Johnson was sworn in as president, Jackie stood beside him in her symbolic suit, and someone took a picture.

Just before the plane was due to land in Washington with its terrible cargo, Mary Gallagher stepped back into Jackie's bedroom compartment to make sure no personal items to be packed up remained there. On the bed lay one of Jackie's gloves. In the innocence of morning, she'd chosen her shortest length, fashioned, with one little pearl button at the wrist, from kid leather that was pure white, soft and spotless. By nightfall, the glove had become macabre, blackened all over by blood. Since she'd tugged it off, finger by finger and thrown it from her, the glove had dried and stiffened to the actual shape of Jackie's hand, so that it looked as if her hand were still trapped in that dark surround. The glove had been tossed onto a newspaper which bore the bold, black headline: "DALLAS WELCOMES JFK."

It was close to four a.m. when Jackie, dazed, sedated, still numb with shock, finally took off her pink suit. Provi at once bundled it into a bag and out of sight. The actual suit would end its days in the attic of Jackie's mother's house. Her mother, in her orderly way, with an eye to posterity, had placed the Chanel suit in a box, written "November 22nd, 1963" on top, and stored it with one other box, dated "September 12th, 1953," which contained Jackie's white bridal gown.

Two images of the suit would also be preserved, one in the famous photo taken at Johnson's swearing-in aboard Air Force One, the other in the Zapruder video footage. That obscene contradiction of Jackie both elegant and bloodied, costumed half in brightest pink and half in darkest crimson, would never fade or die. It seems ironic that a dress manufacturer, a man, who, like Jackie, cared mightily for clothes, was the innocent creator of this special static kind of hell from which there was no going backward or forward in historical time. Since she'd come to national prominence three years before, Jackie's relationship with the camera had been a love-hate one, as contradictory as everything else about her. She wanted attention, but only of the right kind, under her strict control. She loved posed photos of herself because they were usually beautiful, hated candid ones because they were sometimes ugly. After November 22, the real Jackie would go forward to other events, other garments, but the image of Chanel-suited Jackie disheveled and defiled would supersede all others, would fix itself forever in the very center of America's collective unconscious, and there, no matter what she did or said, it would remain.

Born thirty-four years before the event which stained her life, in Southampton, Long Island, on July 28, 1929, Jackie was the eldest daughter of Janet Lee and John Vernon Bouvier III. Her bassinet was beige wicker, elaborately beruffled in peach *point d'esprit*, as befitted a baby born to silver-spoon gentility. As a child, Jacqueline Lee Bouvier was a strange mixture of silk and iron, gentle and clinging one minute, stubborn and intractable the next. Her mother Janet, a small, busty woman with fierce, dark eyes, was a conventional female garbed in clothes of conservative cut and color, in grays, browns and beiges, but made from the finest materials. Her shoes were plain with medium heels but were fashioned from the softest leathers. Janet punctuated her ordered life with embroidered linen sheets, French soaps, engraved invitations. Jackie's father, on the other hand, known as "Black Jack Bouvier," more because of the tint of his skin than his soul, was rather wild and unpredictable, a gambler, spendthrift, dreamer and womanizer. While still at Yale, he had routinely commandeered three or four pretty girls per night, and then kicked them out of his room as he used them up. While on his honeymoon with Janet, he'd carried on a romance with tobacco heiress Doris Duke. He was handsome, debonair, suave as silk; all women adored him. He was also always in debt, borrowing from friends, prodigally spending money he didn't have on clothes for himself and his little daughters, Jackie and Lee, who was born on March 3, 1933. Black Jack's suits were custom-made by Bell, his shirts by Tripler and Sulka, his shoes by Peel's of London, his cravats by Turnbull and Asser. Her dandified daddy would be Jackie's first and most important clothes mentor. Her mother disciplined her and taught her social graces; her father spoiled her and taught her how to indulge herself with material things. Jackie tolerated her mother and adored her father. Neither of them gave her enough of their time.

When Jackie was seven, in September 1936, her mother parted company from a husband who couldn't properly provide and couldn't stop straying. After that, Jackie only saw him on weekends or during vacations. She felt pulled in two different directions and her lifelong conflicts and insecurities began. Where did she belong? In her mother's world, conforming to polite society's rigid standards of behavior and unremarkable clothes? In her father's world, flouting convention, grabbing style with both hands, living with more panache than prudence? Jackie became, according to a cousin, "an odd mixture of tomboy and dream princess." She climbed trees and high-jumped on her pony, but she also retreated from her bifurcated world into a private dreamscape. The cousin recalls that Jackie (like Elinor Glyn) even manufactured a crown, and announced one day that she was running away to become "queen of the circus."

When she was nearly eleven, in 1940, her parents finally divorced. In response to her pain at this irrevocable event, Jackie emotionally detached herself, once and for all. From then on she would be more onlooker than participant in life, with expression of her feelings permanently blocked. Norman Mailer, with the perceptive eye of all good novelists, said of adult Jackie that there was "something quite remote in her – not willed, not chilly, not directed to anyone in particular but distant, detached as psychologists say, moody and abstracted." Another novelist, Pearl Buck, found her "withdrawn, as though she were not altogether among us." Friends described her as "cool and aloof" and "an absolute ice princess." Later in life, Carly Simon would notice her friend Jackie's habit, in those rare instances when Jackie's conversation veered close to something personal, of expressing herself in the third person rather than the first. "One does feel..." or "one does wish..." Jackie would murmur softly. After the scarring left by her parents' divorce, it was as if Jackie's soul wore a permanent slip, the kind of white cambric shift nuns used to wear to take their baths, never exposing the nude body even to their own eyes. In addition to her psyche's modesty-cover, Jackie was extremely volatile in her affections, warm one day, icy the next. As her future official designer put it, you never knew where you stood with Jackie, or on which foot to dance. Her personality was like a pair of Siamese twins trying to walk in opposite directions all at once. Underneath the cool exterior, there was plenty of turmoil.

Her mother saw to it that Jackie learned to be a lady at all the right private schools: Miss Chapin's, Holton Arms and Miss Porter's School in Farmington, Connecticut, where Jackie enrolled in September 1944, when she was fifteen. She boarded there, spending half her free time with her father and half with her mother. On visits to her father, who had an apartment in Manhattan, he and Jackie shopped for wonderful, extravagant clothes at all the best stores: Saks, Bergdorf's, Bonwit Teller's, while he kept up a running commentary on how a woman should dress with flair and flamboyance. He would stop in front of a mannequin and say: "Too plain. That dress needs a sensational scarf." He criticized the quiet clothes her mother bought for her, naturally, and got her out of them as quickly as possible and into something daring and dramatic. Then Jackie, in her daring and dramatic guise, went to stay with her mother, who frowned and ranted, and put her back in mufti.

Her mother, in 1941, had married wealthy Hugh Auchincloss, considerably higher on the social scale than Black Jack Bouvier, and pursued her social agenda at Merrywood, a fine estate in Virginia, and at Hammersmith Farm in Newport. Merrywood was a Georgian-style, ivy-covered mansion on forty-six acres of grounds, with eight bedrooms, indoor badminton court, Olympic-sized swimming pool, two stables, delightful gardens, and riding paths winding lazily through its woods. Merrywood's rooms all had buttons labeled "M" and "P" for maid and pantry. At Hammersmith Farm, Janet Auchincloss employed, among her twenty-five servants, one whose sole job was to empty the wastebaskets. At Merrywood and Hammersmith, Jackie moved in an aura which was all patina and polish, with a carefully staged bow to the stately past, when true decorum reigned.

At Miss Porter's, in Farmington, where her classmates soon nicknamed her Jacqueline Borgia, Jackie became a master manipulator, skilled, by various devious means, at getting what she wanted. Her first concern was money, and how to get enough of it by guile and wheedling. The other girls all had generous allowances but Jackie had only the fifty dollars per month she received from her father. Whatever became the fashion fad of the moment, worn by all her peers, Jackie refused. When they opted for white poplin raincoats, she would swagger about in a sweeping wool cape.

After graduating from Miss Porter's in the spring of 1947, Jackie made her debut at a formal dinner-dance at Newport's Clambake Club, wearing a white tulle gown with off-the-shoulder neckline and bouffant skirt, bought for fifty-nine dollars from a New York department store. In spite of this modest beginning, society columnist "Cholly Knickerbocker" – who was really Igor Cassini, brother of Jackie's future designer, Oleg Cassini – named Jacqueline Bouvier Deb of the Year, calling her, with great prescience, a *regal* brunette. Jackie's father had taught her well. "Although shy and extremely private," wrote Igor, "she stood out in a crowd. She had that certain something."

By the time she entered Vassar College in the fall of 1947, Jackie had a strange if unconventional beauty. She was 5'7" tall, so flat-chested that she wore padded bras, with big hands and feet, slightly bowed legs and football-player shoulders. Her figure was more androgynous than feminine; there was nothing cute or soft or cuddly about her. The total effect, however, was somehow arresting and charismatic. Her too-wide-apart, light-brown eyes gave her the look of a startled deer; her too-large head with short curly hair on a long neck gave her the look of a proud lioness. She had a commanding presence – until she spoke. Her voice, in public, was soft, whispery, sounding, as fashion editor Eugenia Sheppard put it, "like a dear little girl who has been running and doesn't want to be late." The contradictions which surfaced in Jackie's clothes began in her person: female and male; deer and lioness; woman and girl. In addition to these striking ambiguities, what gave Jackie, even as early as 1947, her "star" quality was that she seemed somehow larger-than-life, almost a caricature of herself, not quite real. The camera, which feeds on exaggeration and contrast, would always love her. Later in life, Jackie would hype herself even more by means of oversize hairdo and sunglasses. After she became famous, as Truman Capote wickedly noted, "Mrs. Kennedy was the most popular inspiration" for drag-queen contests. At one such, there were a dozen Jackie look-alikes, including the winner. "In life," concludes Truman, "that is how she struck me – not as a bona fide woman, but as an artful female impersonator impersonating Mrs. Kennedy." Like novelists Mailer and Buck, Capote has caught her essence.

Jackie spent her junior college year, 1949, studying at the Sorbonne in Paris, learning the French language and acquiring a love of French history and couture. She considered this "the high point of my life, my happiest and most carefree year." It was the French equivalent of Wallis Windsor's "lotus year" in China. For Jackie to feel that life blossomed for her most fully at age twenty strikes one as rather sad, and makes Jackie worthy of our compassion. Not wanting to return to all-girl Vassar, Jackie moved to better husband-hunting terrain and spent her final college year at George Washington University in Washington, D.C. Jackie always preferred the company of men to women, and never had a close female friend. Confidences were exchanged only with sister Lee, but since Lee was smaller, prettier, and had an even better clothes sense, one bolder and more experimental, there was plenty of rivalry and jealousy between the sisters, too, which would grow as the years passed.

In the fall of 1951, Jackie was thrilled to win *Vogue* magazine's *Prix de Paris*, entitling her to six months as junior editor in Paris and six in New York. However, her mother persuaded her to turn it down. Jackie, after all, was headed for marriage with some suitably wealthy and socially prominent man, not for a lifetime career. In the context of her style, nevertheless, entering the contest served Jackie well. She had to write four technical papers on fashion and lay out an entire issue of the magazine. The fact that she'd won over 1500 contestants gave her new confidence in her own taste in clothes. A few weeks later, she turned up at the Washington home of her mother's dressmaker, Mini Rhea. Mini had surprised her own mother at age ten by cutting out a dress for herself without a pattern, and had been creating clothes ever since. She had opened her Washington salon in 1947, attached a bronze plaque beside her door which said "Mini Rhea, Custom Dressmaker" and quickly acquired the patronage of Washington and Virginia's female élite.

On her first visit to Mini, Jackie dashed in, laden with fashion magazines and a sketch pad. "Mother recommended you highly, Mrs. Rhea, and said you'd be able to understand what I want," said Jackie breathlessly. She made a quick sketch for an evening dress, to be made from French-imported heavy white embroidered satin. Jackie loved the dress when it was finished, and from then on kept Mini busy. "I have a terrific idea for a gown," Jackie would say, her pencil making a few scanty lines. She brought only the best imported fabrics, in dramatic colors: black, white, pale yellow and, of course, hot pink. "This feels good; it will make up well," she would murmur, fingering one of her chosen fabrics, always one with body, never one that was soft and clingy. The fabric had to disguise her body, not reveal it. As Jackie flew in and out of Mrs. Rhea's establishment, with armloads of dressgoods and copies of *L'Officiel* and *L'Art et La Mode*, she was mastering her own peculiar language of clothes. The object of her style was not primarily to express her personality but to first grab attention, and then to reduce the number of clues by which the world could read her. From the fifties on, Jackie's apparel spoke with a forked tongue, broadcasting a message that was both blatant and cryptic, and always contradictory.

One day in November 1951, while standing in front of Mrs. Rhea's full-length mirror in the muslin model which Mrs. Rhea always made before the actual dress, Jackie pushed away the proffered muslin sleeves. "I definitely look better with this sleeveless effect," Jackie said, peering at her image in the mirror. Mrs. Rhea protested that no one was wearing sleeveless dresses; they weren't in fashion. But Jackie ordered the dress made without sleeves, refusing Mrs. Rhea's suggestion of a jacket. "No. That would be losing the whole point," explained Jackie. "I'll just have the dress." The whole point was firstly to fool the eye by minimizing her football shoulders, and secondly to present the world with less than it expected, withholding one vital ingredient of a dress, namely sleeves. This Zen attitude towards apparel was the very opposite of Marlene Dietrich's generous desire to fully gratify, or even satiate, the eye. Jackie's approach was closer to Elinor Glyn's clothes philosophy of using veils, which both obscured reality and inspired imagination. In conversation, Jackie talked slowly, with long silences between the phrases, so that friends would think she was finished speaking when she had merely paused. Her sleeveless dresses were like the gaps in her speech: both showed her reluctance to give, and left room for imagination to fill the space with whatever material it pleased, however improbable or inaccurate.

In December 1951, through stepfather Hugh Auchincloss' connections, Jackie got a job as roving reporter and photographer on the Washington *Times-Herald*, earning $42.50 a week, raised to $56 in March 1952, when she got her own by-line. Her favorite working outfit was a black turtleneck sweater, wide black belt and straight plaid skirt. Sometimes she wore shirtwaist dresses, adding low-heeled shoes and a big black shoulder bag full of flash bulbs, pencils, notebooks, make-up and gloves. Jackie still found time for frequent trips in her black convertible to Mini Rhea, bringing fabrics or ready-to-wear outfits which required Mini's "magic dart" to take in the bustline. Since Mini charged from $35 to $100 per dress, and since Jackie liked plenty of new ones, she needed her rich stepfather "Uncle Hughdie" to indulge her habit.

Jackie first met Jack Kennedy on May 8, 1952, at a dinner party for eight hosted by mutual friends Martha and Charles Bartlett, the latter Washington correspondent for the *Chattanooga Times*. Jack liked Jackie's intelligence, offbeat humor and gentle, fawning ways. Her soft doe eyes stared into his as he held forth, while her head, over and over, nodded in solemn, silent sympathy. When the party broke up, he pursued her as far as her car, then said an abrupt goodnight when he found another admirer slumped on the backseat, awaiting her.

By Christmas 1952, Jackie was writing a column based on the question "Can you give any reason why a contented bachelor should get married?" and ordered Mini Rhea to make her a really "fantastic" ballgown for Christmas dances to be attended on the arm of the handsome, newly elected senator from Massachusetts. Jackie instructed Mini to make her gown from eight yards of bride-like white satin, and to attach three petticoats under its very full skirt. To draw all eyes, Jackie added a floor-length stole, cut from two and a half yards of crimson velvet. No one in Washington had ever worn a long stole. Sometimes, Mrs. Rhea would ask Jackie how the senator had liked a certain dress. "I don't believe he noticed," she would reply with a sad little smile.

Jack's main attraction for Jackie was his money; his father Joe had just been publicly proclaimed the eleventh richest man in the United States, worth about four hundred million dollars. She also liked Jack's intelligence, power and the fact that he was twelve years her senior. Jackie's main attraction for Jack was her breeding; socially she was many notches above the Irish-Catholic Kennedys. He thought her "fey" and liked her volatility, which kept at bay his *bête noire*, boredom.

Jack and Jackie were well-matched in more than name, both essentially cold-hearted, afraid of emotional intimacy. Jackie was far more of a dreamy romantic than Jack; during courtship, she found him disappointing. He'd learned from his father to use women, not to woo them. Jack was far too focused on his own driving ambitions to take time for romance. When he and Jackie were separated, he sent no love letters and only one postcard, mailed from Bermuda, with the trite message, "Wish you were here. Jack."

In June 1953, Jackie was in England for Queen Elizabeth II's Coronation, sending back such choice tidbits to the *Times-Herald* as the fact that the crown now had a secret mark on it so that Elizabeth wouldn't put it on backwards as poor King George VI had when he was crowned in 1937, following brother Edward's defection in Wallis' direction. Jack proposed to Jackie via a transatlantic phone connection full of static and met her when her ship docked in New York with an emerald and diamond engagement ring. The betrothal was announced on June 25 in the *Times-Herald* from which Jackie had, with great alacrity, already resigned.

"I'm in Newport now all the time and most of my trousseau I get in New York by going to wholesale houses," wrote Jackie on July 28 to Mini Rhea, who had gone to Baltimore to work for a dress company there. "Then the rest of it I'll get this winter after I'm married," added Jackie cannily. By then she'd have a rich husband to foot the bills.

The September wedding held in Newport was the usual large society event. Its only dark cloud for Jackie was that her father got so drunk in his hotel room that he couldn't give her away. (Joe Kennedy, with his usual flair for public relations, told the press that Black Jack had the flu.) Jackie's wedding gown was completely out of character, Jack's choice, not hers. Made by Washington dressmaker Ann Lowe from fifty yards of ivory tissue silk, it was a busy mass of ruffles, tucks and stitchings. The very full skirt had eleven rows of ruffles at the hem, with large circles of ruffles above, not to mention sprays of flowers. Even Empress Eugénie would have thought it far too fussy. With her elaborately patterned heirloom rosepoint lace veil, Jackie had wanted a simple, modern gown, but Jack, who lacked Jackie's natural good taste, had insisted on "something traditional and old-fashioned." The resulting creation made Jackie look like Scarlett O'Hara suffering from a severe case of ruffle-mania.

Jackie's going-away outfit, as she departed on a Mexican honeymoon, was a gray Chanel suit. With it she wore the diamond bracelet which Jack, with no words of endearment, had casually dropped into her lap at the bridal dinner, and the diamond pin given her by Joe Kennedy whom Jackie had already, and permanently, charmed.

It wasn't long after the marriage that Jack started complaining about Jackie's spending on expensive clothes. "She's breaking my goddam ass," he fumed to a friend. At first, Jackie tried to pay for all the mounting bills for apparel and furnishings out of her monthly allowance. When the pile got alarmingly high, she sent the invoices to the Kennedy family accounting office in New York.

By 1956, she was happily buying maternity outfits, having already suffered one miscarriage, but on August 23, Jackie was rushed to Newport hospital – typically, Jack wasn't with her – and gave birth, by Caesarean section, to a stillborn baby girl.

To her great sorrow, her father died the following summer. Jackie covered his grave with bachelor's buttons, but was probably too focused on her grief to note the irony of that particular flower for a man who had never stopped acting the carefree bachelor. Four months later, her gloom lifted when a healthy daughter, christened Caroline Bouvier, was born on November 27, 1957, again by Caesarean section.

In those pre-White House years, Jackie dressed in couture acquired either directly from France or from Chez Ninon, a New York salon which did expensive custom-copies of French originals. Rarely, Jackie went to Ohrbach's in New York for much cheaper copies, such as their "Givenchy" double-breasted red coat, to wear when campaigning with Jack, who kept telling her (wrongly, as it turned out) that middle America could be won over only if she didn't look too rich or too fashionable. On the hustings, Jackie put on her modest apparel, and her mask. It was as if, as one perceptive journalist noted, she pulled "some invisible shade down across her face and cut out spiritually" from whatever was taking place on the platform and in the crowd. "We were to see that expression a hundred times in the years to come," he adds.

On the campaign trail in 1960, when John Fitzgerald Kennedy ran for President on the Democratic ticket against Republican Richard Nixon, whose wife Pat was no style-setter, Jackie, who, by July, was obviously pregnant, appeared in outfits by Cardin, Givenchy, Balenciaga and Chanel. The fashion trade paper *Women's Wear Daily* caused a furor in the Democratic camp when it reported on July 13 that Jacqueline Kennedy and mother-in-law Rose had spent $30,000 that year on Paris couture. In a story headed "That Fancy Fashion Fuss," *Life* magazine quoted Jackie as protesting: "I couldn't spend that much unless I wore sable underwear." *Women's Wear Daily* then reported on September 1 that Jackie had been told "that for political expediency, 'no more Paris clothes, only American fashion.'" She would find her own clever way to circumvent that peremptory command.

At seven a.m. on the morning of November 9, Jack woke to find himself elected, by a slim margin, President, the youngest one in history, and Jackie realized, with an excited flush and an apprehensive shiver, that she would be First Lady, the second youngest in history. Jack's triumph over Nixon proved the effectiveness of style. "We're going to sell Jack like cornflakes," Joe Kennedy had boasted at the start of the campaign. Sitting nude beside his Palm Beach swimming pool, keeping well out of sight of the masses, Joe had been the mastermind, spending day after day on the phone, putting his son into the White House by means of the world's smartest and most expensive ad campaign. It was precisely then in American society that political principles gave way to entertainment, integrity to popularity, and reality to the image. Beginning in the early fifties, television had helped to make the image supreme, and America had accordingly elected its first authentic pop President and First Lady after viewing the Kennedy-Nixon debates, wherein Kennedy looked like a young Greek god and Nixon like an all-night card shark in need of a shave. John Fitzgerald Kennedy's carefully packaged exterior, far more than his wife's, belied the reality beneath. The American public perceived only the boyish good looks, the six-foot-tall upright figure, the dazzling smile, the Irish charm, the shining rhetoric. They couldn't perceive what was deliberately hidden: the father's iron hand, the son's ailing physical body, harsh machismo, neurotic lust for power and compulsive sex drive. When America went to the polls on November 8, they cast their vote for the politics of style, which, ever since that fateful day in 1960, has largely replaced the politics of substance.

Just before the election, Jackie had received a note from acquaintance Oleg Cassini asking if he could help design her First Lady wardrobe. If, with an eye on the politics of style, she had to wear "only American fashion," Oleg was her man. He was, after all, only a modest second-string American designer, and he was a real ladies' man. Jackie knew that she could both control and charm him. On November 17, Jackie wrote to Oleg, telling him to "get started designing me something, then send me some sketches." If she liked them, she would hire him to do her entire wardrobe, appointing him the first ever official White House designer. "What I need are dresses and coats for daytime; dresses suitable to wear to lunch. I don't know if you design coats, but I now see that will be one of my biggest problems as every time one goes out of the house, one is photographed in the same coat. Then, for afternoon, cocktail dresses suitable for afternoon receptions and receiving lines – in other words, fairly covered up." She would also need "some pretty, long evening dresses" with "the covered-up look." She asked him to use the same materials used by Balenciaga and Givenchy and clearly spelled out her style demands: "Even though these clothes are for official life, please don't make them dressy as I'm sure I can continue to dress the way I like – simple and young clothes, as long as they are covered up for the occasion."

Nine days after the election, one can see here that Jackie is terrified of the media glare to come, of losing her hidden, carefully guarded, private self. Three times in a short letter she uses the phrase "covered up." This would be Jackie's main agenda as she entered the White House: her clothes, before all else, in three senses of the word, would be a cover-up, hiding her physical body, her psyche and her ongoing undercover dealings with the French couture. Her letter to Oleg also clearly informs him that *she* will dictate fabrics and designs; she will ride into high style with both hands firmly on the reins.

Eight days later, although he wasn't due for another month, Jackie gave birth to a son, John Fitzgerald Jr., and, as before, had a difficult delivery and slow recovery. For the rest of her life, Jackie's children would be her main comfort and delight. In their growing-up years, Caroline and John would be dressed in crisply tailored unisex coats and caps purchased from Rowes in London's Bond Street which, since the 1920s, had been outfitting the offspring of those born to the purple and those who wished they had been.

From her hospital room, while recovering from John's birth, Jackie sent a peremptory summons to Oleg Cassini, who was on holiday in Nassau. He rushed to the nearest store, bought paper and pencils, and began sketching possible designs. Born April 11, 1913, Oleg was the son of White Russian parents, the Count and Countess Loiewski. At eighteen, he had gone to work in Paris for Patou, and two years later started a small couture business of his own in Rome, much like the successful one his mother had run in Florence. Oleg came to the United States in 1936 with twenty-five dollars in his pocket. In 1940, he went to Hollywood, working first under Edith Head, who had succeeded Travis Banton at Paramount, then at Twentieth Century Fox. Oleg married actress Gene Tierney in June 1941, having made her, on their very first date, change her too-fussy gray chiffon dress for something simpler. Gene had had an affair with Jack Kennedy in 1947, while still married to Oleg, whom she divorced in 1952. Oleg got engaged to Grace Kelly and was stunned when she later chose instead to wed Prince Rainier.

Cassini's usual designs were skin-tight, sexy numbers to which he gave names like "Missionary's Downfall" and "The Natives are Restless Tonight." He hated a loose silhouette so much that he once sent a model down a runway in a burlap "sack" dress whose attached hood, when she pulled it up around her, spilled forth potatoes. Having sketched frantically in Nassau for two days, Oleg turned up at the Georgetown hospital where Jackie was recuperating from John Jr.'s birth with twenty sketches and accompanying fabric swatches. They talked excitedly of creating "an American Versailles." Jackie was dreaming of a real court on the banks of the Potomac, led by a queen who would, like Empress Eugénie, dictate taste to a nation, and be remembered by posterity for so doing. Jackie thought of former First Ladies: Mamie Eisenhower in her too-young rosebud-pink frou-frous; Bess Truman with her upholstered-matron look; Eleanor Roosevelt with hats like old squashed cushions. Jackie determined to outclass them all, to be another Marie Antoinette, Josephine or Eugénie. There would, however, be a difference between Empress Eugénie and Jackie. The French empress and Worth had worked in tandem; the American queen would order, Cassini would obey. Jackie had always looked to France for style in both apparel and décor and she wasn't about to change now. Oleg would make her, under his own all-American label, copies of French couture: line by line, fabric by fabric.

When she left the hospital, Jackie flew to the senior Kennedys' house in Palm Beach to recover her strength, and, on December 13, dispatched pages of detailed instructions to Cassini.

Color swatches of each evening gown were to be sent to Mario at "Eugenia of Florence" for matching pumps; to "some man" at Koret for "matching evening bags, simple envelopes or squares"; to Marita O'Connor at Bergdorf Goodman "who does my hats and gloves." Oleg was to check with Jackie before he cut the "orange organza dress" since it was the only one she "wasn't sure of." And perhaps the jersey dress could have "a beautiful jersey medieval cloak?" The letter goes on and on. Jackie, like the Duchess of Windsor, was fanatical about detail, and for much the same reasons. Both women used the wealth acquired from husbands, through the conduit of their personal style, to gain their own kind of authority and power. Jackie headed one paragraph: PUBLICITY. "One reason I'm so happy to be working with you is that I have some control over my fashion publicity," wrote Jackie. "I refuse to have Jack's administration plagued by fashion stories of a sensational nature." In other words, there were to be no more exposés of the French originals which she would secretly keep on buying. The great Closet Cover-Up, long before the more serious ones of Watergate and Iran-Contra, had already begun. Jackie began another paragraph headed COPIES. "Just make sure no one has exactly the same dress I do," she cautioned Oleg. "I want all mine to be originals and no fat little women hopping around in the same dress."

As Jackie languished in bed, members of her style team, in various locales, were already feeling the whip and learning their high-jumps. Secretary Mary Gallagher was flown to Palm Beach, but never saw the sun. She worked round the clock taking dictation, typing, telephoning. Mary conveyed to Marita at Bergdorf's the message that she was to make three pillbox hats for the Inauguration ceremony in black velvet, garnet velvet and beige jersey. The First Lady would decide later which one to wear. Tish Baldrige, Jackie's new social secretary, a friend from Miss Porter's, was to ask Tiffany's to lend the First Lady spectacular diamonds for the Inaugural Balls. Tell them, said Jackie, that "if it [her request] gets in the newspapers, I won't do any more business with Tiffany. If it doesn't, we'll buy all State presents there." Jackie sat up straighter against her pillows; she was feeling better, no doubt about it.

Back in Manhattan, Oleg Cassini had never been so busy. He hired a *première*, an assistant to research fabrics and colors, a draper, a cutter and eight seamstresses, and set them to work exclusively on the First Lady wardrobe. He added three mannequins shaped like Jackie, one live model, and a scout abroad to scour France and Italy for possible fabrics. Some of Oleg's creations Jackie rejected outright. A red wool hunting coat, for example, over which he'd labored, was spurned because she decided its fabric was too heavy. Other costumes she sent back for revisions. "She always knew what she wanted," said Oleg. "I propose and she disposes," he sighed, from under the First Lady's rather large thumb.

The parade of lackeys in and out of the Palm Beach house accelerated. Rose Kennedy noted in her diary that Richard Avedon arrived to photograph Jackie; a New York hairdresser came to do her hair; a fitter, staggering under a pile of boxes, came from Cassini's workroom. Stockings came from Garfinkel's, underwear from Bonwit Teller, nightgowns – "long, not too décolleté" Jackie had decreed – from Elizabeth Arden. Rose's house, not a large house, began to look like one large clothes cupboard.

On January 18, 1961, two days before the Inauguration, Jackie left Palm Beach by plane for Washington, wearing a black-and-white tweed suit with a short, loose jacket, long black kid gloves, black alligator purse and high-heeled alligator pumps. She wore a red suede beret on her bouffant brown hair. The hat signaled the start of her new life, for the old Jackie had been hatless. "I can't get excited about hats," she'd told Mini Rhea.

"Let's say they're fine for church." But when, during the election campaign, reporters had asked Jackie if she was willing "to make concessions to the role of First Lady," she had answered, "Oh, I will. I'll wear hats."

Jackie took with her to Washington her Palm Beach masseuse, New York hairdresser Kenneth and his assistant, Rosemary Sorrentino, who straightened Jackie's curly hair. Jackie had been going to thirty-three-year-old Kenneth Battelle since 1955. He had worked in Lily Daché's New York beauty salon for six years before opening his own earlier in 1960. When Jackie first went to him, he thought her curly hair, with its "feather cut," too short for her head and body size. So he gave her the bouffant style, longer, fuller and straighter, which would be hers, with minor variations, for the rest of her life – a style which, as soon as America saw it, would sweep the nation. Jackie kept this hairdo because physically and psychologically, it suited her perfectly. The big hairdo on her larger-than-normal head gave her a commanding presence and aura of assertive power. All this space, it said, is mine. There was nothing softly alluring or feminine about Jackie's hairdo; it didn't tempt little teasing winds or male fingers to run through it. Her hair, back-combed and sprayed, became a shining, protective helmet, a carapace, a lacquered shell, an enveloping cloak. Like her apparel, Jackie's hair said: "Look at me! But don't get too close."

Shortly before eight p.m. on January 19, while swirling snow began to blanket Washington in its own pristine cover-up, the presidential couple emerged from their Georgetown house with Jackie carefully holding her skirts clear of snow before stepping into a limousine. She was wearing a Cassini gown in heavy white satin, shiny and slippery as ice, inviting the eye to glide over it without stopping. The cut was simplicity itself, on princess lines, with high neck, short sleeves and no trim at all except one large rosette on the left hip. (Jackie would later battle unsuccessfully with the Smithsonian Institute, wanting them to display this gown rather than the one she would wear next evening to the Inaugural Balls. When the latter dress was installed, the traffic of an enamoured public made a large hole in the heavy-duty, guaranteed-indestructible carpet.)

It seems significant that both this gown and the one for next evening's balls were white. White denoted a void; an absence; a virginal reluctance to commit; a page in history's book still blank. White refused definition, refused color, refused everything.

Jackie arranged her pure white self carefully in the limousine, and then, with Jack beside her, was driven off to a reception for Eleanor Roosevelt; a concert at Convention Hall; and an all-star variety show at the National Guard Armoury, arranged by Frank Sinatra and Peter Lawford, where ten thousand Democrats paid one thousand dollars each for the privilege of seeing their new First Lady, and hearing Ethel Merman belt out "Everything's Coming Up Roses."

Meanwhile, Oleg Cassini, realizing how cold it would be the next day, and that Jackie's cloth coat for the noon Inauguration Ceremony outdoors had only a thin silk lining, raced about Washington until he found a clothing store which, by dint of working all night, added a warm inter-lining so that Jackie wouldn't freeze to death.

When she woke next morning, Washington's mantle of thick snow, like her two white gowns, obscured what lay beneath, and conspired with silence. Every tree limb wore a sparkling diamanté sleeve. The temperature dropped to twenty degrees as if to make a consonant beginning for an Ice Princess' reign. Jackie donned a simple beige dress, and matching beige cloth coat with its new lining. She refused to wear the norm, which was fur. "I don't know why," she would say later, "but perhaps because women huddling on the bleachers always looked like rows of fur-bearing animals." Her beige coat had only a small ring of sable at the neck, and little-girl patch pockets. With it, she would carry a sable muff, her homage to the Victorian past, when ladies were dutiful and decorous. As always, as noon crept nearer, Jackie kept Jack waiting, trying on her three pillbox hats, finally rejecting the black and garnet velvet ones in favor of the beige which matched her coat. As she anchored it securely to her bouffant hair, Jacqueline Bouvier Kennedy crowned herself Queen of America, the first one the nation had had since pre-Revolutionary days when ugly Queen Charlotte had shared the British throne with half-mad King George III. Jackie settled on the pillbox shape for almost all her White House hats for two reasons. Firstly, it sat on the back of her head and didn't interfere with her large hairdo. But more importantly, a pillbox hat, more than any other shape, looked like a crown. Jackie smiled at her image in the mirror, did up the buttons on her coat, plain fabric buttons but greatly exaggerated in size, put on little galoshes with fur tops, a pair of long beige gloves, and grabbed her muff. Then she drove off with the top-hatted president through the snowy streets to her manifest destiny.

At the ceremony, Cassini thought that the other wives in their fur coats "looked like bears roaming around," whereas Jackie looked "so neat and pretty and young. She became a bombshell right away." The Kennedy administration was off to a cold but classy start.

It was her appearance that evening, however, which put Jackie squarely and permanently in the spotlight. She herself had designed her gown for the Inaugural Balls, which Bergdorf Goodman had made for a reputed three thousand dollars. It was a full-length sheath of white silk *peau d'ange* with sleeveless hip-length bodice. Richly embroidered in silver and brilliants, the bodice asked to be noticed but then thwarted such attention by means of an overlay of white silk chiffon which veiled and partially obscured its glitter. Over the gown, Jackie wore a Cassini floor-length cape in the same white silk *peau d'ange*, its shining surface similarly hidden by a chiffon overlay. Like her sable muff, the cape looked back to a more romantic period in history. With it Jackie wore gloves befitting a queen which would become her formal-dress signature: twenty-button white glacé kid. Provi soon learned how to take in their seams so that the gloves stayed tightly in place on Jackie's thin but sinewy upper arms.

When she floated into the Red Room of the White House, where the Kennedys were already installed, Jack gazed at her dumbstruck. "Your dress is beautiful," he said. "You've never looked lovelier." At the Mayflower and Statler Hotels, the crowds cheered Jackie to the roof, and Rose Kennedy felt upstaged, even though she was wearing a lot more sparkle in a beaded Molyneux gown made for her 1938 presentation at court in England. "I was delighted to find," Rose tells us proudly in her autobiography, that "I had not changed in any dimension and I could wear it without alteration." "Turn on the lights so they can see Jackie," ordered the president in one ballroom, realizing that for the politics of style, his wife was his major prop. At the National Guard Armoury, Jackie's third and last appearance, she literally stopped the show. When she and the president took their front-row box seats, the crowd stopped dancing and surged forward to stare and cheer. Jackie smiled uncertainly, unbelieving. Were they really cheering *her*, and not Jack? When a reporter asked a young woman in the crowd why everyone was so obviously taken with Jackie, she replied, "We want to see what she's wearing and how she wears it." They saw and were overwhelmed. The American nation, watching Jackie's image on television, first in her pillbox crown and then in her cape and spangles, recognized a queen, and began, at once, to worship and adore.

"I always lived in a dream world," Jackie would later tell Pat and Richard Nixon, referring to her White House years. She was playing, as she had as a child, Queen of the Circus, where appearance ruled and truth was often banished; where her consort did sleight-of-hand tricks while his court jumped through hoops and the masses looked on and marveled.

When, at midnight on Inauguration night, Jackie in her white cape swept, in full sail, fresh from her triumph, into the White House, she imperiously told the chief usher, Mr. J.B. West: "I'll sleep in the Queen's Room." The new President's private rooms on the second and third floors were not yet ready for occupancy, but Mamie Eisenhower, the out-going First Lady, was shocked that Jackie would so peremptorily install herself in the room where only reigning queens traditionally slept. What Mamie didn't yet know was that Jacqueline Kennedy *was* a reigning queen. Sister-in-law Ethel, Bobby Kennedy's plain, down-to-earth wife, on the other hand, had detected Jackie's regal potential from the beginning. "Call me Jacqueline," Jackie had told the Kennedy wives on first meeting, giving the name its French pronunciation (*Zshock-leen*). "Rhymes with queen," grinned Ethel.

On Monday, January 23, Jackie met the members of the White House domestic staff. They were ushered into her presence three at a time while she perched on the corner of the antique desk which had been her father's and was therefore a precious possession. The First Lady wore jodhpurs, white silk blouse and brown boots. Perhaps, as Jackie kept one large hand planted on the French-Empire desk, she thought of France's Second Empire where another lady who loved riding clothes had ruled a court using style as her whip. Provi had already arranged in Jackie's closets plenty of riding habits for following the hunt from the Virginia country estate leased to the Kennedys, Glen Ora, where Wallis Windsor had once flirted with a rich but elusive beau.

Jackie's habits were for real riding, but presaged ones into which designer Ralph Lauren would later put Americans who'd never been near a horse but who wanted to suggest they might well high-jump their way, any day now, given their wealth, into aristocratic terrain.

Jackie was nervous that day as she sat on her father's desk. At thirty-one, she was younger than most of the staff, and was still feeling exhausted from John's birth followed too soon by hectic planning and upheaval. Those first days in the White House, as she recalls, were "not a happy time in my life." She felt "torn to pieces, pulled so many ways at once," and her psyche fluttered helplessly, "like a moth banging on the windowpane."

In one-to-one encounters, Jackie was always shy and guarded, trying to hide the inviolate inner self and the lack of solid self-esteem. With a crowd, however, she could play her regal role, and that role could serve as effective disguise. As one woman journalist noted, Jackie in the White House "posed a lot. It was all theater. She was good at playing the role," and J.B. West noted that in public she was always "elegant, aloof, dignified and regal." "She'd be more at home in Buckingham Palace," sneered one female reporter as Jackie made her usual stately progress around the room at a White House reception, carefully avoiding all reporters, carrying her gold cigarette case and holder, and handing her gold lighter to the nearest man when she felt the need to smoke. (She had ordered photographers never to take her picture with cigarette in hand.)

Her new role as Queen of America was one more fantasy escape, fed far more by insecurity than confidence. Even with her mask in place, however, Jackie still felt vulnerable and exposed. Her relations with the press, particularly its female contingent, were never cordial. Perhaps, as a former reporter herself, she felt envious of their successful careers. She feared mightily that they might somehow penetrate her disguise and, in response, she became even more regal and secretive as their scrutiny increased. A queen, after all, keeps her distance from her subjects, or tries to. Jackie was a truly detached and "cool" First Lady, refusing, among her many refusals, to engage, to lower herself into the political fray.

Underneath that imaginary ermine, however, there was plenty of turmoil and tension which sometimes surfaced in the form of childish temper tantrums and floods of tears, particularly when she was crossed. According to J. B. West, Jackie had a "will of iron, with more determination than anyone I have ever met." Woe betide anyone who wouldn't do her bidding. Then the soft-as-silk voice would rise to drill-sergeant shrillness. One suspects that Jackie would have liked to have shouted "Off with their heads!" as Lewis Carroll's Queen of Hearts did.

The source of much of Jackie's tension was Jack. She hadn't been married very long before she realized that her husband was one of those men, like his father Joe, who, as an acquaintance graphically put it, "would spawn with anything that twitched." Sometimes Jackie would find a pair of lace panties in the president's bed. She would tell him icily, holding them at arm's length, as far from her body as possible, that they were definitely not her size. She couldn't control her husband, neither his sexual antics nor his political agenda. She couldn't control the press which were invading her private space. What she could control was her immediate environment. She focused, almost compulsively, on bringing style and refinement to décor, to the White House social scene and, most of all, to her own person.

Jackie had never been so busy. She dressed each morning in trousers and turtleneck sweaters of lightweight jersey, ordered in bulk from Jax-Manhattan in New York. After a brisk walk around the grounds, she worked all morning at her desk, dictating, ordering, polishing the White House image, and her own. She lunched in her bedroom on a toasted cheese sandwich, then undressed, put on a nightie, and got into bed for a nap (trying not to think what Jack was doing in his bed). The First Lady ordered maids to change her sheets twice daily, once in the morning, and again after her nap.

Gradually, the queen's magic began to take effect. Remembering the homespun, Puritan garb of its past, America had always been suspicious of good taste; now, under Jackie's leadership, good taste became the "in" thing. It was suddenly all right to care about flower arrangements, string quartets and *boeuf en croûte* (Jackie had hired a French chef). Style was in; dowdiness was out; culture was in; philistinism was out. At White House parties, Lawrence Welk was superseded by Pablo Casals. "There is no doubt," wrote Ted James, columnist for *Women's Wear Daily*, in April 1964, "that Mrs. Jacqueline Kennedy probably did more to uplift taste levels in the United States than any woman in the history of our country." Jackie garbed the whole White House, which was looking really shabby, in elegance and consistent style, looking to history for inspiration. She chose the era of President James Monroe (1817–25), began assembling French Empire furnishings, and hired a French decorator, Stephane Boudin, who also worked for the Duchess of Windsor, to help her. Beauty blossomed everywhere in the White House, in silken window swags, well-turned mahogany legs and charming arrangements of meadow flowers cascading from well-wrought urns.

Much more important than the White House's image, however, was Jackie's own. *Time* magazine, shortly after the Inauguration, correctly assessed her "political role" as "mostly visual." Jackie's life in the White House became a series of photo opportunities. Since the image, not the real Jackie, was all her public was going to get, the image must dazzle.

All her clothes during the White House years were based on the dictum that less is more, or, as Diana Vreeland puts it, "Elegance is refusal." Jackie's day clothes refused prints, complicated cuts, and fussy trims. Plain suits had boxy jackets with 3/4 length sleeves and straight skirts. Dresses were often A-line and sleeveless. If she wore a brooch, she eschewed a necklace or bracelet. Spectacular earrings were often her only jewelry.

Evening gowns were straight columns of fabric, with bateau neckline and no sleeves, made from opulent fabrics which could stand alone. One day Jackie discovered that she could effectively counter her too-square jaw and shoulders by a diagonal line across her front, and the one-shoulder evening gown was born – but only after she'd asked Jack's permission for something so daring. Eventually, she talked Jack into letting her bare both shoulders, and ordered Oleg to make her strapless gowns which, like so much else in her closet, gave a double message. The bare top promised sensuality while the all-enveloping skirt denied it. When Jack told her that some new Cassini dresses made her look like a gypsy, Jackie sent them back. Other thirty-something women in those years were starting to dispense with girdles and bras, hats and gloves. America's queen, notwithstanding, buttoned her neat suit jackets, anchored her pillboxes and pulled on her white gloves. And baby-boom young women, then in their teens, took note.

Jackie was ecstatic when she learned that she'd made it onto the Best-Dressed List for 1960 (and even more thrilled when she topped the list in 1961). She was well into Operation Cover-Up, pretending to dress American while smuggling in French couture. Somehow John Fairchild, who was rapidly turning his family's paper, *Women's Wear Daily*, into one widely read and well regarded, discovered that in Paris Givenchy was making clothes on his Jackie dummy and that her sister Lee was transporting them to the U.S. in her luggage. *WWD* ran the story on its front page.

"Jesus, Jackie," yelled Jack. "The New Frontier is going to be sabotaged by a bunch of goddammed French couturiers!" But Jackie kept on buying abroad. One Givenchy bill came to over four thousand dollars. She cajoled Mark Shaw, a staff photographer for *Life*, into passing on to her pre-publication photos of the Paris fashion openings. Jackie then chose which designs she wanted, and passed the word to the relevant couturier. She also had a spy in Paris, Letizia Mowinckel, who regularly scouted the salons, reported in detail to Jackie and relayed her orders.

Clothes kept pouring into the White House in positive avalanches of cloth, much as Empress Eugénie's finery had inundated the Tuileries Palace. Oleg Cassini made Jackie more than three hundred outfits during her two years in residence. News pictures taken during the first sixteen months of the administration show Jackie in nearly four hundred different costumes, costing an estimated $50,000, two-thirds of Jack's trust fund income, and half the presidential salary, which he, to his wife's annoyance, had turned down. "Goddam, Jackie," shouted Jack, waving one department store bill in her face, "how could you spend $40,000 at one go?" Jackie looked puzzled, and replied that she really didn't know; she hadn't purchased "any furnishings or fur coats or anything." Another bill for a fresh influx of pillbox hats came to $3900. What Jack never seemed to realize was that Jackie's kind of "spending" was the female equivalent of his daily "spending" between some woman's thighs. The First Lady's expenditures for gracious living in the White House for 1961 came to $105,446.14 and rose to $121,461.61 for 1962.

If the design of her attire, like her speech, dealt in blank spaces, her closets didn't. When Jackie's second floor dressing-room closets were full, her apparel overflowed to the third floor, and onto racks in Provi's bedroom and in storage rooms. Sometimes, after a fresh burst of Jack's rage and thunder, Jackie ordered clothes from Chez Ninon or Bergdorf's, wore them once, and returned them for a refund. Occasionally would come an afternoon session of clearing out, when Jackie would let fall two large piles of suits, coats, dresses, blouses, slacks: one to be given to her female staff; the other to go, via Mary Gallagher as front, to resale shops. Jackie was almost as meticulous about her wardrobe as Wallis Windsor. One day, Mary Gallagher found Provi and her ubiquitous ironing board in Jackie's bedroom, where Provi was pressing Jackie's pantyhose. "Mees Kennedy likes to find her stockings in nice, neat pile," explained Provi as she meekly folded a dozen pairs and carried them to a drawer.

Jackie badly needed the rush of confidence her clothes gave her during her first four months in the White House when she was trying to pin down her style and her role. It wasn't until she and Jack made their State visit to Paris and Vienna at the end of May that Jackie felt firmly ensconced and enthusiastically endorsed on her invisible, yet tangible, throne.

On the morning of May 31, Paris welcomed Jacqueline Kennedy with even more warmth than they'd welcomed Empress Eugénie on her wedding day 108 years before. President and Mme. De Gaulle met the Kennedys at Orly Airport, then joined them in a motorcade through the wide streets of Paris, accompanied by the mounted *Garde Republicaine*. As the open limousine containing the president and First Lady moved slowly forward, the sun shone through dappled trees along the river Seine to sparkle on black-satin horseflesh, golden trumpets, brass helmets exuberant with scarlet plumes. Thousands of Parisians lined the streets shouting, "*Vive Jacqui! Vive Jacqui!*"

They loved her! Jackie could hardly believe her ears. In her sunshine-yellow coat buttoned to one side, and matching pillbox, she raised her chin higher, and flashed her famous smile. She knew that the crowds had loved her at the Inaugural Balls, but that was in America; that was to be expected. This was in the city which had always been her mecca of good taste and culture, the city closest to her soul.

The dream continued. She stayed with Jack at the Palais des Affaires Etrangères, a large château overlooking the Seine, slept in a bed last occupied by Belgium's Queen Fabiola, bathed in a silver tub in a mother-of-pearl bathroom, drove about beloved Paris in a limousine escorted by plumed cavaliers. The Parisians clearly adored her, this lady with a French name and lineage who spoke their language, knew their history and was dressed in what looked like their couture. For the reception at the Elysée Palace, Jackie donned a pink and white straw lace gown ostensibly designed by Cassini but which bore a remarkable resemblance to one in Pierre Cardin's spring collection.

Next evening came the climax, at the state banquet held at Versailles. Jackie had sent a lock of hair a week before to hairdresser Alexandre so that he could make a chignon to match her hair. Now he anchored it to the top of her hairdo, and added a diamond tiara. Famous make-up artist Nathalie lightened Jackie's Florida-tanned skin with make-up and applied a pale orange lipstick. Jackie stepped into a Givenchy gown – she didn't have to dissemble on the origins of this one, since wearing French couture complimented her hosts. The dress was a white satin sheath with bodice embroidered in blue and red. When Jackie saw herself in the large gilt mirrors which gave Versailles' Hall of Mirrors its name, she gasped with the wonder of it all, for what she saw was a young and beautiful reigning monarch. The dream caught her up in its pink-gold glimmer, as she looked down the long table festooned with pale-peach flowers at antique vermeil candelabra and table service. No wonder General de Gaulle seated beside her fell completely under her spell. She had never been more sparkling or sure of herself.

"She is a wow!" teletyped United Press International while *France-Soit* ran the headline "Apotheosis at Versailles!" It was precisely then, in June 1961, that Jackie stopped being just a famous man's wife and decorative accessory and became an international celebrity in her own right, a new star on the world stage. It was during the Paris idyll that Jackie began to really enjoy her First Lady role.

America's adulation increased when they saw that their own cult figure had become a world-class one. Jackie's impact on the American public, by being primarily visual, and more or less mute, left plenty of gaps for imagination to fill. American society during Jackie's thousand days in the White House wove the myth of their own royal princess in her snow-white palace. Ever since they'd thrown their tea into Boston harbor and declared themselves a republic, Americans had been hungry for crowns and courts, for all the pomp and parade of royalty. The republic was founded solely on reason, leaving imagination to long, to positively lust, for all the story-book splendor it had renounced in the rational phrases of the Declaration of Independence. Now, at long last, the American public had a beautiful young aristocrat in the White House on which to exercise its fancy. Jackie's clothes obsession meant that America's collective unconscious was kept well fed with visual stimuli of exactly the right sort. In the White House, according to the shaping myth, which of course bore little resemblance to reality, reigned a comely maiden with exquisite manners and raiment and her handsome, healthy consort who adored her and never strayed from her side. (The public didn't know that both Kennedys in Paris had been dosed by Dr. Max Jacobson, a New York doctor who accompanied them, with amphetamines to give them pep.)

"Jacqueline Kennedy has given the American people from this day on one thing they had always lacked – majesty," noted one British journalist. Jackie's American public couldn't get enough of her. By the end of 1961, a Gallup poll reported that she was the most admired woman in America, a position she'd keep for five consecutive years. "Jackie is undisputed top *femme* in the world," screamed *Variety*. "Her every seam is the subject of hypnotized attention," declared *Life* magazine. "Jackie brings glamour to America," decided the *New York Daily News*.

If, in Jackie, American women found a focus for their dreams, they also found a fashion model worth imitating. Hollywood designer Edith Head pronounced Jackie "the greatest single influence [on fashion] in history," which is probably an exaggeration, but certainly no woman in the western world since Empress Eugénie had been more quickly or eagerly copied. James Brady, editor of *Women's Wear Daily*, wrote: "As a consumer, as distinguished from a designer, Jackie has been the greatest influence of any woman of her time." *WWD* dubbed the regal First Lady "Her Elegance" and appointed a Washington correspondent early in 1961 who did nothing but keep track of what she was wearing.

Jackie's charisma began at her hemline and swirled round the world, catching Oleg Cassini in its wake. This was gratifying for a designer previously not overly successful. In the winter of 1962, Saks Fifth Avenue bought the entire Cassini collection, and dressed their windows with mannequins who bore a remarkable resemblance to Jackie. On October 25, 1961, fashion reporter Eugenia Sheppard wrote: "According to Tobe's most recent coast-to-coast survey, the best-known name in American fashion is Oleg Cassini." An enterprising Danish firm began to produce Jackie dummies and had already received orders from thirty-three countries before the U.S. Embassy put its foot down. Dr. Oscar J. Becker, a rhinoplastic surgeon at the University of Illinois College of Medicine, told a medical specialist's gathering early in 1962 that Mrs. Kennedy's name topped the list of ladies whose faces were most in demand. She had "nosed" out Princess Grace of Monaco and Elizabeth Taylor.

After Jackie appeared in sleeveless A-line shifts, dressmaker suits, low-heeled pumps, white gloves, one-shoulder evening gowns, English riding clothes, minaudières for evening bags, chain-handled purses, so did American women. "The Jackie look" spread from the U.S. across Europe and even penetrated the Iron Curtain, for ads appeared, in the Leningrad magazine *Mody*, that featured Jackie's clothes on Jackie clones. When she wore belts, the top executive of the belt trade told Cassini that the entire industry had been rejuvenated. Because Jackie wore hats, the almost moribund American hat industry found in her pillbox a miraculous cure, as every woman in the country wanted a pill-box hat. The shape had been invented by Balenciaga, but once Jackie had made it the supreme hat trick, Cassini, Halston and Givenchy all came forward, with no modesty at all, to claim the pillbox as their own invention.

"It's amazing how many women ask for the Kennedy hat," said an Ohrbach's buyer in April 1961. "Even older women. They put the hat on the back of their heads, look in the mirror and you can just see what's going through their heads. They're having the time of their lives seeing themselves as Jackie Kennedy." When Jackie went to London in June that year Reuters reported that British milliners were working day and night to fill orders for pillbox hats. Jackie didn't pluck her style innovations out of thin air, but rather from avant-garde European fashion magazines. Then she added the potent alchemy of her star quality and sprinkled the resulting gold dust around the globe, as she and Jack made their State visits to Canada, France, Austria, Venezuela, Colombia and Mexico. For each day of these trips, Jackie would wear three or four complete outfits, making nine coordinating items (hat, coat, dress or suit, shoes, stockings, handbag, gloves, underwear) for the incomparable Provi to assemble, pack and list in a big ledger which, like her ironing board, was seldom out of her sight. Jackie just loved all the presents acquired from mesmerized Heads of State; no First Lady had ever received so many, about two million dollars worth – almost as impressive a heist as that of the Prince of Wales, who'd acquired from a doting empire spectacular jewels eventually passed on to his greatest jewel: wife Wallis. From the President of Pakistan, Jackie received a diamond, emerald and ruby necklace worth $100,000; from the Emperor of Ethiopia, a leopard coat worth $75,000; from King Moulay Hassan of Morocco, a gold belt encrusted with jewels. These and all the other presents reinforced in Jackie's psyche the belief, established in childhood by her father's bounty, that approval and consumer goods went hand in hand. (Because she took these gifts with her when she vacated the White House, Congress passed a law stipulating that future First Families couldn't keep any gifts worth more than a hundred dollars.)

Jackie consolidated her world-wide image as pop star with her television special "A Tour of the White House," fittingly broadcast by CBS on Valentine's Day, 1962, viewed by eighty million Americans, and distributed to 106 countries, including, in spite of the Cold War, six behind the Iron Curtain. Jackie was simply dressed in a deep-red nubby wool two-piece dress, low-heeled shoes, with her pearls worn as she liked to wear them: half-hidden, like her personality, tucked inside the neckline of her costume. America was surprised by her voice, which, like her self-conscious stance before the camera, her big hands with bitten nails clasped in front of her, showed that in spite of the Paris triumph, the frightened little girl was still there – and would visually surface later in her life. The only harsh critic of her performance was Norman Mailer. In an article for *Esquire*, he called Jackie's voice "a quiet parody of the sort of voice one hears on the radio late at night" from "girls who sell soft mattresses." Mailer thought the First Lady moved like a wooden horse and looked like "a starlet who will never learn to act."

On March 9, without Jack, Jackie and sister Lee left New York's Idlewild International Airport on a trip to India and Pakistan, with an entourage which included a hairdresser, Provi, Secret Service agents and a press secretary, Jay Gildner, who kept insisting that "Mrs. Kennedy does not regard this trip as a fashion show." The television cameras caught the First Lady's huge steamer trunks being loaded onto the Pan-American jet. Provi had been packing and listing for days. Included were forty-eight pairs of gloves and a wig, in case the First Lady's bouffant hairdo collapsed in Indian humidity.

Jackie climbed aboard in her Somali leopard coat, custom-made by New York furrier Ben Kahn. Ted Kahn, a Harvard classmate of Jack's, had brought skins to the White House in the previous October. Jack had wanted Jackie to choose conventional mink; Jackie had wanted something wilder and more original. After Jackie was photographed for *Life*'s cover in her leopard coat, which probably cost about $6000, the price of one jumped to $40,000 and the animal went on the endangered species list where it still remains. This is serious fashion influence. Jacqueline Kennedy almost single-handedly cleared the jungles of these big cats.

It was hard for Lee not to feel jealous of her famous sister. After divorcing Michael Canfield, whom everyone, including the Duke of Windsor, believed to be the illegitimate offspring of his brother, the Duke of Kent, Lee had married Prince Stanislas ("Stash") Radziwill, rich Polish aristocrat and London business tycoon. Fashion rivalry between the sisters had surfaced when Jackie wrote to her Paris scout Letizia Mowinckel: "You are so sweet to write me such a long letter about all the heavenly clothes in Paris," purred Jackie. "What I really appreciate most of all is your letting me know before Lee about the treasures. Please always do that – now that she knows you are my 'scout' she is slipping in there before me. So this fall, do let me know about the prettiest things first."

Jackie wore twenty-five different outfits in her first twelve days in India, many of them in bright shades – hot pink, orange, turquoise – which could hold their own with the glaring sun. The Associated Press for the first time handed question-and-answer forms on fashion to Jay Gildner, so that he could describe every item of the First Lady's apparel, even her shoes. At the Rome airport, where Jackie had a brief stopover, the world learned that she wore a charcoal day dress with chunky belt, and a short white satin evening dress with jet-beaded overblouse for Countess Mimi Pecci-Blunt's dinner party. Jackie's Indian garb included a hot pink rajah coat, a green silk dress worn with a little-girl white hairbow, and a turquoise sleeveless shift in which she sighed over the romantic beauty of the Taj Mahal. A male NBC reporter informed the American nation that in his opinion an apricot silk dress and matching coat were the prettiest ensemble. Keyes Beech, reporter for the *Chicago Daily News* got the biggest scoop. "This reporter is now able to lift the veil of secrecy from Jacqueline Kennedy's feet," he wrote excitedly, after a visit to the Mahatma Gandhi Memorial, where Jackie had to leave her shoes outside before entering sacred ground. The enterprising Beech had sneaked a look at the size: 10A. "Having no tape measure, I was unable to measure the exact length of the heels," he added earnestly. "However, my rough estimate would be two inches."

Initially, the American press was wildly enthusiastic about their new First Lady's young, distinctive, dignified image. They were bedazzled by her fashion sense, her beauty, her star quality. To do justice to all her outfits, they had to learn the technical language of fashion, the difference between a pleat and a placket, between taffeta and twill. The whole media had to become fashion reporters, and in so doing, they raised the consciousness of the whole nation as to female dress and image. As time passed, however, journalists became frustrated by Mrs. Kennedy's reserve and refusal to reveal herself. In growing desperation, they realized that they had to go on reporting her clothes in excruciating detail because it was all they had. There was nothing else to write about on the subject of the First Lady.

Indians turned out to see Jackie in greater numbers than had greeted Queen Elizabeth, and dubbed her "Amerika Maharani" – Queen of America. Jackie's Indian trip, one long fashion show (despite Jay Gildner's claims), was filmed, shown in American movie theaters as a short and spread her influence even further. When the international press became highly critical of her flaunting so many expensive outfits before a people suffering great poverty, Jackie told Jay Gildner to stop passing out the question-and-answer fashion forms. If the press questioned her wardrobe, snapped the First Lady, "tell them it's second-hand and that I bought everything at the Ritz Thrift Shop." The queen's oversized head, it seems, had been turned by too much adulation; the queen was proving herself both spoiled and insensitive.

On March 26, Jackie sent a smug note to Oleg Cassini: "This is just to tell you that all your clothes were an absolute dream and I was delighted with them. The white coat is ESPECIALLY lovely and really looks outstanding. They are all now in rather a pathetic condition after 3 weeks of 1 night stands, and well worn. I only wish I'd gotten more, but next time I'll know better." Jackie's clothes mania was getting out of hand, but would not peak for another seven years. One might have expected that massive approval would have resulted in less apparel, not more. What inner conflicts were driving her to buy, buy, buy?

Following the Indian trip, Mary Gallagher found her secretarial duties were mainly clothes-related as she issued checks; returned rejected garments to Oleg in New York; arranged for La Guardia's flight manager to expedite more Cassinis en route to Washington. "The heavens seemed to have opened up – it simply *rained* clothes!" remembers Mary. When the Cassini shipment duly arrived at the White House, Jackie tried everything on, dropped each garment to the floor for Provi to pick up and dictated to Mary changes to be made in the garments chosen as to style, color or fabric. Meanwhile, Seventh Avenue manufacturers were busy making sari evening dresses inspired by those the First Lady was wearing, custom-made from a trunkful of saris garnered on her India trip. For the next four years, sari dresses in America would be big sellers.

By the spring of 1963, Jackie was pregnant again and couldn't fit into anything really stylish. Lane Bryant, the leading manufacturer of maternity wear, again advertised their "First Lady Maternity Fashions." Patrick Bouvier Kennedy was born by Caesarean section at Otis Air Force Base hospital on August 7. He weighed only 4 lbs. 1 oz. and died on the third day of his little life. Jackie was too ill and distraught to attend his burial.

To help her recover her spirits and strength, acquaintance Aristotle Onassis invited Jackie (without Jack) to cruise the Mediterranean with him and a party of friends on board his yacht *Christina*. Ari had been born in 1906 in Smyrna, Turkey, had landed in Buenos Aires on September 21, 1923, with sixty dollars in his pocket, had prospered in the tobacco trade and got rich fast. By 1963, he'd amassed a fortune estimated at five hundred million to one billion dollars, made love to Gloria Swanson, Greta Garbo, Evita Peron, Veronica Lake and many other women, owned a fleet of more than one hundred ships, a casino at Monte Carlo, and lavish homes on three continents, including one on his own island, Skorpios, in the silver Ionian sea. Ari cared nothing for clothes. His suits were tailored by an elderly Greek in out-of-date styles. Nor was Ari physically attractive, being short, with greasy black hair, liver-colored skin and a fleshy nose, but he had an erotic energy that women found irresistible. Marlene Dietrich summed him up well: "I really admired Aristotle Onassis," she writes in her memoir. "Unlike most rich people, he wasn't boring. He sparkled with *joie de vivre* and possessed a generosity from which everybody profited." Marlene also liked his sense of humor, and thought him "an extraordinary human being." In December 1946, Ari had cannily married Tina Livanos, daughter of a rival Greek ship-owner even richer than he was. He and Tina, for an annual rent of $48,000 had, from 1950 to 1953, rented the Château de la Cröe at Antibes, where Wallis and Edward Windsor had spent part of their bejeweled life. In June 1960, Tina divorced Ari, who sought consolation in the arms of opera diva Maria Callas. He'd invited Jackie to cruise on the *Christina* in 1961, but she'd turned him down. Now, feeling fragile since her baby's death and in need of extra cossetting, Jackie accepted.

Ari planned his conquest of the First Lady with the wisdom of Socrates, and great insight into Jackie's character, just as if he were luring a timid fawn into a very well-baited trap. First, he hired extra crew to see to her every whim, engaged a dance band and two hairdressers, invited sister Lee so Jackie would feel at home, and Italian fashion designer Irene Galitzine so she could talk clothes to her heart's content. Then, having on previous meetings divined Jackie's overwhelming need for privacy, just before she stepped aboard, Ari went below and stayed well out of sight, biding his time, never appearing until the *Christina* reached the island of Lesbos. Then he greeted his special guest, volunteered his services as guide to the island, and enchanted Jackie utterly by being so charming, energized, and knowledgeable about Greek history and myths. He waxed eloquent about the god Apollo's first love, Daphne, and about the shy goddess Diana, who had thwarted Actaeon. Jackie drank it all in, as the ship floated on an impossibly blue sea. She admired the way the *Christina*'s lapis lazuli fireplaces matched the sea's color, relaxed in the beauty salon where, as always, her hair was set every two days, ignored the garish bad taste of most of the ship, particularly the bar stools upholstered with the scrotums of whales. Long after everyone else had gone to bed, Jackie sat with Ari on the poop deck, under a black-velvet sky spangled with stars. Ari was a romantic word-spinner, in a way that Jack had never been, not even in courting days.

On the final evening of the cruise, Ari snapped his tender trap shut with the sound of a jewel case's click. He presented Jackie with a diamond and ruby necklace that could be converted into two bracelets. "Oh, God," moaned sister Lee, insanely jealous. "It's so splendid I can't believe it." It was worth at least $50,000. Lee at once wrote to her brother-in-law, Jack, to tell him so, adding, "Ari has showered Jackie with so many presents I can't stand it. All I've gotten is three dinky little bracelets that Caroline wouldn't even wear to her own birthday party." Back in Washington, Jack was fuming at the First Lady's trip with this particular shark. One of the guests on board the *Christina* was Franklin D. Roosevelt Jr., then undersecretary of commerce. Members of Congress railed lest Ari, through Franklin, should try to curry favor with the U.S. Maritime Administration. They needn't have worried; Ari had a different agenda.

Back in Washington, Jackie was already looking forward to Christmas in the White House. "I know it's too expensive for words," she murmured to Jack's secretary, Evelyn Lincoln, one day in early November, but would Evelyn please inform the president that what Jackie wanted for Christmas was a chinchilla bedspread worth about four thousand dollars. There would, alas, be no 1963 Christmas in the White House, no present from Jack.

On November 22, in Dallas, Texas, Jackie found herself thrust into the middle of a Greek tragedy, turned to stone by the sight of a head far more frightening than Medusa's, staring in horror at the blood and brains which defiled her shocking pink Chanel suit, and forever bruised her soul.

Jackie woke the next morning, Saturday, after a few hours of drugged, disturbed sleep, with Friday's detachment from her husband's assassination wearing off, and the full horror seeping like a slow-spreading stain through her being. She knew that only her habitual attention to detail could keep her sane. She began to plan the State funeral, and what she would wear; she asked Provi to find her a widow's black veil. "Very few people call for them anymore," explained a funeral director whom Provi contacted. She offered her mistress a black lace mantilla instead, the closest thing to a mourning veil she could lay her hands on. No, said Jackie firmly, that wouldn't do. Was the picture floating in her mind that of the British Royals at King George VI's funeral in 1952? The Queen Mother, Queen Elizabeth II and Princess Margaret had all worn semi-sheer, shoulder-length black veils over face and head. Such veils were associated with royalty, and Jackie was determined to have one. She ordered Lucinda Morman, a White House maid skilled at making quick repairs and alterations to Jackie's clothes, to make one at once on her sewing machine.

Jackie got through the next few days leaning on the conventions of dignity and decorum learned from her mother, reinforced by the proprieties of Merrywood and Hammersmith Farm. Jackie knew, in some small part of her splintered mind, that she was about to play Queen Jacqueline's most terrible and climactic scene. She resolved to do so with consummate grace, and not a single stumble.

For her world-wide audience, as American television broadcast its black-and-white requiem for John Fitzgerald Kennedy, this would be Jackie's finest hour. Millions watched on Monday, November 25, as Jacqueline Kennedy, widowed at thirty-four, marched slowly in procession from the Capitol Rotunda, where the slain president had lain in state, to St. Matthew's Cathedral for the burial service. She was wearing a black suit with boxy jacket and knee-length skirt. The jacket's only trim were two very large black buttons which formed a mute elegy for the big beige-fabric ones aligned with hope and promise which had fastened her Inauguration coat two years before. Covering Jackie's face was her extra-long mourning veil which, like all her clothes, gave forth a conflicting message. By being rare and anachronistic, the veil drew attention to its wearer; by concealing the face, it foiled that focus. The very real veil bodied forth that invisible one which Jackie had always worn before her public. Anchoring the veil to her head was a black pillbox hat, but not in her habitual shape, which was proudly upstanding. This pillbox had lost its daring and its rule; it was squashed, depressed into a mere memory of a crown. Jackie's flattened hat served as epitaph for what its wearer had forever lost.

After the burial service, Jackie emerged from the cathedral's dark arch to stand on the steps, holding the hands of her children. "Hail to the Chief" sounded in her ears for the last time; she quietly prompted her little son, in one of history's most poignant, memorable and truly dramatic gestures, to salute the American flag atop his father's coffin as it was borne away.

At that precise moment, as she stood straight-backed on the steps, Jacqueline Bouvier Kennedy was raised in the world's eyes from star to saint, from celebrity to icon, from object of desire to object of worship. From now on, there would be two Jackies: one real, one mythical. This ultimate dichotomy would last until her death, and the mythical half would go beyond, acquiring ever more gloss as time passed and the shadowy outline of the real, very private Jackie grew fainter. People around the world, glued to their television sets on November 25, 1963, garbed Jackie in the well-worn fabric of two major myths. Firstly, they saw her as desolate romantic lover, for in all great love stories (which is what the public thought the Kennedy marriage was), one or both principals must die: Juliet awakens to a dead Romeo; Sir Lancelot prays over a dead Guinevere. And there on the cathedral steps stood Jacqueline Kennedy, young, comely, and bereft, a slim, black, silent presence, without forward motion, without a mate. Secondly, the masses mythologized Jackie by girdling her in the robes of a *mater dolorosa* who, like the Blessed Virgin, had held her slain Lord and master in her arms.

Jackie thus proffered an ideal of beauty that went far beyond raiment to morality. She responded to a horrible random accident, a thunderbolt descending from some dark and evil place, with the stoicism, emotional restraint and dignified silence which were already deeply ingrained in her character. Now the whole world saw those traits, suffered with her, and was redeemed by her comforting gift of conventional form and consummate style.

After the funeral, as was inevitable, numbness departed and Jackie fell apart. Her eyes darted; her speech slurred; she feared everyone and everything. "I'm a freak now," she moaned to relatives and friends. "I'll always be a freak." On November 29, she summoned journalist Theodore A. White to her Hyannis Port summer home, and herself gave a mighty push to the process just begun of turning history into myth. Clad in beige sweater and black-trimmed slacks, Jackie talked about the assassination and about her slain husband. She instructed Teddy White, in writing his story for *Life* magazine, to describe the magical thousand and one nights of the Kennedy administration as time spent in Camelot, the legendary home of King Arthur. "Jack's life," she told White, had "more to do with myth, magic, legend, saga and story than with political theory or political science." Jackie sprinkled her magic dust in White's eyes, and through him conveyed it to a nation. She talked about how Jack loved the words from the musical *Camelot* written by his Choate and Harvard classmate, Alan Jay Lerner: "Don't let it be forgot, that once there was a spot, for one brief shining moment that was known as Camelot."

Ignore the reality, swallow the myth. Ignore John Fitzgerald Kennedy's suspect Mafia links, his compulsive womanizing, his Addison's disease, his addiction to amphetamines, his tendency to hide the truth. Like all good queens, Jackie judged her people accurately, and knew how to manipulate them. She knew how sentimental her nation was, how, before all else, it loved a golden hero and a golden myth. So she gave it to them, sitting on the sofa talking softly to a member of the press, while gray sea pounded beyond the windows. Deft weaver of dreams ever since her childhood, Jackie gave to the man who'd never given her one really romantic moment or word, the ultimate romantic gift. She crowned him King, created him, by association, quite as pious, virtuous and honest as good King Arthur. She'd already shared her superb taste and style with a grateful nation; now she unfurled her imagination into a magic carpet, doing it, not in her usual chary, grudging way, but with great prodigality and generosity. When White's *Life* editor wanted to remove the fourth mention of Camelot from his article, White consulted Jackie. No, no, he mustn't, she told him. "It stays in." No one must remove a single thread from her delicate tapestry. (Later, biographers and historians would hack it to pieces.)

Ten days after she'd lit the eternal flame – her idea – on her husband's grave at Arlington Cemetery, Jackie moved out of the White House. But she left a legacy to her successor, Lady Bird Johnson. After Jackie's reign, no First Lady could afford to be negligent about clothes. Poor Lady Bird – one of those "Texas broads" Kennedy had disparaged – had to smarten up, and was hounded by *Women's Wear Daily* to disclose the names of her designers. Lady Bird proved herself equal to the task, for in 1966 she would make it onto the Best-Dressed List.

In the following months, having moved into a borrowed Georgetown house, Jackie became deeply depressed. She looked terrible: haggard, disheveled and – proving how serious her depression was – lost all interest in clothes. She stayed much of the time in bed, took anti-depressant pills by day and sleeping pills by night, while the horror of the assassination, over and over, reeled through her mind, one image at a time: the pink, perfect circles inside Jack's skull... crushed rose petals dripping blood... When she could drag herself out of bed, Jackie climbed listlessly into some black garment. For a year she dressed only in black. "The poor woman was crying every time I saw her," remembers Ken O'Donnell, Jack's special assistant. When, one year after the trauma, in November 1964, journalist Dorothy Schiff lunched with Jackie, the former First Lady wore a brown cotton skirt with black stockings, and a white silk blouse over an inappropriate slip which plainly revealed, through the blouse's semi-transparent silk, its too-dark presence. Jackie had grown very thin; her eyes looked dull and her hair "dusty." "It was hard talking to her. She let silences go on. She is odd and different, very much less the queen than she was," noted Dorothy. "I think she was scared of me, in a funny sort of way." Now that she'd hung her Camelot filaments in every American mind, Jackie knew that she must be even more guarded than before with the press. Perhaps her silences lengthened because she was thinking carefully before she uttered each phrase, lest some impulsive word tear a hole in her creation.

If Jackie looked poorly, she also felt poor, since she had only about $200,000 a year to live on. Bobby Kennedy gave her an extra $50,000 a year and Joe Kennedy, his speech reduced since his stroke three years before, to two highly characteristic words: "shit" and "no," nevertheless still paid Jackie's clothing bills.

Jackie fled Washington's miasma of memories and moved to New York in 1964, buying for $200,000 a fifteen-room apartment on Fifth Avenue at 85th Street. Fourteen of its twenty-three windows overlooked the soothing greens of Central Park and Jackie had the whole fourteenth floor to her very private self, sharing it only with her children and servants. Slowly, she began to climb out of her dark hole back to sanity and sunlight, using style as her ladder. She hired Billy Baldwin to decorate her apartment with the Louis XIV furniture she loved. She summoned the new *wunderkind* on the fashion scene, Mario Valentino, to her apartment. He was a dashing Italian from Milan who'd hired a real Princess, Orsetta Torlonia, to direct his Rome salon. He came at once to Jackie, bringing his entire couture collection, an assistant, a fitter and a live model. Jackie anointed him her couturier-in-chief, and kept him very busy for the next five years making her brightly colored outfits to replace her mourning garb. Style saved her, and brought her back from the dead.

For the rest of her life, it was as if Jackie never took off that darkly obscuring veil which she'd made manifest at Kennedy's funeral. After the early 1970s, she granted journalists no more interviews. She decided that publicity, like her clothes, mustn't be ugly or revealing. She herself would try, with no success at all, given the public's ongoing appetite for news of her, to tailor it to her own measure. As with her friends, Jackie blew hot and cold with the media, and was, as in most things, ambivalent. Sometimes she wanted privacy; sometimes she wanted coverage – but only of the right sort. When in New York, she often told her secretary, faithful school chum Nancy Tuckerman, to inform *Women's Wear Daily* that Mrs. Kennedy would be lunching at La Côte Basque or at La Grenouille on a certain day, should they care to send a photographer.

Magazines soon discovered that if they put Jackie on the cover, sales dramatically increased, just as they had in her White House days. Between 1963 and 1966 *Life* and *Look* put her three times on their covers, and at least thirty-five movie magazines per month also used a Jackie cover. It seems fitting that, as the years passed, Jackie seemed to exist primarily on a cover, for "cover" had always been the operative word for her style. Whether on a magazine or on her person, covers fulfilled their function: they hid more than they revealed. The stories inside the magazines had much speculation and few facts. Jackie's continued silence was twofold. She herself didn't speak, and neither did those many photographs of her. She forced her adoring public, just as had Gloria Swanson and Clara Bow in their silent films, to focus on the image alone and weave their dreams around it. It was as if Jackie knew what Elinor Glyn knew: imagination thrives on mystery, and loves to be teased. Modern American society likes to package its heroes and heroines in simple forms and a few, primary colors so that it can consume them easily and quickly. No celebrity ever conspired to help them in their devout devouring as much as Jackie. America can be fickle in its affections; celebrities appear and disappear from its consciousness with astonishing rapidity. Jackie would live another thirty-one years after she stopped being First Lady and for all that time the world would keep her, like a startled deer in a car's headlights, in a fierce, unrelieved glare. Since then, almost one biography a year has been written about her, and in the years before her death *The Reader's Guide to Periodical Literature* had more listings for Jackie than for any other living woman. Almost all these books and articles spread out, one more time, the same few shreds and patches of anecdotal material. As in a simple children's fairy tale, repetition strengthened the myth.

In the continuing spotlight, Jackie put on a new and different guise. When catapulted into the White House's center ring, she'd searched through history's grab-bag and come up with the role of queen. Now she rummaged in her own past, and reverted to little girl. Jackie's look grew younger, more playful, more frivolous – and much closer than her royal role to her actual psyche. She bicycled or jogged in Central Park in tight pants, poor-boy sweaters that looked as if she'd outgrown them, and no make-up. *Women's Wear Daily* ran the headline "Jackie Has the Knack of Looking Darling" – and about ten years old. In the fall of 1966, Jackie asked Marita O'Connor at Bergdorf's to make her a beret "just like the children wear" and illustrated her note with precise sketches of little girls in stem-topped tams. She had already looked in vain in the children's department of stores for what she wanted but, naturally, couldn't find one big enough for her overlarge, adult head. On July 20, 1966, *WWD* reported on page one that with her shorter skirts and "that long heavy hair," "SHE'S A REAL GIRL."

WWD featured a double-spread of Jackie photos taken outside Manhattan's Lafayette Restaurant on December 4, 1966. They showed Jackie in a skirt several inches above her knees. Jacqueline Kennedy was wearing mini-skirts! The news flashed round the globe. She thus single-handedly revived a fashion first launched in the late 1950s by English designer Mary Quant and English model Twiggy and aimed at the very young. Thanks to Jackie, the mini skirt swept across the fashion scene with the same force as Dior's mid-thigh "New Look" of 1947. Everyone who had the legs to wear a mini-skirt did; those who didn't either wore one anyway or felt suddenly old and dated.

Jackie's girlish mini-skirts and mini-dresses represented one more refusal; this one, a refusal of adulthood. Girls didn't have to face up to adult decisions and dilemmas or be strong and self-reliant. Alice-in-Wonderland hair, cute little tams and mini-dresses show how Jackie's beleaguered psyche was trying to curl up and suck its thumb. Marlene Dietrich could have told her how sexy and alluring bared legs could be; Jackie used hers to run after a new father figure who could spoil and indulge her ever-needy, never-satisfied id.

Coco Chanel, for one, disapproved of Jackie's new look. "She wears her daughter's clothes," sneered Coco. "A woman in her position should be more dignified." Like the Duke of Windsor, Jackie was something of an arrested adolescent. She was never happier than when playing games and romping with her two young children; she had chosen as first husband not a contemporary but a man twelve years older; her notes to friends are full of teenage gush. Carly Simon would later refer to Jackie as "the eighth-grader she really was." Journalist Norman Podhoretz once described her as "the brightest sixteen-year-old in America."

Jackie was also enjoying her return to the age of dating; she was seen in New York night spots with Mike Nichols, Lord Harlech, Pete Hamill, Roswell Gilpatric, and ran about town in a double-breasted black mink coat cut like a school-girl's reefer.

When Bobby Kennedy was murdered on June 4, 1968, Ari Onassis flew at once to Los Angeles – he had also flown to Washington when Jack was assassinated – to find Jackie in a state of panic and disbelief, so disoriented that she seemed to be confusing Bobby's murder with Jack's. In the past five years, Jackie, who always needed a strong man in her life, had relied on Bobby for guidance and fatherly advice. Bereft once more, she switched her little-girl needs to Onassis, and, after the funeral, invited him to Hammersmith Farm.

By autumn, Jackie had decided to marry the persuasive Onassis, to stage her further retreat from the public by jumping off the impossibly high pedestal on which they'd placed her, viewing her as a permanent *mater dolorosa* living only through her children and forever grieving her lost knight. Jackie hadn't been able to erase that womanly-woman widow image by dressing in mini-skirts, tams, skinny pants and poor-boy sweaters. Now she would do it, once and for all, through her actions. On October 17, Jackie walked out of her Fifth Avenue apartment, holding ten-year-old Caroline by one hand, and seven-year-old John by the other, and flew off to Greece. She boarded the plane in a gray jersey mini-dress. Her 1953 going-away suit for marriage to Jack had been gray. Was gray, for Jackie, the color of marriage?

On that same day, Ari went to Zolotas, his favorite Athens jewelry store, and bought Jackie diamond earrings and a ruby-encrusted gold bracelet. He had already picked out her $1.25 million engagement ring, a heart-shaped ruby surrounded by diamonds. Jackie's pre-nuptial agreement with Ari gave her three million dollars outright, plus annual interest on a one million dollar trust for each of her children until they reached twenty-one. Ari was trying to buy himself favor with U.S. banks, who'd blacklisted him ever since World War II, because he wanted to negotiate loans. Marriage to a former First Lady would hopefully improve his image. Jackie, as always, was trying to buy herself the attention and approval she'd been denied as a child. In addition to a bottomless purse, Ari could give her privacy and protection. She would be safe from murderers, prying press, and an idolatrous, nosy public on Skorpios, Ari's five-hundred-acre Greek island whose breezes brought her the mingled, heavenly scents of pine needles, orange blossoms, eucalyptus leaves and endless fields of lavender.

The wedding took place at 5:15 p.m. on October 20, 1968, in the island's tiny, white-washed chapel, while a cold, driving rain turned the sea from turquoise to gray. Jackie wore a two-piece beige Valentino creation of chiffon and lace, its skirt three inches above her knees. (Next day, Valentino received thirty-eight orders for an identical dress, which he describes as his "most famous" one.) Jackie's hairdo flowed to her shoulders, with one little-girl braid down the back and a wide, beige little-girl hair ribbon on top. Even with elevator shoes, Ari, in nondescript navy suit and crimson tie, was shorter than his bride.

The American reaction to the marriage was one of horror. How *could* their princess marry a toad? Jackie was immediately demoted from saint to sinner, and when the February 1969 Gallup Poll's list of most admired women came out, Jackie had plummeted to seventh place, replaced as number one by the new *mater dolorosa*, Robert Kennedy's widow, Ethel. The rest of the world was just as disapproving. "Jackie – How Could You?" demanded a Stockholm newspaper. "John Kennedy Dies Today for the Second Time" sighed one from Rome. However, once they'd all recovered from their initial shock, everybody realized that Jackie as pop-culture idol was hotter than ever. Her life was proving to be a fine soap-opera saga, full of the usual wealth, family dynasties, adultery, murder, multiple marriages, all centered on a beautiful heroine who was the pawn of powerful men. *Women's Wear Daily* switched from "Her Elegance" to "Jackie O. and Daddy O." Jackie and Ari soon became the most famous couple in the world, even more renowned than Liz Taylor and Richard Burton.

As soon as she was married, Jackie started a prolonged, frenetic orgy of shopping and spending. Three days after the wedding she summoned New York's Billy Baldwin to Skorpios to begin redecorating everything in sight. She wheedled Ari into giving her five million dollars worth of jewels during the first year of marriage. Every two weeks, he presented her with a bouquet of flowers which had yet another bracelet hiding coyly in its petals. As a child might, Jackie asked "Daddy O." to bring her back a present every time he went away on business. "She is like a diamond, cool and sharp at the edges," said a seemingly besotted Ari, "fiery and hot beneath the surface." He literally put his money where his mouth was by giving her, for her fortieth birthday in 1969, a forty-carat diamond (one for each year) set in a Cartier ring worth one million dollars. He also gave her a solid gold belt appropriately adorned with a lioness' head.

"She is like a bird," said Onassis indulgently. "She wants the protection of the nest, yet she wants, as well, the freedom to fly." Jackie flew, always, straight into the nearest store. Style became the panacea for all her psychological insecurities, but it was style in fever form, completely out of control. She had shown symptoms of galloping consumption ever since childhood; now it became a serious malady.

If her greed expanded, so did her hairdo. It puffed out into the kind of overblown shape one sees when delirious. Sunglasses became bigger, too, and broadcast the usual double message: their exaggerated size begged for notice; their dark lenses masked the expression of Jackie's eyes. Of course, the rest of the female world put on oversized, wrap-around, tortoise-rimmed sunglasses too, and soon every drugstore had displays of them for $1.98 and up. Once, Jackie was spotted in Washington's National Gallery looking at paintings in a trenchcoat, slacks and her habitual sunglasses. This proves that her psyche's need for such a symbol was greater than her passion for art. No one can see true color through a darkly veiled eye.

In the beginning, Ari was quite willing to indulge his bride's addiction to shopping and, in the honeymoon phase of their marriage, was spending about $1.6 million per month on her. "God knows Jackie has had her years of sorrow," he said. "If she enjoys it, let her buy to her heart's content." The trouble was, Jackie's heart never *was* content, no matter how voraciously she fed her need for material things. For the other women in this book, the pleasures of style came mainly from wearing clothes; for Jackie, they came from acquiring them. Ari's chief accountant, Costa Gratsos, was shocked at her extravagance: "It was a bit sickening. Jackie not only had the interest from her newly replenished $3 million, she had a $30,000 monthly allowance, plus charge privileges," but all this was never enough. Jackie became an accomplished speed shopper. She could be in and out of any store in the world in ten minutes or less, having run through at least $100,000. "She had an eye for immediately spotting the most precious and expensive object wherever she goes," sighed Ari, as his disenchantment grew. She ignored price tags; she just pointed. Sometimes, at Valentino or Givenchy showings, Jackie would buy almost the whole collection, not just the models that suited her. Her consumptive fever was now seriously affecting her style. Truman Capote recalls how sometimes when they were together in New York, Jackie would walk into a store, order three dozen identically styled silk blouses in all the colors available, give an address, and walk out. She seemed dazed, hypnotized, in a trance. In one binge at Bergdorf's, she bought thirty-six pairs of shoes. When she went to Teheran, Iran, on a nine-day stay, Jackie's total bill, for hotel accommodation, room service, Persian rugs, lamps, antiques, sheepskin jackets and tubs of golden caviar, came to $650,000. When it became clear to Ari that Jackie, incredibly, couldn't stay within her $30,000 allowance, he railed and ranted, much as Jack had, and scaled it back to a mere $20,000.

Two years into the marriage, it began to fall apart. While Jackie was in New York early in May 1970, Ari spent four nights in a row with his former love, Maria Callas, confiding his growing dissatisfaction with his wife, her chilly indifference, her spendthrift ways, her impenetrable armor. By 1974, he had decided to divorce her. "I've had it up to here," he told his attorney. "I cannot understand her. All she does is spend, spend, spend – and she's never in the same place as I am. If I'm in Paris, she's in New York. If I go to Skorpios, she goes to London. She's never with me," he concluded with a deep sigh. He felt hurt, abandoned, but Jackie just kept her distance, kept on shopping.

What was Jackie feeling? Disappointed, betrayed, unloved? We have only those little-girl clothes and that rampant consumerism to give us clues. Twice she had married and twice she had erred, choosing powerful older men primarily for their wealth. Jack had focused not on her but on his fierce pursuit of power; Ari had at least given her romance and empathy, but somehow it wasn't enough. No matter how many clothes she bought, her inner discontent and strange hungers were unassuaged. The lack of proper nurturing and praise from madly social, selfish parents had left scars on Jackie's personality that would never heal.

Before he could divorce Jackie, who in their seven years of marriage had spent forty-two million dollars, or almost seven million per year, Ari died, on Saturday, March 15, 1975, of myasthenia gravis, a muscle-wasting disease. He expired at the American Hospital at Neuilly-sur-Seine where, in another eight months, Wallis Windsor would lie supine upon her peach-colored, crested Porthault sheets. Jackie wasn't with Ari at the end; she'd gone skiing in New Hampshire. She flew to Paris for the funeral, where, a day or two later, fashion editor James Brady spied Valentino in the lobby of the Hotel St. Regis. "What are you doing in Paris?" asked Brady. "Jackie Onassis phoned me in Italy," Valentino told him, "and asked me to meet her. She said she needed a new black dress for the funeral and so I brought something along and fitted it on her." Did Jackie ask herself, as once again, in black widow's weeds, she followed a husband's coffin, if perhaps she wore, like the mark of Cain, some invisible, cursed stain which had precipitated the deaths of two husbands, and three offspring, as well as a father and a brother-in-law?

Ari's will, as per the pre-nuptial agreement, left Jackie only $200,000 in tax free funds, with another $50,000 tax free for Caroline and John until they reached the age of twenty-one. Jackie knew she couldn't possibly support her clothes habit on that paltry sum, so she contested the will. After eighteen months of legal haggling, Ari's daughter Christina, whom Jackie had tried unsuccessfully at the beginning of her marriage to convert to stylish garb, angrily told her lawyers to give her rapacious, wicked stepmother a settlement of twenty-six million dollars, and good riddance.

After the notoriety of the court battle, Jackie retreated even further from the world's clamor into her inscrutable shell. She gathered around her a small but protective coterie of friends, such as Bunny Mellon and the Duchess of Windsor's rival Jayne Wrightsman, and swore them all to silence on the subject of their famous, Sphinx-like friend.

By the fall of 1975, as Jackie, aged forty-six, faced each gray dawn, she asked herself what on earth she was going to do with the rest of her life. Various fashion houses approached her to represent them or to create a collection under her own sure-to-sell label. But Jackie turned her back on beautiful images and opted for the written word instead. She went to work for New York publisher Viking, turning up each day in the protective coloring of sweaters and slacks, "dressed just like the rest of us," according to her assistant, Rebecca Singleton. Not quite; all the sweaters were finest quality cashmere; all the trousers had couture labels sewn into their waistbands. While at Viking, she edited such elegant coffeetable books as *In The Russian Style* (1976), based on a show of Imperial Russian eighteenth- and nineteenth-century costumes, artifacts and icons mounted at New York's Metropolitan Museum. Jackie and the Met's Director, Tom Hoving, went to Russia together to gather material. There he gasped at her beauty when Jackie materialized before him modeling an evening outfit which poor, doomed Empress Alexandra had worn to the opera. Of shimmering white silk, its gown, muff and hooded cape were trimmed with white swans-down. It must have reminded Jackie of her own queenly versions of white gown and cape in those early days at Camelot.

Jackie left Viking in the fall of 1977 after a falling out with its publisher, Thomas H. Guinzburg, and in the following spring went to work at Doubleday three days a week, editing art and photography books. Her annual salary was a mere ten thousand dollars, an amount she sometimes spent at Ungaro's shop on Madison Avenue during her lunch break.

In the early 1980s, Jackie found a new designer, and a new man. She switched her fashion loyalties from Ungaro and Valentino to Carolina Herrara. Like Oleg Cassini, Herrara, whose father had twice been Venezuela's minister of foreign affairs, had the kind of social background of which snob Jackie could approve. Carolina had started designing in 1981, and believed in clothes that were "simple and pure" in "great materials and colors." Jackie began to appear in such arresting outfits as a fuchsia wool suit, white crepe dinner gown well-sequined in silver, and a jacket with broad black and white stripes. When daughter Caroline, on July 19, 1986, at Hyannis Port, married Edward Schlossberg, whose father had founded a Manhattan textile company, Jackie wore a plain, long-sleeved dress in pale pistachio crepe, and was photographed in a most characteristic pose: with her head resting on a strong masculine shoulder; in this case, it belonged to the last surviving Kennedy brother, Ted. Caroline had followed her mother's example by marrying a much older man; her new husband was forty-one; she was twenty-eight.

Jackie's own safe haven was wealthy, protective, gentle Maurice Tempelsman. She'd known him, a loyal Democrat, for thirty years. An Orthodox Jew, separated but not divorced from his wife of thirty-odd years, Lily, Maurice was a Belgium-born financier and diamond merchant who now helped Jackie parley her holdings into an estimated $200 million. "I noticed that Jackie deferred to Maurice all the time," commented a dinner guest in 1989, after Tempelsman had come to live in Jackie's Manhattan apartment. "Maurice," she'd say, "should we have coffee here [in her red-lacquered library] or in the living-room?" "We'll have coffee here," he'd reply in a loud, assertive tone, and Jackie would look relieved. She needed a man as she needed clothes: to add substance and structure to her ailing soul.

For the rest of her life, she kept her cover, via structuralist clothes and disarming sunglasses, and continued to adorn all the best glossy magazines. In 1987, in the first revival of her 1960s look, the French magazine *Madame Figaro* put her on its cover, as did *Life*, *Vogue* and *Vanity Fair* in 1989. "For thirty years, she has been fashion dynamite, setting trends, breaking rules, and putting her stamp on American style," enthused the *Philadelphia Enquirer* on July 23, 1989. When New York's Henri Bendel showed versions of "the Jackie suit" at the opening of its new store in 1991, the originator herself was there to smile her icon's smile and modestly pronounce the revival "silly." She'd had her face worked on twice by plastic surgeons, but as Jackie entered her sixties, her hands, as hands inevitably do, broadcast her true age by means of prominent veins and liver-spots. Jackie borrowed a trick from

Elsie de Wolfe Mendl and the Duchess of Windsor, and took to wearing white gloves for all social occasions. Glove manufacturers rubbed their hands in glee as sales escalated.

During the Christmas holidays of 1993, when Jackie was sailing in the Caribbean, she began to feel unwell and couldn't shake a persistent cough. When she returned to New York, doctors diagnosed her as suffering from a form of cancer known as non-Hodgkins lymphoma. She began receiving chemotherapy and steroid drugs, but failed to improve. This was the final paradox which succeeded so many others in her life: the beauty of an elegant woman coupled with the beast called cancer, destroying her from within.

As she lay dying in her Fifth Avenue apartment, she watched herself, according to a family report, on television. She died at 10:15 p.m. on May 19, 1994, with Maurice and both children at her bedside. She was two months short of her sixty-fifth birthday. It seems fitting that someone so fixated on youth would never officially become a senior. With one eye, as always, on posterity, Jackie had asked to be buried at Arlington cemetery next to Jack and his eternal flame. On the days between death and funeral, huge crowds kept sentimental vigil outside her apartment building.

Following the funeral, New York's *Daily News* published a special ten-page supplement with two pages devoted to Jackie's favorite shopping places. *Time*, *Newsweek*, *U.S. News and World Report*, *New York*, *Life* and *Vanity Fair*, for the very last time, put her on their covers. All but one magazine chose a nostalgic 1960s picture of Jackie Kennedy. Only *Vanity Fair* opted for a contemporary photo of Jackie Onassis. Myths, like old soldiers, never die; in the American consciousness, Jackie had fixed herself forever in the misty towers of Camelot. All the articles that flooded newspapers and magazines worldwide, all the television specials, trotted out the same old bits of motley, the same old amorphous, well-quilted clichés. After writing 630 pages of his biography, *A Woman Named Jackie* (1989), C. David Heymann throws up his hands in despair, and admits defeat. On the final page, he asks: "What is Jackie really like?" And the answer is: "We may never truly know."

Her cover-up had been complete, one of the most successful and long lasting in American history. She covered up her body in a way that also covered up her essential being and prevented us from accurately reading her. She let the myths enshroud her, obscuring everything beneath. Jackie, we never knew you, because we looked at you through a double disguise, ours and yours: our gauzy filaments of wish and sentiment, your carapace of confusing signals. Did Jackie keep herself hidden because she knew, in her innermost being, that the real woman would disappoint and bore us, that she was really not unique or even unconventional, but just one more jet-set rich bitch starved in body and spirit?

The fashion shows that took place in Milan in March 1995, of the next fall's ready-to-wear, noted *Time* magazine on April 17, "showed a dramatic shift in direction. In a fashion world that has seemed, in recent years, increasingly remote, self-involved and obsessed with stunts, it was a remarkable about-face. Call it a return to elegance." The article goes on to say that two ghosts haunted the collections: that of Audrey Hepburn and Jackie Kennedy Onassis. Even Karl Lagerfeld, designer of the Chanel collection, who in previous years had shown vinyl micro-skirts in neon colors and tacky, bare-midriff tops with maribou trim, returned to full sobriety with dressmaker suits with 3/4 length sleeves in muted tweeds, which looked like they'd be good for the long haul and for ordinary street wear, rather than for dancing on a bar-room table or swinging from a trapeze. The Jackie look, we can see now, never really died; it just went onto a store-room rack, bided its time, and reappeared as strong and influential as ever.

Go to any theater lobby or cocktail party or upscale restaurant. You will find plenty of Jackie clones, in plain sleeveless shifts or neat little suits, clutching their chain-handle bags. Jackie's image burns with an eternal flame, but, like the Emperor's clothes, it's cut more from fancy than fact, and hung in our minds upon a willing suspension of disbelief.

Does it matter? Everything she wore was stunning, memorable, gorgeous, truly beautiful. So let's leave her garments empty, strung out upon a myth, blowing and billowing in history's wind. As part of his oration at Jackie's funeral, Ted Kennedy said it best: "For those of us who knew and loved her, she graced our eyes."

Wrapping It Up

We've peered into a great many closets and hat boxes and jewel cases in tracing the stylish lives of five remarkable women. Empress Eugénie matched her crinoline's expansion to that of the Second Empire, and bravely survived their mutual collapse. Elinor Glyn used a tiger skin as magic carpet to riches, royal friends and two rewarding careers. Marlene Dietrich tossed her furs so generously in all directions that her glamour still wraps us round. The Duchess of Windsor made her stately progress through life in the light of a thousand hard, clear gems. Jacqueline Onassis muffled her body and personality in double-faced fabrics but still managed to spark a splendid myth.

"It is by style," novelist Henry James once wrote, "that we are saved." From what? Answers to that question lie in the preceding pages: saved from too much reality, from banality, bad taste, boredom, poverty, ugliness, low self-esteem, repressed creativity, gender confusion and sexual vulgarity. Saved from the full impact of painful self-knowledge and of the cruel, random blows of fate.

Of course it is by style, to misquote James, that we are damned as well. These five lives demonstrate, in varying degrees, how style can be a shield, a disguise, an obsession, a despot, even a destroyer of character and soul. But on the whole, if style is applied to one's life with due regard for moderation and other priorities, benefits, not bad side-effects, accrue. The sheer poetry of style, its loveliness and lilt, sing louder than the pain.

What are the positive attributes of style? First comes creativity. The art of dress is the only art available to every single woman. Since we all have to get dressed every morning of our lives, we might just as well turn the task into a positive pleasure and do it with loving care, originality and flair. Eugénie, Elinor, Marlene, Wallis and Jackie have already shown us how.

The second advantage of style is fantasy, the kind of idealizing which uplifts and energizes the psyche. I believe that all of us, every time we read about a glamour goddess like Marlene or dream about a cult figure like Jackie, are searching for our own highest good and greatest beauty, for a special, luminous self, as Plato defined it in the *Symposium.* The life-stories here can reactivate imaginations grown sluggish from lack of exercise since the advent of television. (The average American viewer now reclines with an anesthetized imagination before the full-color dots of a television set for seven hours a day.) By flipping through these pages, every woman can let her fancy leap round the idea of being, as Dodie Smith once put it, "naked, with a chequebook."

The heroine of Paul Gallico's charming novel *Mrs. 'Arris Goes to Paris* can show us exactly how to fantasize in cloth. She is a poor, hard-working cleaning woman, untraveled, unsophisticated, with red, raw hands and "wispy hair down about her ears," habitually dressed in cheap cotton and soiled apron. When Mrs. 'Arris sees "a bit of heaven" in lace and chiffon hanging in her employer's closet, "something inside her yearned and reached for it" with a powerful, purely feminine craving. She keeps on scrubbing and slaving until she saves enough money to buy a Dior black-velvet gown which she will never wear but which will keep her happily dreaming and enraptured for the rest of her life.

We can name Mrs. 'Arris an honorary woman of style. Like our five, she understood how beauty and luxury in attire, even in modest amounts, can not only redeem the dullest individual life but also give a whole society a sophisticated gloss. The level of civilization is always directly related to the amount of aesthetic attention paid to dress. Whenever culture reaches full flower, as in Renaissance Italy, or Elizabethan England, clothes for both sexes, among the wealthy elite, are splendid and sumptuous in the extreme: richly brocaded, gem-encrusted, sable-trimmed. Mrs. 'Arris knew instinctively, as did Eugénie, Elinor and the others, that every life can use a little luxe. These women knew all about putting on the Ritz, dressing *up* to an occasion, not down, as women tend to do today. Formality in dress is in retreat, casual wear in the ascendant and the gamut of choices available in steep decline. One wears denim to clean out the septic tank and denim to go dancing with one's lover. We have no time now, we say, to indulge in style; no time to buy it; no money to have it custom-made; no room to store it; no place to wear it. Gone are the days when women like Marlene cared enough about style to have three fittings on a nightgown. Haute couture is on the way out with its high-flying fantasy, its intricate construction, its highly skilled workmanship. Women have moved on to other things. But we can still revel and rejoice in style's heyday, when its devotees started off naked with a checkbook and attired themselves in rainbow raiment fit for goddesses and queens.

In addition to lessons in creativity, fantasy and luxury, the best-dressed five can lead us towards a fresh definition of what it means to be female. All of them, in varying degrees, embraced and exemplified through clothes something which women today have lost sight of: the mystery which forms a crucial part of the female anima. Starting in the 1960s, North American feminists gathered their forces, put on their man-tailored suits and began to chant, "Why can't a woman be more like a man?" Perhaps it's time to ask, "Why can't a woman be more like a woman?" Without taking style to foolish or self-destructive extremes, why can't she still manage to incorporate in her life some measure of the romantic glamour which Elinor and Marlene bodied forth so easily and gracefully in floating scarves and hats with little veils?

The stylish five can also demonstrate the importance of play and whimsy to modern lives of relentless routine and drive. Elizabethan playwright and poet Ben Jonson, living in an age when every gentleman wore lace ruffles, wrote that rich apparel "makes continual holiday where it shines." We can all respond to the siren song of style, which plays, in quick-step spirit, with the most serious question of human consciousness, namely, "Who am I?"

There's another lesson here, and it's a moral one. Outer beauty can produce inner. The woman of style can embody true elegance, using that word as Jane Austen used it in her novels, to mean a refined co-ordination of body and soul. Of course, elegance may be only skin-deep, as it was for Wallis Windsor. But I agree with Anne Hollander that rags "create a tattered condition of soul" and that the habit of fine clothes "can actually produce a true personal grace" which spills over into courtesy and civility.

It is also worth noting that style for all five ladies peaked not in youth but in middle-age. I hope their examples can help bring the mature woman back into fashion's spotlight. She disappeared – "Mrs. Exeter" was her name – from the pages of American *Vogue* in 1962 and hasn't been seen since, her reign usurped by fashion models who've been growing ever younger. In the 1960s, almost half the American population was under the age of twenty-five, so the fashion trade was right to woo them. But by the year 2000, thirty per cent of all adult American women will be age fifty or over. This powerful group will number forty-two million, and every one of them who remains free of cancer and heart disease will live to celebrate her ninety-second birthday. In light of these amazing demographic changes, it's high time to lead glamour back to the fountain of age, and Elinor Glyn, who "never looked more beautiful" than when she was seventy-plus, is just the person to do it.

Five women put on the habit of style, and took their vows. In its service they were dedicated, infinitely patient through long hours of fittings, disciplined enough to starve themselves to keep the line. Once the Duchess of Windsor asked Mainbocher to make the skirt of a new creation tighter over the hips. "But your Royal Highness," he protested, "if I do you won't be able to sit down." "Then I won't sit down," sighed the Duchess. There speaks a true disciple of style. We can admire the passion and tenacity of this quest for perfection. Five style-setters did it their way, and kept the faith. They walked in beauty and in light, leaving a trail of glossy images to inform, inspire and gladden every eye.

Watch them dance across the page, and feel their dazzle. Eugénie and Jackie waltz and twirl at the center of a Court, beaming their bright messages around the world. Elinor and Marlene snake their hips on the Hollywood Hotel dance floor, swirling chiffons and pale fox borders. The Duchess of Windsor clinks the ice of her diamond bracelets in some Paris night club, and manages to do the twist without disarranging a single hair of her sleek coiffure. From a respectful distance, we can only stand and marvel and applaud each one for the way she looks tonight.

Acknowledgments

I am indebted, first of all, to Professor Peter Clarke of St. John's College, Cambridge, an eminent historian who, over a leisurely breakfast in June 1994, not only gave me the book's title, but also suggested I include Empress Eugénie. His wife, on the other hand, my fellow-biographer Dr. Maria Tippett, was, at the same breakfast, adamant that Jackie Onassis get a chapter. Thank you to both these friends for their warm interest and help. I am also grateful for information received from Sir Anthony and Lady Susan Glyn.

As always, I received helpful and efficient service from the staffs of the four libraries where I did my research: The Robarts Library, at the University of Toronto; the Metropolitan Toronto Reference Library; the Royal Ontario Museum Library; the Four Arts Society Library in Palm Beach, Florida.

Friends and relatives who contributed to this book in all kinds of helpful ways include Warren Collins, Dr. Louis Bodnar, Robert Cramer, Gerard Gauci, Brenda Gwyn-Williams, Norma Harrs, Don and Anna Little, Dr. Dorothy Millner, Shirley Mowbray,

Joan and Michael Pierson, Mary Scott and Diana Wurtzburg. My son Tim, always my best critic and most knowledgable companion, read the manuscript carefully and offered his usual insightful comments.

My editor at Random House of Canada, Diane Martin, greatly improved the manuscript and gave me constant encouragement, as did Charles Spicer, senior editor at St. Martin's Press in New York. Copy editor Tanya Wood corrected my inconsistencies and caught every error. I am also grateful to David Kent, President, and Douglas Pepper, Vice-President, of Random House of Canada, two men of style who proved to be amazingly knowledgable on the subject of feminine fashion. My heartfelt thanks to all of the above.

M. F.
Toronto, Canada.

PHOTO CREDITS

1, 2, 3, 4, 5, 6, 7, 8, 21, 22, 23 and 24 reproduced by Metropolitan Toronto Reference Library; 9, Sir Anthony Glyn, reproduced from his book *Elinor Glyn*; 10, 11, 12, 13, 17, Elspeth Chowdharay-Best; 14 and 15, Film Stills Archive, Museum of Modern Art; 16, National Portrait Gallery; 18, 19, 20, Dietrich archive, private collection; 25, Richard Avedon; 26, Pictures, Inc.; 27, International News Photos; 28 and 33, Windsor Archive, Mohamed Al-Fayed; 29, © Horst P. Horst, courtesy: Jane Corkin Gallery, Toronto; 30, Roger Schall; 31, Kenro Izu; 32, Cecil Beaton Archive, Sotheby's, London; 34, Molly Thayer, Magnum Photos; 35, Paul Schutzer, *Life* magazine, © Time, Inc.; 36 and 39, Wide World Photos; 37, Yale Joel, *Life* magazine, © Time, Inc.; 38, Camera Press; 40, Henri Dauman, Magnum Photos; 41, Allan B. Goodrich, John F. Kennedy Library, Boston.

Note: Every effort was made to trace copyright holders; in the event of an inadvertent omission, please contact the publisher.

Bibliography

I. MAGAZINES AND NEWSPAPERS

American Mercury
The Beaver
Cosmopolitan
Connoisseur
Godey's Lady's Book
Good Housekeeping
Harper's Bazaar
Harper's Magazine
Harper's Weekly
Ladies Home Journal
Lady's Circle
Lady's Realm
Life
Literary Digest
Look
New Republic
Newsweek
New Yorker
New York Times
Ms
Observer
Palm Beach Daily News
People Weekly
Putnam's Monthly
Saturday Review
Time
The Times [London]
Vanity Fair
Vogue [U.S.]
W
Wilson Library Bulletin
Women's Wear Daily

II. BOOKS – FICTION

Capote, Truman. *Answered Prayers. The Unfinished Novel.* New York: Random House, 1987.

Edwards, Anne. *Wallis: The Novel.* New York: William Morrow, 1991.

Gallico, Paul. *Mrs. 'Arris Goes to Paris.* New York: Doubleday, 1958.

Glyn, Elinor. *His Hour.* Auburn: The Author's Press, 1910.

The Letters of her Mother to Elizabeth. London: John Lane, 1901.

The Price of Things. Auburn: The Author's Press, 1919.

The Reason Why. London: Duckworth, 1914.

Red Hair. Auburn: The Author's Press, 1905.

The Seventh Commandment. Auburn: The Author's Press, 1902.

Three Weeks. Introduction by Cecil Beaton. London: Duckworth, 1974.

Remarque, Erich Maria. *Arch of Triumph.* New York: Appleton-Century, 1945.

III. BOOKS – NON-FICTION

de Acosta, Mercedes. *Here Lies the Heart.* New York: Reynal and Company, 1960.

Airlie, Mabell, Countess of. *Thatched With Gold.* London: Hutchinson, 1962.

Alsop, Susan Mary. *To Marietta from Paris, 1945–1960.* Garden City: Doubleday, 1975.

Amory, Cleveland. *The Best Cat Ever.* Boston: Little Brown, 1993.

Anscombe, Isabelle. *A Woman's Touch: Women in Design from 1860 to the Present Day.* New York: Penguin Books, 1985.

Antoine. *Antoine.* New York: Prentice-Hall, 1945.

Aronson, Steven M.L. *Hype.* New York: William Morrow, 1983.

Aronson, Theo. *The Golden Bees: The Story of the Bonapartes.* Greenwich: New York Graphic Society, 1964.

Atherton, Gertrude. *Adventures of a Novelist.* London: Jonathan Cape, 1932.

Bach, Steven. *Marlene Dietrich: Life and Legend.* New York: William Morrow, 1992.

Baldrige, Letitia. *Of Diamonds and Diplomats.* Boston: Lanewood Press, 1968.

Baldwin, Billy. *Billy Baldwin Remembers.* New York: Harcourt, Brace Jovanovich, 1974.

Ballard, Bettina. *In My Fashion.* London: Martin, Secker & Warburg, 1960.

Barschak, Erna. *The Innocent Empress: An Intimate Study of Eugénie.* New York: E.P. Dutton, 1943.

Barthes, Roland. *The Fashion System.* New York: Hill and Wang, 1983.

Barthez, Dr. E. [Antoine Charles Ernest] *The Empress Eugénie and her Circle.* London: T. Fisher Unwin, 1912.

Basinger, Jeanine. *A Woman's View: How Hollywood Spoke to Women 1930–1960.* New York: Alfred A. Knopf, 1993.

Beaton, Cecil. *The Glass of Fashion.* London: Cassell, 1989.

The Happy Years: Diaries 1944–48. London: Weidenfeld & Nicolson, 1972.

The Parting Years: Diaries 1963–74. London: Weidenfeld & Nicolson, 1978.

The Wandering Years: Diaries 1922–39. London: Weidenfeld & Nicolson, 1961.

The Years Between: Diaries 1939–44. London: Weidenfeld & Nicolson, 1965.

Bell, Quentin. *On Human Finery.* London: Hogarth Press, 1976.

Bender, Marylin. *The Beautiful People.* New York: Coward-McCann, 1967.

Bergler, Edmund, M.D. *Fashion and the Unconscious.* New York: Robert Brunner, 1953.

Bertin, Célia. *Paris à la Mode: A Voyage of Discovery.* London: Victor Gollanz, 1956.

Bicknell, Anna L. *Life in the Tuileries under the Second Empire.* New York: The Century Company, 1895.

Birmingham, Stephen. *Duchess: The Story of Wallis Warfield Windsor.* Boston: Little Brown, 1981.

Jacqueline Bouvier Kennedy Onassis. New York: Grosset and Dunlap, 1978.

Blackwood, Caroline. *The Last of the Duchess.* New York: Pantheon Books, 1995.

Bloch, Michael, ed. *Wallis and Edward. Letters 1931–1937: The Intimate Correspondence of the Duke and Duchess of Windsor.* New York: Summit Books, 1986.

Blunden, M. *The Countess of Warwick: A Biography.* London: Cassell, 1967.

Bouvier, Jacqueline and Lee. *One Special Summer.* New York: Delacorte Press, 1974.

Bradlee, Benjamin C. *Conversations with Kennedy.* New York: W. W. Norton & Company, 1975.

Brady, James. *Superchic.* Boston: Little Brown, 1974.

Brodsky, Alyn. *Imperial Charade: A Biography of Emperor Napoléon III and Empress Eugénie.* New York: The Bobbs-Merrill Company, 1978.

Brody, Iles. *Gone With the Windsors.* Philadelphia: John C. Winston, 1953.

Bryant, Traphes, with Frances Spatz Leighton. *Dog Days at the White House.* New York: Macmillan Publishing Company, 1975.

Buck, Pearl S. *The Kennedy Women: A Personal Appraisal.* New York: Cowles Book Company, 1970.

Buckle, Richard, ed. *Self-Portrait with Friends: The Selected Diaries of Cecil Beaton 1926–1974.* New York: Times Books, 1979.

Burchell, S. C. *Upstart Empire: Paris During the Brilliant Years of Louis Napoléon.* London: Macdonald, 1971.

Capote, Truman. *Truman Capote: Conversations.* Edited by M. Thomas Inge. Jackson: University Press of Mississippi, 1987.

Carette, Madame [A.] *My Mistress, the Empress Eugénie.* London: Dean and Son, n.d.

Carlyle, Thomas. *Sartor Resartus*. London: Chapman and Hall, n.d.

Carr, Larry. *Four Fabulous Faces*. New York: Arlington House, 1970.

Carter, Ernestine. *Magic Names of Fashion*. London: Weidenfeld & Nicolson, 1980.

Cassini, Oleg. *In My Own Fashion: An Autobiography*. New York: Simon and Schuster, 1987.

Channon, Sir Henry. *Chips: The Diaries of Sir Henry Channon*. Edited by Robert Rhodes James. London: Weidenfeld and Nicolson, 1967.

Chaplin, Charles. *My Autobiography*. London: Bodley Head, 1964.

Chase, Edna Woolman and Ilka Chase. *Always in Vogue*. New York: Doubleday, 1954.

Cheshire, Maxine. *Maxine Cheshire: Reporter*. Boston: Houghton Mifflin, 1978.

Clinch, Nancy Gager. *The Kennedy Neurosis*. New York: Grosset & Dunlap, 1973.

Cooper, Diana. *The Light of Common Day*. London: Rupert Hart-Davis, 1959.

Croce, Benedetto. *The Aesthetic as the Science of Expression and of the Linguistic in General*. Cambridge: Cambridge University Press, 1992.

Curtis, Charlotte. *First Lady*. New York: Pyramid Books, 1962.

D'Ambès, Baron [pseud.] *Intimate Memoirs of Napoléon III*. Trans. by A. R. Allinson. 2 vols. London: Stanley Paul, n.d.

Davenport, Millia. *The Book of Costume*. New York: Crown Publishers, 1948.

David, Lester. *Jacqueline Kennedy Onassis: A Portrait of Her Private Years*. New York: Birch Lane Press, 1994.

Davies, Marion. *The Times We Had: Life with William Randolph Hearst*. New York: Bobbs-Merrill Company, 1975.

Dickerson, Nancy. *Among Those Present*. New York: Random House, 1976.

Dietrich, Marlene. *Marlene*. Trans. from the German by Salvator Attanasio. New York: Grove Press, 1989.

Douglas, Susan J. *Where the Girls Are: Growing up Female With the Mass Media.* New York: Random House, 1994.

Dubois, Diana. *In Her Sister's Shadow: An Intimate Biography of Lee Radziwill.* Boston: Little Brown, 1995.

Etherington-Smith, Meredith and Jeremy Pilcher. *The It Girls.* London: Hamish Hamilton, 1986.

Evans, Dr. Thomas W. *The Memoirs of Dr. Thomas W. Evans: Recollections of the Second French Empire.* Edited by Edward A. Crane. 2 vols. London: T. Fisher Unwin, 1906.

Fairbanks, Douglas Jr. *The Salad Days.* New York: Doubleday, 1988.

Fairchild, John. *The Fashionable Savages.* New York: Doubleday, 1965.

Fisher, John. *Call Them Irreplaceable.* London: Elm Tree Books, 1976.

Fleury, Comte [Maurice]. *The Memoirs of the Empress Eugénie.* 2 vols. New York: D. Appleton and Company, 1920.

Flügel, J.C. *The Psychology of Clothes.* London: Hogarth Press, 1930.

Fraser, Kennedy. *The Fashionable Mind: Reflections on Fashion.* New York: Alfred A. Knopf, 1981.

Frischauer, Willi. *Jackie.* London: Michael Joseph, 1976.

Gaines, Jane and Charlotte Herzog. *Fabrications: Costumes and the Female Body.* New York: Routledge, 1990.

Galella, Ron. *Jacqueline.* New York: Sheed and Ward, 1974.

Gallagher, Mary Barelli. *My Life with Jacqueline Kennedy.* Edited by Frances Spatz Leighton. New York: David McKay, 1969.

Garland, Madge. *The Changing Form of Fashion.* London: J.M. Dent & Sons, 1970.

Gernsheim, Alison. *Fashion and Reality.* 1840–1914. London: Faber and Faber, 1963.

Glyn, Anthony. *Elinor Glyn: A Biography.* London: Hutchinson, 1955.

Glyn, Elinor. *Romantic Adventure.* New York: E.P. Dutton, 1937.

Glynn, Prudence. *In Fashion: Dress in the Twentieth Century.* London: George Allen & Unwin, 1978.

Goldwyn, Samuel. *Behind the Screen.* New York: George H. Doran, 1923.

Gombrich, E.H. *The Sense of Order: A Study in the Psychology of Decorative Art.* Oxford: Phaidon Press, 1979.

Griffith, Richard. *Marlene Dietrich: Image and Legend.* Museum of Modern Art, Film Library, 1959.

Guedalla, Philip. *The Second Empire.* London: Hodder and Stoughton, 1937.

Guiles, Fred Laurence. *Marion Davies.* New York: McGraw-Hill, 1972.

Hardwick, Joan. *Addicted to Romance: The Life and Adventures of Elinor Glyn.* London: Andre Deutsch, 1994.

Hart, Kitty Carlisle. *Kitty: An Autobiography.* New York: Doubleday, 1988.

Hartnell, Norman. *Royal Courts of Fashion.* London: Cassell & Company, 1971.

Haskell, Molly. *From Reverence to Rape: The Treatment of Women in the Movies.* 2nd edition. Chicago: University of Chicago Press, 1987.

Hastings, Selina. *Nancy Mitford.* London: Papermac, 1985.

Head, Edith and Paddy Calistro. *Edith Head's Hollywood.* New York: E.P. Dutton, 1983.

Hegermann-Lindencrone, Lide. *In the Courts of Memory 1858-1875: From Contemporary Letters.* New York: Harper & Brothers, 1912.

Henrey, Robert, editor. *Letters from Paris 1870-75.* London: J.M. Dent & Sons, 1942.

Heymann, C. David. *A Woman Named Jackie.* New York: Lyle Stuart, 1989.

Higham, Charles. *The Duchess of Windsor. The Secret Life.* New York: McGraw-Hill, 1988.

Marlene: The Life of Marlene Dietrich. New York: W.W. Norton & Company, 1977.

Holden, W.H., ed. *Second Empire Medley.* London: Technical and General Press, 1952.

Hollander, Anne. *Seeing Through Clothes.* New York: Penguin Books, 1988.

Sex and Suits. New York: Alfred A. Knopf, 1994.

Johnson, Leo A. *A History of Guelph 1927-1977.* Guelph: Guelph Historical Society, 1977.

Keenan, Brigid. *The Women We Wanted to Look Like.* New York: St. Martin's Press, 1978.

Kelley, Kitty. *Jackie Oh!* Secaucus, N. J.: Lyle Stuart, 1978.

Kennedy, David. *Incidents of Pioneer Days in Guelph.* Toronto: n.p., 1903.

Kennedy, Rose. *Times to Remember.* Garden City: Doubleday, 1974.

Koestenbaum, Wayne. *Jackie Under My Skin: Interpreting an Icon.* New York: Farrar, Straus and Giroux, 1995.

Konig, René. *The Restless Image: A Sociology of Fashion.* London: George Allen & Unwin, 1973.

Kroeber, A.L. *Style and Civilizations.* Ithaca: Cornell University Press, 1957.

Kübler, George. *The Shape of Time: Remarks on the History of Things.* New Haven: Yale University Press, 1962.

Kurtz, Harold. *The Empress Eugénie 1826–1920.* Boston: Houghton Mifflin, 1964.

Lambert, Eleanor. *World of Fashion: People, Places, Resources.* New York: R. R. Bowker, 1976.

Lang, Berel, ed. *The Concept of Style.* Philadelphia: University of Pennsylvania Press, 1979.

Langley-Moore, Doris. *The Woman in Fashion.* London: B.T. Batsford, 1949.

Langner, Lawrence. *The Importance of Wearing Clothes.* New York: Hastings House, 1959.

Lasch, Christopher. *The Culture of Narcissism.* New York: W.W. Norton & Company, 1978.

Lasky, Jesse L. *I Blow My Own Horn.* With Don Weldon. London: Victor Gollancz, 1957.

Laver, James. *Clothes.* London: Burke Publishing Company, 1952.

Costume and Fashion: A Concise History. London: Thames and Hudson, 1982.

Style in Costume. London: Oxford University Press, 1949.

Taste and Fashion from the French Revolution to the Present Day. London: Harrap, 1945.

Lavine, W. Robert. *In A Glamorous Fashion: The Fabulous Years of Hollywood Costume Design*. New York: Charles Scribner's Sons, 1980.

Leamer, Laurence. *The Kennedy Women*. New York: Villard Books, 1994.

Legge, Edward. *The Comedy & Tragedy of the Second Empire*. London: Harper & Brothers, 1911.

The Empress Eugénie and Her Son. London: Grant Richards, 1916.

Lesley, Cole. *The Life of Noel Coward*. Harmondsworth: Penguin Books, 1978.

Lifton, Robert Jay, ed. *The Woman in America*. Boston: Houghton Mifflin, 1964.

Loliée, Fréderic. *Women of the Second Empire: Chronicles from the Court of Napoléon III*, compiled from unpublished documents. Trans. by Alice M. Ivimy. London: John Lane, 1907.

Loos, Anita. *A Girl Like I*. New York: Viking Press, 1966.

Lorenz, Konrad. *Behind the Mirror: A Search for a Natural History of Human Knowledge*. Trans. by Ronald Taylor. New York: Harcourt Brace Jovanovich, 1977.

Lurie, Alison. *The Language of Clothes*. New York: Random House, 1981.

Lynam, Ruth, ed. *Couture: An Illustrated History of the Great Paris Designers and Their Creations*. New York: Doubleday, 1972.

Macaulay, Rose. *Personal Pleasures*. London: Victor Gollancz, 1968.

Manchester, William. *The Death of a President*. New York: Harper & Row, 1967.

Marion, Frances. *Off With Their Heads! A Serio-Comic Tale of Hollywood*. New York: Macmillan, 1972.

Marlborough, Laura, Duchess of. *Laughter from a Cloud*. London: Weidenfeld & Nicolson, 1980.

de Marly, Diana. *Worth: Father of Haute Couture*. London: Elm Tree Books, 1980.

Martin, Ralph G. *The Woman He Loved*. New York: Simon and Schuster, 1973.

Maurois, Simone André. *Miss Howard and the Emperor.* London: Collins, 1957.

Menkes, Suzy. *The Windsor Style.* London: Grafton Books, 1987.

Metternich, Princess Pauline. *The Days That Are No More: Some Reminiscences.* London: Eveleigh Nash & Grayson, 1921.

Milbank, Caroline Rennolds. *Couture: The Great Designers.* New York: Stewart, Tabori & Chang, 1985.

Miller, Lesley Ellis. *Balenciaga.* London: Batsford, 1993.

Morella, Joe and Edward Z. Epstein. *The "It" Girl: The Incredible Story of Clara Bow.* New York: Delacorte Press, 1976.

Morley, Sheridan. *Tales from the Hollywood Raj.* London: Weidenfeld & Nicolson, 1983.

Mosley, Diana. *The Duchess of Windsor.* New York: Stein and Day, 1981.

Mulvagh, Jane. *Vogue: History of 20th Century Fashion.* London: Bloomsbury Books, 1988.

Murphy, Charles J.V. and J. Bryan III. *The Windsor Story.* New York: Dell Publishing, 1981.

de Navacelle, Thierry. *Sublime Marlene.* London: Sidgwick & Jackson, 1984.

Negri, Pola. *Memoirs of a Star.* New York: Doubleday, 1970.

Nichols, Beverly. *The Sweet and Twenties.* London: Weidenfeld & Nicolson, 1958.

Nystrom, Paul. *The Economics of Fashion.* New York: The Ronald Press, 1928.

O'Connor, Patrick. *The Amazing Blonde Woman: Dietrich's Own Style.* London: Bloomsbury, 1991.

Philipson, Morris, ed. *Aesthetics Today.* Cleveland: World Publishing, 1961.

Potter, Jeffry. *Men, Money and Magic: The Story of Dorothy Schiff.* New York: Coward, McCann & Geoghegan, 1976.

Rhea, Mini. *I Was Jacqueline Kennedy's Dressmaker.* With Frances Spatz Leighton. New York: Fleet Publishing, 1962.

Robinson, David. *Chaplin, His Life and Art.* New York: McGraw-Hill, 1985.
Hollywood in the Twenties. New York: Tantivy Press, 1968.

Rogers, Peter. *What Becomes a Legend Most? The Blackglama Story.* New York: Simon and Schuster, 1979.

Rose, Helen. *Just Make Them Beautiful.* Santa Monica: Dennis Landman, 1976.

Rutter, Owen. *Portrait of a Painter: The Authorized Life of Philip de Laszlo.* London: Hodder and Stoughton, 1939.

Saunders, Edith. *The Age of Worth: Couturier to the Empress Eugénie.* London: Longmans, Green, 1954.

Selznick, Irene Mayer. *A Private View.* New York: Alfred A. Knopf, 1983.

Sencourt, Robert. *The Life of the Empress Eugénie.* New York: Charles Scribner's Sons, 1931.

Sheean, Vincent. *Between the Thunder and the Sun.* New York: Random House, 1943.

Shulman, Irving. *"Jackie!" The Exploitation of a First Lady.* New York: Trident Press, 1970.

Silverman, Debora. *Selling Culture: Bloomingdale's, Diana Vreeland and the New Aristocracy of Taste in America.* New York: Pantheon Books, 1986.

Smith, Jane S. *Elsie de Wolfe: A Life in the High Style.* New York: Atheneum, 1982.

Smyth, Ethel. *Streaks of Life.* New York: Alfred A. Knopf, 1922.

Snow, Carmel, with Mary Louise Aswell. *The World of Carmel Snow.* New York: McGraw-Hill, 1962.

Spanier, Ginette. *It Isn't All Mink.* London: Collins, 1959.

Spoto, Donald. *Blue Angel: The Life of Marlene Dietrich.* New York: Doubleday, 1992.

Squire, Geoffrey. *Dress, Art and Society 1560–1970.* London: Studio Vista, 1974.

Steele, Valerie. *Paris Fashion: A Cultural History.* Toronto: Oxford University Press, 1988.

Stenn, David. *Clara Bow: Runnin' Wild.* New York: Doubleday, 1988.

Sternberg, Josef von. *Fun In a Chinese Laundry.* New York: Macmillan Company, 1965.

Stewart, Robert Alan Maclean. *A Picture History of Guelph.* Vol. 2. Privately printed, 1978.

St. Johns, Adela Rogers. *The Honeycomb.* New York: Doubleday, 1969.

Swanson, Gloria. *Swanson on Swanson.* New York: Random House, 1980.

Tapert, Annette and Diane Edkins. *The Power of Style: The Women Who Define the Art of Living Well.* New York: Crown Publishers, 1994.

Thayer, Mary Van Rensselaer. *Jacqueline Kennedy: The White House Years.* Boston: Little Brown, 1967.

Thomas, Helen. *Dateline: White House.* New York: Macmillan, 1975.

Trent, Paul. *The Image Makers: Sixty Years of Hollywood Glamour.* New York: McGraw-Hill, 1972.

Twain, Mark. *The Autobiography of Mark Twain.* Edited by Charles Neider. New York: Harper & Brothers, 1959.

Vanderbilt, Gloria and Thelma, Lady Furness. *Double Exposure: A Twin Autobiography.* New York: David McKay Company, 1958.

Veblen, Thorstein. *The Theory of the Leisure Class.* New York: The Modern Library, 1934.

Vickers, Hugo. *Loving Garbo.* London: Jonathan Cape, 1994.

Vidal, Gore. *Palimpsest: A Memoir.* New York: Random House, 1995.

Vidor, King. *A Tree is a Tree.* New York: Harcourt Brace, 1952.

[Vizetelly, Ernest Alfred] *The Court of the Tuileries 1852–70.* By Le Petit Homme Rouge. London: Chatto & Windus, 1912.

Vreeland, Diana. *Allure.* New York: Doubleday, 1980.

D.V. New York: Alfred A. Knopf, 1984.

Warwick, Frances, Countess of. *Afterthoughts.* London: Cassell and Company, 1931.

Waugh, Nora. *Corsets and Crinolines.* London: B.T. Batsford, 1954.

The Cut of Women's Clothes. London: Faber and Faber, 1968.

Weibel, Kathryn. *Mirror, Mirror: Images of Women Reflected in Popular Culture.* Garden City: Anchor Books, 1977.

West, J.B. with Mary Lynn Kotz. *Upstairs at the White House: My Life with the First Ladies.* New York: Warner Books, 1973.

Wiliamson, Alice M. *Alice in Movieland.* New York: D. Appleton & Company, 1928.

Wilson, Edwina H. [pseud. for Laura Brookman] *Her Name was Wallis Warfield.* New York: E.P. Dutton, 1936.

Windsor, Duchess of. *The Heart Has Its Reasons.* New York: David McKay Company, 1956.

Windsor, Duke of. *A King's Story: The Memoirs of the Duke of Windsor.* New York: G.P. Putnam's, 1947.

Wollheim, Richard. *Art and Its Objects.* 2nd edition. Cambridge: Cambridge University Press, 1980.

Worth, Jean Philippe. *A Century of Fashion.* Boston: Little Brown, 1928.

Ziegler, Philip. *Diana Cooper: The Biography of Lady Diana Cooper.* Harmondsworth: Penguin Books, 1983.

King Edward VIII. New York: Ballantine Books, 1992.